CU00866000

THE LIFE OF
BRIAN

THE LIFE OF
BRIAN

Celebrating the life and times of a football genius

By Tim Crane

FootballWorld

Published December 2004 by
Football World
Tel: (01708) 379 877
Website: www.footballworld.co.uk

Printed by Lavenham Press, Lavenham, Suffolk

Distributed by Vine House Distribution Ltd
Waldenbury, North Common, Challey, East Sussex,
BN8 4DR, England.
Tel: (01825) 723398
Email: sales@vinehouseuk.co.uk

Set in Times Roman

ISBN 0-95-48336-4-3

To Emily

My first for my first

Acknowledgements

A book of this stature needs a team and I had a team of Mackays and McGoverns and Shiltons and Robertsons behind me.

The following people provided crucial compass points towards a path of knowledge on all things Brian Clough. I offer hearty thanks to them for their contribution in preserving what must be shared with generations to come – the incomparable greatness of Brian Clough:

The following are not in any particular list of importance but do form a particularly important list: Contributors are not all listed here as their inclusion in the book will hopefully suffice as the biggest thank you I can offer.

The fans and players of Middlesbrough, Sunderland, Hartlepools United, Derby County, Brighton & Hove Albion, Leeds United and Nottingham Forest for their recollections and warmth.

Steve Goldby – www.ComeOnBoro.com

Marcus Alton – www.brianclough.com

Karl Pridmore – www.the-eye.com/nffc.htm

Stephen O'Malley, Editor – 4thegame

Darren Bowser – Arsenal-land

Todd Street – NFSDU Forum

Robert Nichols – *Fly Me To The Moon* and *Middlesbrough Evening Gazette*

Daniel Wynne – Tottenham Trust

Lesley Callaghan – Marketing and Communications Director, Sunderland FC. www.safc.com

Darren Griffiths – Media & Public Relations Manager, Everton FC

Jon (JF) – mancity.net

Steve Jones (aka Kipper) – www.bluekipper.com
Tim Gopspill – The Journalist Magazine
Mick Everett – Charlton Athletic FC www.cafc.co.uk
Jeff Willits – Derby County FC www.dcfc.net
Helen Robinson – *The Derby Telegraph*
Jon Crampin, *FourFourTwo* Magazine's book reviews editor
Simon Binns – Middlesbrough fan
Martin Knight – Author of *The Real Mackay, Ossie* and
Scoring At Half Time
Martin Neal – *Middlesbrough Evening Gazette*
Danny Francis & Susie Muir – Football World, publishers of this book

Thanks to Empics, Getty Images, The Northern Echo and The Brighton
Evening Argus for their superb photographic contributions.

Special mention is sprinkled on my mother and my sisters, Sally and
Jackie, for a lifetime of laughter and to my uncle Sid, a sorely missed
shining light.

To Stuart Liddell for his natural affinity with friendship

To Helen Kensett for her support, fun and enthusiasm

To Tony McDonald for guidance and selflessness

To Terry Connelly for his rainbow coloured character

And finally, every team needs a Dave Mackay and we had one in, well,
er . . . Dave Mackay actually.

Contents

Foreword

By Dave Mackay

He always called me David. I liked that. It was Brian Clough's way of immediately awarding dignity to his players. The first brick in the house of confidence he built around a player.

He had his own ideas on how he wanted his teams to play and, in turn, those ideas brought phenomenal success. It was his idea to make me a sweeper, which was a big departure from the midfield role I had always performed at Hearts and Spurs and for a man with tired legs it was most welcome. It was also a masterstroke, because it put three years on my career. It also worked on a financial level, because Cloughie bought me for £5,000 and sold me for £20,000.

All this after a general consensus in football that my career was over after the nine years I had spent at Tottenham and, believe me, I was part of that consensus! The man saw things that remained invisible to others.

My initial meeting with him was at White Hart Lane after a Spurs training session at Cheshunt. We sat on the grass in the corner of the stadium, the area where the players used to run out, and I listened about a Derby team I had hardly heard of from a man I barely knew. The meeting lasted no longer than 20 minutes and I'll always remember what he said: "David, if you come to Derby County we will win the second division."

He fired promises and predictions at me like a machine gun. Such was the confidence and determination of the man, I bought into it 100 per cent.

Looking back, there were so many bold decisions that could have gone wrong. He could have been criticised for playing me out of position, for instance, and the stories about cases of drinks on the team bus before

1

THE LIFE OF **BRIAN**

Brian congratulates his skipper, Dave Mackay (above), after he led Derby to the second division title in 1969. Facing page: The mutual respect was still obvious many years later.

crucial games could have given the press a field day. There would have been a push to annihilate instead of knight him!

That was the fine line you walked with Cloughie. He was unorthodox and that often upsets a lot of people. Brian found it easy to upset people. But his contribution has made many more people very happy, he has left behind so many great memories.

He treated me like a God. I always had Monday off while the other players were in for training. He put me up in the Midland Hotel, next to Derby station, because I was still living in London at the time and he wanted me to enjoy some time with my family. He knew the power and benefit of a loving family more than anything. He often told players that: "David Mackay decides what we do in training." He couldn't have put me any higher and the respect I had for him was tremendous. And don't forget, he was a younger man than me.

His partnership with Peter Taylor was a glorious one. As I have said before, Peter found the players and Brian set them on fire. Like all good partnerships, whether marital, business or otherwise, they knew each other back to front, could anticipate the other's thoughts and, most importantly, they gave each other space to breathe. It was because of their closeness that they fell out so dramatically. I am convinced that if Peter had not died so prematurely they would have healed their wounds and become muckers again in retirement.

2

When I got into management myself we had the disharmony at Derby as the backdrop but it never diminished the regard we had for each other. After all, I wouldn't have sold John McGovern and John O'Hare for £130,000 to just anyone, you know! The unsettled Derby fans called themselves the BBC (Bring Back Clough). How I wish we could.

When I was managing in the Middle East, Brian brought his team to play a pre-season friendly and he invited my wife and I out for dinner. He never forgot people. It was one of his finest assets. It was fully deserved to see and read the outpouring of affection people had for the great man after he died.

I find it extraordinarily poignant to be asked to pen this foreword. At the time of writing I have just had published my own autobiography in which I reflected on the only two English managers I ever played under: Bill Nicholson and Brian Clough. How lucky I was to be part of *their* story. Two totally different men with a common aim: to play good football, to win and to entertain the punters at the same time. A simple ethic but one that is not so visible today. They were both lovely and important men in my life and when they both passed away almost as soon as my book hit the shelves, I felt bereft and knew that era had most certainly come to an end.

Brian Clough was a genius, a one-off. There will never be another Cloughie!

Dave Mackay, November 2004

Introduction

Brian Clough aroused all the passions. He left an indelible mark on millions, filled trophy cabinets with football's richest prizes and made dreams come true for a privileged band of players and a vast army of fans.

He was everything a devotee of the great game could wish for – forthright, outrageous, controversial and wonderfully successful.

Assisted by Peter Taylor, Cloughie took teams to the great theatres of football at home and abroad and returned with points and trophies under his arm. He was driven by a philosophy, which had its roots in his playing days at Middlesbrough and Sunderland and had at its epicentre a winning style earned through hard graft and desire.

He was the catalyst for reshaping the way people thought about the game and he oversaw a renaissance of managerial ideas which will always prevail in small or large measure in the great game we call football.

He bucked trends, smashed convention and laughed at the orthodox – and the fans loved him for it.

The supporters of every team he played for or managed, with the possible exception of Leeds United, feted him. And in the words of John McGovern, even they must look back and think: "Maybe we should have persevered with him."

He was both dashing and brilliant, a master thinker of the game and in possession of a heavyweight personality which has long been given God-like status by the hoards of Cloughites around the world.

The Life of Brian is a quest for more. More Cloughie quotes from press conferences, more detail of his scoring feats from his prolific playing days and more from the fans who lapped it all up along the way. This book has sought to provide deeper insight into the 42-match unbeaten streak at

Nottingham Forest and more background to his two championship-winning seasons, at Derby County in 1972 and Forest in 1978 and the glorious European Cup-winning campaigns that followed.

More is offered on the pure drama of his 44 days at Leeds, from his managerial beginnings at Hartlepool and his brief sojourn at Brighton.

The more I searched, the more I found – in copious, entertaining chunks. There is simply too much for one book, or even several volumes and I hope *The Life of Brian* will provide a lasting tribute to this great man's immense contribution to the beautiful game.

Tim Crane
London, November 2004

Chapter 1
Middlesbrough

Hey, Young Man! – The Boro Goal Machine

They were brought up on goals at this club and brought up on great players; the George Hardwickes, Wilf Mannions, Mickey Fentons and George Camsells graced this ground for many years, so when I came along and started scoring goals, it was just the norm.

Brian Clough

I took great pride in telling my players how good they were. If one of my players scored a goal, I used to say: "I once put them in but I didn't put them in quite as good as that". The fact I scored five times more didn't make any difference.

Brian Clough

I always feel happy for goalscorers because they have the hardest job in the business.

Brian Clough

What a fantastic goalscoring record Brian Clough achieved in his comparatively short time as a player. He holds the record for reaching 250 goals faster than any other player in the history of the game. It is safe to say that feat will never be emulated.

Although predominantly a right-footed player, he also scored many with his head and left foot. His goalscoring achievements are all the more impressive given that he did not take the penalties, a responsibility which normally fell to Lloyd 'Lindy' Delapenha and, later, William Harris.

At Middlesbrough contemporary reports provide evidence of very bad luck in front of goal and a somewhat average supply from midfield and the flanks, which could have improved his impressive goal tally even further.

Brian Clough made his debut for Middlesbrough against Barnsley at home on September 17, 1955. He was third choice behind Wayman and McPherson in the first team but had caught the eye by scoring 15 in nine games for the reserves that season.

The Boro line-up for the Barnsley game, a 1-1 draw courtesy of a goal by Fitzsimons, was: Ugolini, Bilcliff, Stonehouse, Harris, Robinson, Dicks, Delapenha, Scott, Clough, Fitzsimons and Mitchell.

Clough still stands as the only Middlesbrough player to have scored five goals in a competitive match since the Second World War. It came against Brighton on August 23, 1958. For the record, he scored eight against the Seagulls that season.

His hat-trick tally of 16 is four ahead of George Elliott on the all-time list at Middlesbrough and seven shy of the club's ultimate hat-trick hero, George Camsell.

But for the defensive shortcomings of Middlesbrough during this period Brian Clough would have undoubtedly been part of a promotion-winning side.

Middlesbrough's manager throughout Clough's time at Ayresome Park was Bob Dennison, who held his young forward in very high regard. On December 15, 1956, Stan Cullis, legendary Wolves manager, visited Stoke's Victoria Ground for the visit of Boro, to run his eye over Clough. After the game Bob did not talk about his striker except to say: "We are building a team for Middlesbrough, not some other club".

Clough will always enjoy legendary status at Middlesbrough and the 197 league goals he scored during his nine years at Ayresome Park form the bulk of his 251 Football League career goals.

The need to preserve in print an account of this phenomenal league goals-to-games ratio is well overdue and hopefully the information to follow will evoke a wealth of great memories for fans who saw Cloughie make his mark in the North-East.

THE LIFE OF **BRIAN**

So we'll start with the first of his 197 league goals for Middlesbrough, at home to Leicester in October 1955 . . .

Season 1955-56

Goal 1 – October 8, 1955 v Leicester City (h), won 4-3
A combination of youth and local lads are fielded in this game in which Clough scores his first goal for Middlesbrough. Right-back Barnard, 21, left-back Stonehouse, 21, outside right Day, 18, and centre-forward Clough, 20, are all Teessiders with youth on their side. Clough, Fitzsimons, Delapenha (pen) and Harris secured the victory.

Goal 2 – October 15, 1955 v Lincoln City (a), won 2-1
It is strongly asserted in the press that William Day, 18, of Connaught Road, Middlesbrough, will join the ranks of the great players born on Teesside.
Tripps had put Lincoln level after Delapenha had opened the scoring on 40 minutes. Clough gained more confidence with a forceful display and a good winning goal.

Goal 3 – February 11, 1956 v Bristol City (h), won 2-1
Following a defeat at home to Liverpool the previous week, there are several changes to the team. Clough has been in and out of the squad and will end up playing only nine games since his debut. This is his third, and final, goal of the 1955-56 season. He converts a Fitzsimons pass into the net for what proved to be the winner. As early as the sixth minute Clough set up Delapenha for the opener, before Atyeo equalised 20 minutes later.

Season 1956-57

Goals 4 & 5 – August 21, 1956 v Bury (a), lost 2-3
At Gigg Lane, Clough and Sam Lawrie replace Boro's injured players Cooper and Day at centre-forward and outside-right respectively.
Sam Lawrie played direct, progressive and speedy football. He laid on both goals and had a superb header brilliantly saved a few seconds from the end. Clough, who scored twice, was desperately unlucky not to complete his hat-trick. He led the 'giant' Norman Neilson a merry dance.

Goals 6 & 7 – August 25, 1956 v Barnsley (a), won 3-1
At 21, and with only a handful of league appearances behind him, Clough is learning fast and in the process is helping himself to a healthy tally of

goals. Four from his two games this season is a fine return and he is unlucky not to have at least twice as many to his credit. He is establishing a reputation of being a bustling, strong, opportunist with a commendable work ethic.

Goal 8 – August 29, 1956 v Bury (h), drew 2-2
A flying leap by Bury keeper, Adams, could not rob Clough of his well taken goal. It was an unstoppable power drive with his left foot and took his goal haul to five in three games. It made it 2-0 on 39 minutes after Burbeck had put Middlesbrough ahead on 22 minutes. Once again the defence could not defend their lead and The Shakers left with a point.

Goal 9 – September 1, 1956 v Leicester City (a), drew 1-1
Clough gave a wholehearted performance, always harassing and bustling the defence and several times beating the experienced centre-half, Jack Froggatt, in the air and on the ground. Clough scored in the 46th minute but Leicester City's bustling centre-forward, Willie Gardner, equalised five minutes from the end.

Goals 10 & 11 – September 4, 1956 v Grimsby Town (a), lost 2-3
Boro are beaten by the weaker team after falling 3-0 behind. Clough's goals were well taken. The first, in the 53rd minute, came after Delapenha sent Fitzsimons through who pinpointed a pass for Clough to slam home. The second was a result of a cross from Delapenha, which Clough netted from close range. There was no time to complete the comeback.

Goal 12 – September 8, 1956 v Bristol Rovers (h), won 3-2
Clough is going from strength to strength. He played a vital part in this victory in front of 20,000 at Ayresome Park. What a fine goal he scored and it is noticeable how the accuracy of his passing has increased and how he has added more maturity to his play. Clough, in a relatively short time, has made big strides.

Goal 13 – September 12, Grimsby Town (h), won 2-1
Boro fans celebrated as Clough slashed the ball past Williams after Delapenha's tremendous strike from the penalty spot had put Boro ahead. Town had hit back within five minutes, Crosby chipping in a free kick over a packed line of defenders to score via the crossbar. So Boro were back where they started but this season they have a 21-year-old match-winner called Brian Clough and in the 74th minute this local lad hit a typically opportunist goal. Fitzsimons cut through and the ever alert Clough was on

THE LIFE OF **BRIAN**

hand to blast the ball past the helpless Williams for his 10th goal in seven matches. He has scored in every game he has played this season.

Goal 14 – September 22, 1956 v Liverpool (h), drew 1-1
A Robinson own goal had put the visitors ahead after 15 minutes but with seven minutes left Clough's header beats Liverpool keeper, Younger, who clawed in vain as the ball shot past him on 83 minutes.

Goal 15 – September 29, 1956 v Leyton Orient (a), drew 1-1
Peter Taylor gave a fine goalkeeping display at Brisbane Road. A lively Orient had some of the wind taken out of their sails by a 45th minute strike from Clough who was put through by Delapenha. A 77th minute equaliser from Facey restored parity.

Goal 16 – October 6, 1956 v Port Vale (h), won 3-1
Improving Boro keep climbing after establishing a convincing lead from goals by Delapenha (two penalties, 11 and 31 minutes) and Clough, who fully maintained his great form with a strike on 23 minutes. Port Vale's Stephenson pulled one back on 87 minutes. Esmond Million served as an able replacement for injured Peter Taylor.

Goal 17 – October 13, 1956 v Rotherham United (a), won 3-2
Derek McLean hits his first goal of the season. In only his second appearance for the club, Ronnie Burbeck looked the best forward on view. Clough kept up his great scoring record, albeit against the league's bottom club. The scorers for the home team were Stephenson (8 mins) and Selkirk (84). Clough (24), McLean (27) and Burbeck (89) won it for the visitors.

Goals 18 & 19 – October 20, 1956 v Bristol City (h), won 4-1
This slick Boro display brings their biggest win – Delapenha has his best game for weeks and his best goal for months (75mins). The understanding Clough and Day have built up in the reserves is coming to fruition, the young Clough scoring first on 37 minutes and then linking up with McLean for his second on 55 minutes. Harris ran half the length of the pitch before shooting past Cook on 85. Rogers (74) had earlier reduced the deficit for Bristol City. Promotion is in the thoughts of most Middlesbrough fans.

Goal 20 – November 3, 1956 v Fulham (h), won 3-1
McLean (8), Clough (26) and Burbeck (30) strike Boro into an unassailable lead. Hill (67) was Fulham's only reply. Harris, in defence, underlines his claim for another cap. Fitzsimons has his best game for some time and

Burbeck continues to look like a wonderful bargain. Boro are unbeaten in seven games.

Goals 21, 22 & 23 – November 10, 1956 v Nottingham Forest (a), won 4-0
Brian Clough on how he felt scoring his first league hat-trick, ironically against the team he would later lead to its greatest achievements: "It's wonderful, absolutely wonderful. Lindy Delapenha gave me the first goal, Ronnie Burbeck the second and Arthur Fitzsimons the last. Don't forget that and don't forget the work Derek McLean put in – what a fighter he is. The defence held out well when Forest were on top and I couldn't have done a thing without the lads around me. It is grand to play in the side these days because everyone is fighting and helping you all they can". Scorers: Clough (44, 68 and 79) Fitzsimons (80).

Goal 24 – December 1, 1956 v Lincoln City (h), won 3-0
Delapenha has another skilful, effective performance with goals on 23 and 41 minutes. Not even Lincoln's brilliant keeper, Downey, could stop Clough's power drive on 56 minutes.

Goals 25 & 26 – December 25, 1956 v Doncaster Rovers (h), won 3-2
Boro come from two goals down at half-time to score three times in seven second half minutes. Harris and the prolific Clough (twice) provide the Ayresome Park crowd with plenty of Christmas cheer. Walker and Kavanagh had given Doncaster a great start.

Goal 27 – January 12, 1957 v Bristol Rovers (a), won 2-0
Scott shot Boro into the lead in the 66th minute following some good approach word from Day. In the last minute Clough scored the second but struggles with influenza after this game. Meanwhile, tickets for the cup tie against Aston Villa are sold out within an hour.

Goal 28 – February 9, 1957 v Leyton Orient (h), lost 1-2
Boro have a lot of the play but make little use of it. Both Clough and McLean hit the bar but the forward line lacked a general. Clough opened the scoring on two minutes but Woosnam (20) and Johnston (41) replied for Orient. This defeat means that promotion is now only a mathematical possibility.

Goal 29 – February 16, 1957 v Port Vale (a), lost 1-2
The poor spell continues. Clough scores early after neat work from Scott

and McLean. He also flashes one inches wide of the upright before Vale's defence settle down and put Boro's forward line out of the picture.

Goals 30 & 31 – March 9, 1957 v Swansea Town (h), won 6-2
Boro's young forward line clicked into top gear after last week's poor show in the 2-1 defeat at Bristol City. Clough hit two and might have had four. Fitzsimons (3), Day (9), Harris (11) and McLean (35) add to the rout. McKintosh (59) and a Stonehouse own goal (89) fail to console Swansea.

Goal 32 – March 16, 1957 v Fulham (a), won 2-1
Team spirit is the key to Boro's win but back-to-back victories is still too little too late. Clough, watched by an England selector, heads a good goal soon after the start and often threatened danger. McLean scores the winner in the 29th minute, six minutes after Chamberlain's equaliser.

Goal 33 – March 23, 1957 v Nottingham Forest (h), drew 2-2
Clough makes McLean's goal on 70 minutes and scores the second on 82 minutes but he is too closely marked to pose a constant threat. Higham had put the visitors ahead on 10 minutes, while Barrett almost won it on 79.

Goal 34 – March 30, 1957 v West Ham United (a), drew 1-1
Clough opens the scoring on 18 minutes but Malcolm Allison equalised on 35. Clough was a well-marked man but scored a fine goal and almost hit a last-minute winner.

Goals 35 & 36 – April 6, 1957 v Blackburn Rovers (h), won 2-1
Blackburn attacked spiritedly with a depleted side but with four minutes to go they started to mistakenly mass in defence. Clough scored one lucky goal and one good one with seconds to go to deal Rovers' promotion hopes a shattering blow. It is Blackburn's first league defeat of the year.

Goal 37 – April 20, 1957 v Sheffield United (h), won 3-1
Clough had a busy night and was involved in all three goals. He was impeded twice and Harris converted both penalties on 34 and 51 minutes. On 74, Clough broke through to crash the ball past Hodgkinson in the United goal to make it 3-0. Sheffield Utd replied through Ringstead in the 83rd minute.

Goals 38, 39, 40 & 41 – April 22, 1957 v Huddersfield Town (h), won 7-2
The last home game of the season produces the biggest win. Clough had a field day, scoring four goals, including the indirect free-kick which

deflected off Huddersfield's Quested. Brian has been credited with that goal but, technically, it was an own goal. Clough also provided the passes for the goals by McLean and Fitzsimons. Not a bad afternoon's work by the 39-goal sharpshooter. Harris was Boro's other scorer.

Season 1957-58

Goal 42 – August 24, 1957 v Stoke City (a), lost 1-4
Despite getting off the mark early, Clough lacked adequate support and soon faded as the game developed. High hopes for Middlesbrough's promotion push this season suffer an early blow at Victoria Road and the victory was as convincing as the scoreline suggests.

Goals 43 & 44 – September 5, 1957 v Rotherham United (a), won 4-1
Clough gets back on the goal trail with a brace to put Boro back on the promotion trail. Boro were faster, cleverer and always more dangerous than Rotherham. Clough has been sitting too deep in recent games and the switch to further up the field paid dividends. He shot at every opportunity and was unlucky not to score a hat-trick.

Goals 45 & 46 – September 7, 1957 v Cardiff City (a), won 2-0
But for keeper Vearncombe making many fine saves, this would have been a roasting for Cardiff. The spearhead for all that was positive for Boro was Clough. Quick thinking and despatch by Peter Taylor in goal and the hard work put in by McLean ensured a good supply for Clough, who took his chances well.

Goals 47, 48, 49 & 50 – September 11, 1957 v Doncaster Rovers (h), won 5-0
Clough puts on a gala performance and Boro emerge as serious promotion candidates. It is Boro's first home victory of the season and despite his first class finishing, he insists it was no one-man show. Clough displayed all the

skills. He moved the ball well, linked up with his team-mates, ran himself into the ground and mastered the art of quality marksmanship. The press herald him as the latest in the line of great Boro strikers to follow Mannion, and Camsell. Clough scored his first with his lethal right foot, smacked a 20-yard rasper for the second, a bullet header for his hat-trick and added interest with a fourth. He even set up the opener for Burbeck. All this with barely an hour on the clock.

Goal 51 – October 5, 1957 v Charlton Athletic (h), won 2-0
Boro beat a good side in Charlton. Delapenha was too fast and wily and Clough scored his first goal in almost a month and should have had three. Burbeck had his best game of the season. Fitzsimons also scored.

Goals 52 & 53 – October 12, 1957 v Fulham (h), won 2-0
Clough scored a minute before half-time and full-time to secure two points for Boro. His second was one of the most remarkable goals seen at Ayresome Park for a very long time. Fulham's centre-half, Stapleton, and goalkeeper, Black, were left flummoxed as Clough robbed the former and waltzed past the latter before cracking the ball home. It will be talked about for as long as his second goal against Doncaster. His first was a headed effort.

Goal 54 – October 19, 1957 v Swansea (a), won 4-1
The previous night Clough had scored in the first floodlit game against Sunderland, where Boro ran out 2-0 winners. To follow this up with a 4-1 victory at the Vetch Field was highly impressive. Derek McLean stole the headlines with two well taken goals and on 57 minutes Burbeck scored a very clever goal when he lobbed the keeper from a very narrow angle. With four minutes left to play, Clough ensured he left his mark in Wales. Although he was closely marked by the burly Peake, Clough brought the ball down with his right foot and smacked it home with his left.

Goal 55 – October 26 v Derby County (h), won 3-2
Clough gets off the mark after just three minutes and Boro claim the win after Fitzsimons (17) and McLean (84) finally put paid to Derby's commendable spirit.

Goals 56 & 57 – November 9, 1957 v Lincoln City (h), won 3-1
The Imps are beaten on merit and now Boro are just two points behind the league leaders. Clough had scored on four and 12 minutes after good approach work from McLean. Burbeck added a third on 21. Northcott

replied on 55 minutes as Boro eased off.

Goals 58, 59, 60 & 61 – November 23, 1957 v Ipswich Town (h), won 5-2
Clough's four goals makes him the leading scoring in the country with 20 goals. One came from a perfect cross from Day, which was met by a powerful header. The move was reminiscent of their days in the reserves together and clearly that understanding has evolved in the first team. The pair of them ran the Suffolk men ragged and Day also got on the scoresheet. Ray Henderson's debut is remembered for all the right reasons as Middlesbrough ran out easy winners. Ipswich manager Alf Ramsey had no complaints. "We were beaten by the better team," said the man who would become England's next manager.

Goal 62 – December 21, 1957 v Stoke City (h), lost 1-3
Edwin Holliday makes his debut in this home defeat. Clough was fiercely marked by defender, Thompson, and although he did manage to score on 65 minutes, Boro were already 3-0 down. Kelly got two for Stoke and Coleman the other.

Goal 63 – January 18, 1958 v Liverpool (a), won 2-0
Liverpool are the league leaders and this is Boro's most impressive performance for some time. Holliday gets better with every game and Burbeck – who came in for Billy Day, who failed to obtain army leave – scored a fine goal to seal the win on 87 minutes. Clough was more than a match for Liverpool defender, Molyneux, and opened the scoring.

Goal 64 – February 1, 1958 v Barnsley (h), won 3-1
Clough is maturing quickly and added to his impressive tally. Peacock grabbed a pair for himself and McLean covered a tremendous amount of ground while Burbeck, in for Day, had another good game. Graham replied for the Tykes on 82 minutes.

Goals 65 & 66 – February 15, 1958 v Charlton Athletic (a), lost 2-6
Boro's defence was ripped open and panic set in early. Clough cracked home two good goals in the latter stages of the game (78 and 85 mins) and could have had more. It was, however, too little too late as the game was well and truly lost by then.

Goal 67 – February 22, 1958 v Ipswich Town (a), drew 1-1
A tighter defensive display and only one goal from Clough this week but it was enough to earn a point. Clough was very good indeed and, at 22, is

clearly one of the top three centre-forwards in the country. His goal came on 12 minutes.

Goals 68 & 69 – March 1, 1958 v Swansea (h), won 2-1
The scoreline flattered Swansea who should have been thumped. Brown stifled the threat of Swansea's outside-right, Allchurch, very effectively. Peacock and Holliday enjoyed good games but both squandered chances. Clough scored on seven and 75 minutes. Terry replied on 87.

Goal 70 – March 8, 1958 v Derby County (a), lost 1-2
Boro were clearly off form and woke up too late to salvage a point. Million played very well and kept the score respectable. Clough maintained his scoring sequence on 50 minutes but the game was already lost. He worked tirelessly to bring his colleagues into the game.

Goals 71 & 72 – March 15, 1958 v Bristol Rovers (h), won 4-3
Peacock grabs a hat-trick while the other goal came from Clough, who found it difficult to shake off Rovers' defender, Byle.

Goal 73 – March 22, 1958 v Lincoln City (a), won 3-2
Boro manager, Dennison, is recovering from a fractured cheekbone but takes his place on the bench at Sincil Bank. He sees Holliday shine and Clough maintains his rich vein of form with another well taken strike. Middlesbrough have won 16 points from the last 22 and although they beat moderate opposition here, they are moving up the table.

Goals 74 & 75 – March 29, 1958 v Notts County (h), won 3-1
Probably the likeliest candidates for a place amongst England's forward line at the moment are Bobby Smith, Jimmy Murray and Brian Clough. Of the three, Clough has scored most goals this season and added two more to his tally at the County Ground. It should be conceded that the other two are regularly meeting stronger opposition in the first division.

Goals 76, 77 & 78 – April 7, 1958 v Grimsby Town (h), won 5-1
Grimsby are hit by a whirlwind of goals. How much longer Clough can be ignored by the England selectors is foremost in the minds of many. He opened the scoring in the 15th minute with a superb header direct from Day's corner. Peacock restored the lead after Grimsby had carved an equaliser and then Clough claimed his hat-trick, before Harris secured the fifth from the penalty spot. Three of the five goals came from the industry of Day who returned to his army unit in Germany after the game.

Goals 79 & 80 – April 12, 1958 v Blackburn Rovers (h), lost 2-3
But for Peacock being thwarted by the upright and Clough by the legs of
the keeper, Boro would have had something to show for their fast,
exhilarating football. Clough completely overshadowed his opposite
number, Tommy Johnston, the country's leading goalscorer. Clough scored
twice (32 and 53 mins), was unlucky not to add three more and led his line
with skill. Blackburn's Vernon netted the last minute winner.

Goal 81 – April 21, 1958 v Fulham (a), won 1-0
An outstanding performance topped by Clough driving home Carl Taylor's
centre in the 20th minute. How the ball stayed out after Clough beat
Macedo, only to see it somehow bounce outwards from the inside of the
post, was a mystery. Such a freak angle of contact is very rarely seen.

Season 1958-59

Goals 82, 83, 84, 85 & 86 – August 23, 1958 v Brighton & H.A. (h),
won 9-0.
Brighton are hopeless and when Clough scores his fifth, and Boro's ninth,
the record books are scoured. It is revealed that George Camsell was the
only previous Boro player to notch five in one competitive match. They
came against Villa on September 9, 1935. Brighton manager, Billy Lane,
said: "We will not meet a better side in the division all season. I certainly
pray we don't!". In a post-match interview Clough jokes that it was the
added responsibility of being captain that held him back!

Goal 87 – August 25, 1958 v Sheffield United (a), won 1-0
This was a gallant performance from Middlesbrough's rearguard. A cross
from Harris and a melee in the box involving McLean saw the ball break
loose for Clough to hammer it home with a first-time, left-foot drive. Boro
have a goal average of 10 for and 0 against.

Goal 88 – August 30, 1958 v Grimsby Town (a), lost 2-3
Clough was almost shut out by the resolute defending of Joblin in this hard
match which Boro narrowly lost with just two minutes left. Day and
Clough scored Boro's goals.

Goals 89 & 90 – September 6, 1958 v Liverpool (h), won 2-1
This game was won by a resolute defence and an even more forceful
Clough. Liverpool keeper, Younger, was unable to hold a shot from

Peacock, which Clough pounced on after 35 minutes. He added a second on 57.

Goals 91 & 92 – September 11, 1958 v Rotherham United (a), won 4-1
Clough always threatened danger when he got the ball. He scored twice and teed up one. Rodgerson made his own headlines when also grabbing two with brilliant first-time shots – one with his left foot, the other with his right.

Goal 93 – September 13, 1958 v Stoke City (a), lost 1-3
Stoke City usually put the Indian sign on Middlesbrough so this result was no surprise. The same can be said of Walter Winterbottom whose presence at the game once again sees Clough put in a sub-standard display, despite opening the scoring with a scrappy goal. It is announced that Sunderland's Don Revie would not be signing for Middlesbrough.

Goal 94 – September 17, 1958 v Rotherham (h), lost 1-2
Boro manager Bob Dennison is still looking for an inside-forward. Clough scored a great goal past Rotherham's Quairney in the second half but it is not enough. He also goes close on two other occasions and there is a feeling that the young captain is being let down by his team-mates.

Goals 95 & 96 – October 25, 1958 v Fulham (h), lost 2-3
A very exciting game which once again saw Clough score and end up on the losing side. Middlesbrough sign Ray Yeoman on November 6 and captain Clough welcomes him to the side.

Goals 97, 98 & 99 – November 8, 1958 v Scunthorpe United, (h), won 6-1
Clough scores a jack-knife header on his way to his hat-trick but is upstaged by Peacock, who scores a hat-trick after just 21 minutes. Neill scores Scunthorpe's only reply.

Goal 100 – November 29, 1958 v Bristol Rovers (a), lost 1-3
Boro could not match a Bristol Rovers side with fire in their bellies. It started promisingly when Burbeck's shot was only parried and Clough followed up for a 10th minute opener and his 100th league goal. But it was a rare moment when he escaped the attention of Rovers centre-half, Byle.

Goal 101 – December, 6, 1958 v Ipswich Town (h), lost 2-3
Bill Fernie, signed from Celtic, makes his debut in this home defeat. The Clough-Peacock spearhead had an off day and despite scoring in the first

minute, Clough missed a few others. Burbeck scored Boro's second.

Goals 102, 103, 104 – December 20, 1958 v Brighton (a), won 6-4
Brian 'The Hove Hoodoo' Clough records eight goals against Brighton this
season as Middlesbrough claim the copyright in performing woefully one
day and scintilatingly the next. Boro played some glorious football and
Clough's hat-trick came in a 13-minute spell. He made two of the three
others as he was lauded by the press for his intelligent leadership. Peacock
(twice) and a Bertolini own goal did the rest. It is Boro's first away victory
for more than three months.

Goals 105 &106 – December 26, 1958 v Barnsley (h), won 3-1
Clough leads the way with a terrific right-foot shot which beat Hough in the
Barnsley goal. Day centres for Peacock to hammer home, while Clough
grabs a second as his form reaches new heights.

Goals 107 & 108 – January 1, 1959 v Huddersfield Town (h), won 3-1
Another brace for Clough who heads home Boro's third from a perfectly
placed McLean free-kick in the 52nd minute to clinch a well deserved
victory. Clough and Fernie are working up a fine understanding. Clough is
the leading scorer in the country on 27 goals.

Cloughie tangling with Charlton's Gordon Jago at The Valley in February 1958.

THE LIFE OF **BRIAN**

Goal 109 – February 14, 1959 v Bristol City (a), drew 2-2
Clough wins the penalty, which is converted by Harris. He also scores one
but goals from Atyeo and Etheridge ensured the points were shared.

Goals 110, 111 & 112 – February 28, 1959 v Scunthorpe United (a),
won 3-0
Yet another hat-trick for Clough, which brings his haul for the season to 31.
He also hit the bar and had other chances. He can do anything with a ball
and usually leaves it in the net. The pick of his goals was the third, which
came about when he collected a ball from Taylor and ran half the length of
the pitch before scoring. It was his sixth goal against Scunthorpe this
season.

Goal 113 – March 11, 1959 v Grimsby Town (h), won 1-0
Having twice hit the upright, Clough deserved his goal. Once again he
looked like the only Boro player likely to score.

Goal 114 – March 14, 1959 v Fulham (a), lost 2-3
Johnny Haynes had a fantastic game but the best ball-player on view was
Fernie. Clough scored again but Boro were undone by two goals in a
minute from Haynes and Barton. Harris scored from a lovely free-kick for
Boro which will be talked about for some time to come.

Goals 115, 116, 117 & 118 – March 21, 1959 v Swansea (h), won 6-2
This was a very slick Boro win capped once again by the star performer
Clough. Representatives from Newcastle are watching from the stands and
transfer speculation is rife. It appears that everyone is recognising Clough's
talent except the England selectors. Fernie and a Harris penalty were the
other goals.

Goal 119 – March 30, 1959 v Huddersfield Town (a), lost 1-5
Clough scored to make it 1-3 after the interval but the mini revival was
short-lived.

Goal 120 – April 4, 1959 v Leyton Orient (h), won 4-2
In the 69th minute Clough strengthens his claim for international honours
with a beautifully taken goal from 15 yards out. Earlier, two from Peacock
and another from Harris had established a lead for Boro.

Goal 121 – April 8, 1959 v Liverpool (a), won 2-1
An impressive display in front of 36,288 at Liverpool, where Holliday and

Clough ensure Middlesbrough's third consecutive league win at Anfield. They would continue this fine record over the next two seasons.

Goals 122 & 123 – April 11, 1959 v Derby County (a), won 3-0
Clough gave Boro the lead in the 20th minute. He started a jinking run not far outside the Derby box and beat the unsighted Oxford in the Rams' goal with a rather weak shot. He scored again in the 47th minute and Burbeck netted the other. Clough hurt his knee but returned after a few minutes to finish the game.

Goal 124 – April 18, 1959 v Bristol Rovers (h), drew 2-2
Clough finishes the season on 42 goals, about half of which he has created himself. He equalised in the 63rd minute. Standing with his back to the goal, he received a pass from Harris and in one smooth motion pivoted and blasted the ball into the roof of the net.

Season 1959-60

Goals 125, 126, 127 & 128 – September 5, 1959 v Plymouth Argyle (h), won 6-2
Clough opens his account for the season in some style. His first was a volley from Day's centre, the second a ground shot from a Fernie pass. The third and fourth rounded off a goalfest for the young striker.

Goal 129 – September 9, 1959 v Hull City (h), won 4-0
Clough scores one and has one disallowed and also wastes three easy chances. His goal was a beauty. Receiving a pass from Harris just inside the penalty area, he calmly hammered the ball into the bottom of the net. A Harris penalty and goals from Yeoman and Day finished the rout.

Goal 130 – September 14, 1959 v Hull City (a), drew 3-3
Two goals from Peacock and another from Clough should have been enough but plucky Hull nick a point.

Goals 131, 132 & 133 – September 19, 1959 v Charlton Athletic (h), won 3-0
Clough continues his great form by netting all three. On 27 minutes Fernie's cross finds Clough who slots home easily. On 38, Clough showed just why people view him as an England centre-forward when he drove the ball in from an oblique angle. Another searing ground shot earned Clough his hat-trick on 70 minutes.

Leyton Orient's Sid Bishop can't stop this Cloughie effort at Orient in November 1958.

Goals 134 & 135 – October 3, 1959 v Scunthorpe United (h), won 3-1
Despite Clough's two goals, this game marks the occasion of Fernie's one and only strike for Middlesbrough this season. Harris lobbed the ball into the area for Clough to calmly steer the ball into the net. Great passing between Fernie and Day allowed Clough to smash home his second and Middlesbrough's third. Thomas replied for Scunthorpe.

Goal 136 – October 24, 1959 v Lincoln City (h), won 3-2
McLean scores his first goals of the season, while Clough brilliantly headed home a cross from Day in the 80th minute.

Goals 137, 138 & 139 – November 21, 1959 v Bristol Rovers (h), won 5-1
Clough's third hat-trick of the season is the driving force behind this comprehensive victory. On 15 minutes, Ayresome Park explodes to applaud

a wonder goal from Clough. Picking up the ball in midfield, he beat one man and played it out to Holliday. The winger returned the pass and Clough cracked it home from 25 yards. His second was courtesy of great play from Fernie who set it up for an open goal. Clough, playing at his brilliant best, completed his hat-trick on 46 minutes.

Goals 140 & 141 – December 5, 1959 v Brighton & H.A. (h), won 4-1
In the seventh minute a slip in Brighton's defence allowed Clough to score the easiest of goals. In the second half Clough dived in to head home a cross from Day. Harris (penalty) and Peacock scored the others.

Goals 142, 143 & 144 – December 12, 1959 v Stoke City (a), won 5-2
Clough scores three quick goals in the second half to put the game beyond Stoke. Day and Holliday net the other two.

Goal 145 – December 19, 1959 v Portsmouth (a), lost 3-6
Clough's goal came from a header from close range after a great cross from Day had been touched on by Peacock. Further goals by Day and a Harris penalty is not enough to prevent a rampant Portsmouth taking both points.

Goal 146 – December 28, 1959 v Rotherham United (h), won 3-0
Six minutes from time, Clough is once again in the right spot to leap high above the Rotherham defence to head in Holliday's cross. Holliday nabbed one himself and Harris again scored a penalty – the eighth of 11 goals he would net from the spot this season.

Goals 147 & 148 – January 2, 1960 v Derby County (h), won 3-0
Clough scores his brace in the last five minutes. His first came when he chested down a pass from McLean and blazed a rasping drive past Oxford in the Derby goal. With two minutes left he sailed high above three defenders to score a spectacular goal. McLean scored the other.

Goal 149 – January 16, 1960 v Plymouth Argyle (a), drew 2-2
Peacock and a cannonball from Clough earn a point against the Pilgrims.

Goals 150 & 151 – January 23, 1960 v Liverpool (h), drew 3-3
On six minutes Holliday's cross to McLean is headed down for Clough who struck like lightning to slam the ball home. Liverpool then take a 3-1 lead. Good approach work from Fernie and McLean provided the second Boro goal for Clough, who calmly sidefooted the ball into the net. A Harris penalty earned a point.

THE LIFE OF **BRIAN**

Goals 152, 153 & 154 – February 13, 1960 v Bristol City (h), won 6-3
Another hat-trick from Clough, who opens the scoring after netting
Fernie's pass on seven minutes. His second and third came in the second
half, while goals from McLean (2) and a Harris penalty finish off City.

Goals 155 & 156 – March 12, 1960 v Lincoln City (a), lost 2-5
Clough equalised Lincoln's opener after Holliday had beaten two defenders
and squared the ball for Clough to score easily. By half-time, Lincoln were
4-1 up. In the second half some fine work on the left from Holliday and
Peacock gave Clough his second goal from 12 yards.

Goal 157 – March 19, 1960 v Swansea, (h), won 2-0
Middlesbrough went in front in the 75th minute after Peacock hit it to
Waldock, who calmly slotted it past King in the Swansea goal. Nine
minutes later Clough was on the spot to head in for the second.

Goals 158 & 159 – April 2, 1960 v Ipswich Town (h), won 4-1
Peacock, Holliday and two for Clough secures the points for
Middlesbrough. Clough scores two in a minute after sidefooting into the
net late in the second half and following up with a header from a Holliday
cross.

Goal 160 – April 9, 1960 v Bristol Rovers (a), won 2-0
In the 41st minute a powerful shot from 25 yards gave Clough yet another
memorable moment in a Boro shirt. Despite contemporary reports which
credited Peacock with the other goal, Holloway is often chronicled in
history books as being the second scorer.

Goal 161 – April 16, 1960 v Stoke City (h), won 1-0
Burbeck started the attack which gave Boro the lead in the 35th minute.
Younger fails to clear a shot from Stonehouse and Clough was on hand to
tap home.

Goal 162 – April 18, 1960 v Sheffield United (h), lost 1-2
Clough scores in the dying seconds but to no avail, despite chances galore
for Boro.

Goal 163 – April 23, 1960 v Brighton & H.A. (a), lost 2-3
Clough scored in the 66th minute and, despite an own goal by the Seagulls,
it was still not enough to take anything on the long trek back to the North-
East.

Season 1960-61

Goal 164 – September 3, 1960 v Rotherham United (a), won 2-1
This was a vastly improved display from Clough who has been slow to find
his touch this season. He scored on 20 minutes and Peacock added a second
five minutes later.

Goals 165 & 166 – September 10, Southampton (h), won 5-0
Saints keeper, Reynolds, has a torrid time as Clough regains his top form
to score twice on 19 and 79 minutes. On this form he could play for any
club in the country. Windross on 16, Peacock 47 and Harris 85 completed
the rout.

Goal 167 – September 15, 1960 v Scunthorpe United (a), drew 1-1
Clough hits an upright with Scunthorpe goalkeeper, Jones, nowhere near.
His poor luck continues when centre-half, Howard, impedes him in the area
but Boro go unrewarded. Thomas puts Scunthorpe into the lead to the
delight of the majority of fans at the old Showground. On 74 minutes the
equaliser came when Clough stabbed home Waldock's sliced effort.

Goals 168 & 169 – September 17, 1960 v Leeds United (a), drew 4-4
This thriller at Elland Road typifies the Middlesbrough experience. They
are capable of scoring and conceding a hatful of goals in the same game.
For the record, Henderson, McLean and two from Clough earned Boro a
point. One of Clough's goals came when Purgin failed to hold Peacock's
fierce shot and he was on hand to score.

Goal 170 – September 24, 1960 v Sunderland (h), won 1-0
This was never a classic but provided a great result for Middlesbrough.
Clough came through with an improved performance but was never at his
lethal best. The only goal came on 56 minutes when Sunderland keeper,
Wakeham, failed to hold a backpass from Ashurst and Clough beat Hurley
to it to net the winner.

Goal 171 – October 1, 1960 v Brighton & H.A. (h), drew 2-2
Brian Clough's eighth minute goal couldn't inspire Middlesbrough and
they became increasingly ragged as the game went on. Brighton took
advantage early in the second half with two goals in as many minutes and
looked set to take the points until Henderson's equaliser.

Goals 172 & 173 – October 8, 1960 v Plymouth Argyle (a), drew 3-3

Yet another thriller and Clough was once again the star of the attack. Burbeck, on eight minutes, and Clough (15 and 41 mins) established a 3-1 lead but it wasn't enough despite a wholehearted display.

Goal 174 – October 15, 1960 v Norwich City (h), won 2-0
The first goal came when Henderson collected a pass from Clough and saw his shot deflected into the net. For the second, Kennon failed to prevent Clough's header from flashing just inside the upright.

Goals 175, 176 & 177 – October 22, 1960 v Charlton Athletic (a), drew 6-6
The game of the season but a goal from McLean, a rare brace from Burbeck and another hat-trick from Clough still fails to take both points from a gutsy Charlton side that scored the final equaliser in the 89th minute.

Goal 178 – October 29, 1960 v Sheffield United (h), won 3-1
Clough met an able opponent in Shaw but he hadn't met his match because he scored a fine goal, made another and tested goalkeeper Hodgkinson more than once.

Goal 179 – November 12, 1960 v Swansea Town (h), won 3-1
Clough scores the first vital goal past Town keeper King, has a hand in the second and kept Swansea's defence worried throughout. Peacock scored twice and should have gained a hat-trick.

Goal 180 – December 10, 1960 v Huddersfield Town (h), won 2-1
Despite turning his ankle in a friendly against The Army the previous night, Clough takes his place in the team and climbs high to head home the winner from Burbeck's cross with five minutes left on the clock.
Appleby won plaudits for his many saves, most notably from a wonderful shot on the turn from Massey. McNeil's own goal was an early setback but Harris followed up his missed penalty to equalise.

Goal 181 – December 26, 1960 v Leyton Orient (h), won 2-0
Despite being well held by O's commanding centre-half, Bishop, Clough scored a very fine goal. Burbeck beat a couple of men on the left and put the ball across for Clough, who climbed high to head down into the net on 71 minutes. Kaye unleashed a great left-foot shot for the second, nine minutes later.

Goals 182 & 183 – December 31, 1960 v Liverpool, (a), won 4-3

Clough scores two in this thriller at Anfield, where Middlesbrough maintain their fine record. Peacock and an own goal provide the other goals.

Goal 184 – January 14, 1961 v Rotherham United (h), drew 2-2
Clough scores one of the finest goals at Ayresome Park for a long time. He is almost on the by-line when he shoots and scores from an impossible angle to beat Rotherham keeper, Ironside. Peacock hits the bar a couple of times and Perry and Karkman had twice give Rotherham the lead. A Morgan own goal had gifted Middlesbrough their first equaliser.

Goals 185, 186 & 187 – January 28, 1961 v Portsmouth (a), won 3-0
Clough is the scourge of goalkeepers as he scores all three. Yeoman had a great game and, along with Kaye and Harris, was instrumental in helping Clough to his hat-trick. The goals came in the 14th, 68th and 89th minutes and had all the old assurance Clough has mastered down the years.

Goals 188 & 189 – February 4, 1961 v Leeds United (h), won 3-0
Boro's Number Nine does it again with a brace of goals to excite the Ayresome Park faithful. Jack Charlton is no match for Clough who almost gained his second hat-trick in eight days. When he is in full cry like this, he really is a sight to behold. Peacock added a fine goal into the bargain.

Goal 190 – March 14, 1961 v Leyton Orient (a), drew 1-1
Clough ends his barren spell of five matches by heading a fine goal from Day's centre in the 24th minute. Billy Horner, 18, plays well on his debut at left-half, tackling keenly and always looking for the ball.

Goal 191 – March 25, 1961 v Stoke City (h), won 1-0
Clough collects Waldock's pass on the edge off the area and scores the only goal of the game on 46 minutes. Despite the goal, press reports suggest he is not the player of old. TV coverage of the Grand National contributes to Boro's lowest league gate of all-time – 8,534.

Goal 192 – April 1, 1961 v Lincoln City (a), lost 2-5
Bottom of the division and booked for relegation, Lincoln thump five past lacklustre Middlesbrough. Despite scoring a good goal, Clough was well marked and could not make much impact. The display was described in the local press as "inept and spineless". City's scorers were Smith, Bannister and Chapman (3), while Peacock netted Boro's other goal.

THE LIFE OF BRIAN

Goal 193 – April 3, 1961 v Ipswich Town (h), won 3-1
This was a game to remember. Clough's goal came when he chased a long clearance by Harris and, after Town's Bailey and Nelson got into a tangle, Clough seized on the ball and shot into an empty net to make it 3-1 in the final minute. Yeoman (25 mins) had opened the scoring but Ipswich equalised through Phillips. Day was brought down for a penalty, which Harris (88) duly converted.

Goals 194 & 195 – April 8, 1961 v Luton Town (h), won 2-1
Town keeper Baynham claims Clough to be offside for his goal but his protests are in vain. It made the score 2-1 and Boro never looked back. It was Clough's second goal and he was twice unlucky. He opened the scoring on 34 minutes but Legate (46) equalised before Boro's winner two minutes later.

Goal 196 – April 15, 1961 v Swansea Town (a), lost 2-3
Clough almost salvages a point when he hits the bar in the final minute with Swansea keeper, Dwyer, rooted to the spot. Swansea's left-half, Saunders, scored an absolute gem from 40 yards. It came just a minute after Peacock had shot Boro into the lead following a good run from Day. Davies and Reynolds made it 3-1 to the Welsh side soon after the resumption before Clough clawed back a goal on 60 minutes. It was only a half-chance which he took well and fully deserved after having ran himself into the ground.

Goal 197 – April 22, 1961 v Portsmouth (h), won 3-0
Clough should have repeated his hat-trick feat at Pompey earlier in the year but he had to settle for one and held the line well. Waldock's perseverance was rewarded with two goals, which condemned Portsmouth to relegation.

Cup Goals

1956-57

January 10, 1957 – Charlton Athletic (a), won 3-2 (FAC3 Replay)
Boro add fight to their skill and Ray Barnard, who scored an own goal, said: "It must have looked as though I was trying to pass back to Peter Taylor but I wasn't. I meant to clear the ball but it bounced awkwardly off my leg and bounced into the net. I felt terrible and when Brian Clough smacked in the equaliser on half-time, it was like a ton weight lifted off my shoulders." Clough, in front of England manager, Walter Winterbottom, scored with a strong, left-foot drive.

January 26, 1957 v Aston Villa (h), lost 2-3 (FAC 4)
42,000 showed up for this cup thriller. A half-time lead was cruelly whittled away by a superior Villa side. Harris was the pick of the Boro wing-halfs but Delapenha scarcely took his comeback opportunity. Burbeck has played better and Clough and Scott tried valiantly but with limited success.

1957-58

January 4, 1958 v Derby County (h), won 5-0 (FAC 3)
The average age of Boro's forward line is 20, one of the youngest in the country. This is an unexpected result, as Boro have lost five of their last six league games and haven't won at home since November. Holliday and Peacock (2) steal the headlines with a great showing, while Clough and Day also get on the scoresheet.

January 25, 1958 v Stoke City (a), lost 1-3 (FAC 4)
Boro's young triers go out of the cup after scoring first and looking the better side. Clough scored the opener on 12 minutes but his effort suffered from lack of support and Stoke got back into the game, scoring three times through Wilshaw.

1959-60

January 9, 1960 v Sheffield Wednesday (a), lost 1-2 (FAC 3)
Clough scores but the 5,000 travelling Middlesbrough fans leave Hillsborough disappointed.

1960-61

October 3, 1960 v Cardiff City (h), lost 3-4 (LC 2)
This is the first-ever League Cup tie at Ayresome Park and despite scoring twice, Clough missed three great chances. Cardiff deserved their win but a Peacock header brought respectability to the result. Clough's first goal came when he collected a Peacock pass and ran through to beat Vearncombe. His second came at 1-4, when he slammed home a brilliant shot in the 78th minute.

Chapter 2
England

Two Caps

England Pick Clough At Last!
Northern Daily Mail – **Monday, October 12, 1959**

I am as delighted for young Edwin (Holliday) as I am for myself. This is one of the happiest days of my life and I only hope I can do well on Saturday. I want to succeed for my own sake but also for those wonderful Boro supporters that have always cheered me on. I just hope I don't let anyone down.
Brian Clough on hearing the news of his selection

We wish them the best luck in the world in their first international appearances. Incidentally, I am very happy that it has been proved that if a footballer plays well enough for Middlesbrough in the second division, he can still win a cap for England.
Bob Dennison, Middlesbrough manager

Brian Clough must produce the goods tomorrow against Sweden at Wembley or he will be England's ex-centre-forward
The Middlesbrough Evening Gazette

The day Brian Clough was finally selected to represent his country should have been the dawn of a new era in our national game. The tremendous current of excitement that reverberated around Middlesbrough was tangible.

The selection of Clough's fellow striker, Edwin Holliday, meant that two Middlesbrough players would fill the three-pronged attack preferred by England manager Walter Winterbottom. As added kudos for Middlesbrough, Harold Shepherdson was selected to be the trainer.

The team chosen to play against Wales at Ninian Park, Cardiff on October 17, 1959 was as follows:

Eddie Hopkinson (Bolton Wanderers)
Don Howe (West Bromwich Albion)
Tony Allen (Stoke City)
Ron Clayton (Blackburn Rovers) – Captain
Trevor Smith (Birmingham City)
Ron Flowers (Wolverhampton Wanderers)
John Connelly (Burnley)
Jimmy Greaves (Chelsea)
Brian Clough (Middlesbrough)
Bobby Charlton (Manchester United)
Edwin Holliday (Middlesbrough)
Reserve: Johnny Smith (West Ham United)

England's team to face Wales at Cardiff in October 1959. Back row, l to r: Bobby Charlton, Don Howe, Eddie Hopkinson, Trevor Smith, Tony Allen, Ron Flowers. Front: John Connelly, Jimmy Greaves, Ron Clayton, Brian Clough, Edwin Holliday.

THE LIFE OF **BRIAN**

The match itself took place after a torrential downpour and contemporary reports were unanimous in the view that Clough had seldom seen the ball in the 1-1 draw.

The North-East press were very vocal in suggesting that although he did not score – that honour went to a young Jimmy Greaves, while Moore netted for the Welsh – Clough had done enough to warrant selection for the next match, against Sweden at Wembley later that month, on October 28.

According to the *Middlesbrough Evening Gazette*, "The Middlesbrough captain acquitted himself well. He was intelligent and thoughtful with his distribution. He worked non-stop and was always on the look out for an opening in the Welsh rearguard. He laid on a number of good chances for his colleagues but he waited and waited and waited for a return pass which would put him in with a scoring chance, but he waited in vain".

Brian's father, Joe, had made the nine-hour coach trip to Cardiff along with 40 members of the Wilton ICI Polythene Maintenance Social Section, where Joe Clough worked.

It was announced on the day before the Sweden game at Wembley that the team would remain unchanged and so it was widely perceived that it would be make-or-break for Brian.

Heavy rain before the game made the surface slippery but Clough had a

England manager Walter Winterbottom prior to the Sweden game with (l to r): Ron Clayton, trainer Harold Shepherdson, Brian Clough, Tony Allen, Don Howe, Trevor Smith, Maurice Setters (reserve), Bobby Charlton, Jimmy Greaves, Edwin Holliday.

fine start when he set up the opening goal for John Connelly in the first-half. Bobby Charlton added a second for England but Sweden still ran out shock 3-2 winners. England were described a team that had started brightly but then "faltered, fumbled and fluffed their way to defeat which looked inevitable long before half-time".

The North-East press asked: "Why had not Greaves and Charlton played to the strengths of their centre-forward?"

Consequently, the supporters of Clough agree that he did *not* fail. They reasoned that he didn't get the chance to fail or to succeed. The gravity of the defeat, and the pressure on Winterbottom to make changes, can be measured by the Swedish press, which described the events as "The Miracle at Wembley".

FOOTBALL ASSOCIATION INTERNATIONAL

ENGLAND

v

SWEDEN

WEDNESDAY, OCTOBER 28th, 1959   KICK-OFF 2.30 pm

EMPIRE STADIUM

WEMBLEY

OFFICIAL PROGRAMME   -   ONE SHILLING

Chapter 3
Sunderland
Pain and Glory

They were happy days at Sunderland. I was young, happily married, my
first two kids were born in Sunderland, I was cracking in the goals.
Lovely days. Sunderland people are beautiful.
Brian Clough

My sharpness has gone.
Brian Clough to Peter Taylor after his attempted return from injury

I first encountered Clough at Sunderland when he was coaching the
youth team after retiring through injury.
He was an idol in Sunderland even then.
John O'Hare

Brian Clough agreed to join Sunderland on a quayside in Southampton after returning from a trip with his wife, Barbara, to Cannes. Sunderland boss, Alan Brown, a man who would have a tremendous influence on Clough, the manager, made the trek down to get his man for a transfer fee of £42,000.

Get him he did – and 29 league goals and five cup goals in his first season was the return. Sunderland finished the 1961-62 campaign within one goal of promotion to the first division but lost out to runners-up Leyton Orient on the final day in a super-charged finale in which Liverpool were champions.

Brian's team-mates at Sunderland consisted of Mel Smith, Cecil Irwin, Joe Kiernan, Len Ashurst, Jimmy O'Neill, Jimmy Lewis, Billy Richardson, Charlie Hurley, Jack Overfield, Harry Hooper, Peter Wakeham, Martin Harvey, Keith Hird, Willie McPheat, Stan Anderson, George Herd, Jimmy McNab, Ambrose Fogarty, Ian Lawther, Brian Usher, Dominic ('Nicky') Sharkey, John Dillon, Alistair Murray, John Stidd, Jim Montgomery and Jimmy Potter.

Unaffected by the disappointment of just missing out on promotion to the top flight, Brian was in scintillating form during the 1962-63 season and had scored an incredible haul of 24 league goals by Christmas. Then tragedy struck.

It all came to a disastrous and abrupt end on Boxing Day, 1962, when his goalscoring feats were frozen in the record books after the hideous combination of a brutal winter, a bad ball from Jimmy McNab and the shoulder of Bury goalkeeper, Chris Harker. The incident ended one of the most tremendous, and ultimately the most enduring of records in the game. Like so many of Brian Clough's achievements, this phenomenal record goes largely unrecognised in football yearbooks and encyclopaedias.

Incredibly, 197 of those 250 goals were scored while he was at Middlesbrough, and following is a description of the remaining 53. Just for good measure, Brian scored one final goal – against Leeds United – after his aborted return from injury. It stands as the only occasion when he scored in the top division.

This left his league goalscoring record at 251 from 274 games. Those figures, like the numbers 2 (Take your pick from European Cups, League championships or England caps), 4 (League Cups) 42 (The Streak), 44 (Leeds United) and 93 (Brian's farewell) are inescapably related to the great man. Perhaps the most memorable number with which we associate Brian Clough is captured in his own pithy remark: "I may not have been the best manager there's been but I was certainly in the top one".

But for injury in the 1962-63 season he could have also been Sunderland's

THE LIFE OF **BRIAN**

"top one" striker. It is without question that David Halliday's record of 43 league goals in only 42 appearances during Sunderland's 1928-29 season, to set the club record for a single year, would have come under serious threat from the prolific and hungry Brian Clough.

A crowd of 31,000 Mackems turned out for his testimonial game and the following record of goal achievements is partly the reason why . . .

1961-62

August 19, 1961 v Walsall (a), lost 3-4
Brian Clough enjoys a scoring league debut after some fine approach work from Herd but finishes on the losing side. This high-scoring defeat is in many ways a microcosm of his experience as a player.

He was closely marked and described as 'subdued' in the press. Richard's hat-trick did the trick for Walsall. Clough needs just two more league goals to reach 200. His tally of 198 have been earned in just 215 games.

August 3, 1961 v Liverpool (h), lost 1-4
Herd and Hurley are out injured. Clough scores a brilliant equaliser but Liverpool are just too strong and run out easy winners. Fogarty and McPheat deserved more from their efforts. Clough is on the brink of joining the exclusive '200 Club'.

September 9, 1961 v Leeds United (h), won 2-1
Clough scores his 200th and 201st league goals to take all the points against Leeds. Fogarty squares to Clough who beats Humphries easily on seven minutes. In the 31st minute another through ball from Fogarty isn't dealt with by Hair and Clough pounces to dribble around Humphries for his second. Despite McCole's reply, Leeds were beaten.

September 19, 1961 v Bury (a), lost 2-3
Bury race into a 2-0 lead on 30 minutes. Overfield and Fogarty combine well on the left and when Stokoe slips, Clough races in to place his shot well wide of Adams on 53 minutes. Beaumont makes it 3-1 six minutes later and despite McNab's header (63), Bury held on.

September 27, 1961 v Bury (h), won 3-0
Clough scores his first hat-trick for Sunderland and offers a big thank you to Hooper who had a big hand in all three. On 28 minutes, Hooper sends over a cross and a subtle feint from Clough beats both Stokoe and Adams. Clough was back on his heels as he headed the ball home. Seven minutes

later, Hooper puts in another cross for Clough, who beats Stokoe on the turn and slots past Adams. With three minutes left, Clough collects a pass from Hooper, holds off two powerful tackles before executing a great shot.

October 14, 1961 v Leyton Orient (h), won 2-1
A Roker crowd of 36,780 saw Clough play a stormer. Dunmore put Leyton Orient ahead in the ninth minute but goals on 25 and 52 minutes gave Sunderland victory. Clough looks offside for the first, from Ashurst's cross, but there was no signal and he slotted the ball past O's keeper George. For the second, Herd, Clough and Hooper combined well before Hooper beat Lewis, only to see his shot saved. Clough was on hand to win the game.

October 28, 1961 v Plymouth Argyle (h), won 5-0
Hooper and Herd return after missing a game and Sunderland sweep the Pilgrims aside. Hooper opened the scoring on nine minutes and ended it with a penalty (71). In between, Clough (22, 43 and 54), earns another hat-trick. For his first, Clough collects a ball from Anderson and turns to beat MacLaren with a powerful right-foot shot. For his second the move was started by Herd who won possession and set Hooper away on the right. His decisive cross was met by the head of Clough. Herd was once again instrumental in Clough's third goal, crossing for the forward to hammer home his third hat-trick of the season.

November 25, 1961 v Luton Town (h), drew 2-2
A Hooper penalty (17 mins) put Sunderland in front but a gift goal draws Luton level (58). On 70 minutes, Groves fouls Hooper and although Irwin slices his kick, Ashurst tidies up and puts the ball in the area for Clough to tee up a shot which Standen scarcely saw. Sunderland were still unable to see out the victory.

December 9, 1961 v Swansea Town (h), won 7-2
The Cloughie Show started in the second-half. His first beat King from close range after excellent approach work on the right from Hooper. His second came on 68 minutes when a clearance from Wakeham ran clear of the Swansea defence and Clough got there ahead of Fogarty to slam the ball into the empty net. Clough completed his hat-trick (69) after a brilliant run by Hooper set him up for a great right-foot shot. Fogarty (23, 36 and 89) also claimed a hat-trick while Hooper scored the other on 88 minutes. Reynolds (22) and Williams (64, pen) was the only response from Swansea.

December 12, 1961 v Newcastle United (a), drew 2-2

Clough makes it tough on Newcastle in the 85th Tyne-Wear derby at St. James' Park in front of a passionate 49,120 supporters. Trailing one-nil, Hooper went down the line, beating Wilson and Bell, before crossing for Clough who tangled with McGrath before slotting home. Two minutes later, Newcastle went ahead when McGuigan beat Wakeham. With only five minutes to go, Hooper broke away on the right and hit another excellent centre. McGrath struggled to clear and Clough dashed in to score. Every goal was greeted with swarms of enthusiastic supporters spilling onto the pitch.

December 16, 1961 v Walsall (h), won 3-0

Christmas shopping commitments meant only 22,000 were present for this convincing win. Overfield scored his first of the season when beating Boswell with a cleverly placed shot. He followed it up with a second on 68 minutes after another brilliant run by Hooper. Hooper did most of the work for the third goal (73) when tangling with four defenders and sidestepping a number of tackles before lifting the ball towards the goal. Clough beat the calls for offside to round Boswell and shoot into an empty goal.

March 24, 1962 v Huddersfield Town (h), won 3-1

Clough and Hooper have been out for the last five games but return to some effect against the Terriers. Jimmy O'Neill and Jimmy Davison make way. Clough hasn't scored this year but soon addresses that with a hat trick. His first came on eight minutes when Coddington slips to leave Clough to nip in and score. On 21 minutes Hooper put in a corner, which was headed out to Clough whose shot flew past Wood into the net. Clough's hat-trick was complete on 61 minutes when he finished off a brilliant move between Hooper and Herd. Balderstone on 75 minutes replied for Huddersfield.

March 31, 1962 v Middlesbrough (a), won 1-0

There was plenty of needle in this frenetic Tees-Wear Derby, watched by 35,000, and Clough defeated his former club with a goal on 34 minutes after rising to beat Gates in the air and heading past Appleby's reach in the Boro goal. Clough managed to get the ball into the net a second time from an Overfield centre but was adjudged to be offside. Peacock of Middlesbrough and Anderson of Sunderland have both been called up for England.

April 7 1962 v Southampton (h), won 3-0

Sunderland climb to fourth after this emphatic victory and have only

Liverpool, Leyton Orient and Plymouth in front of them. Clough beats Godfrey on five minutes. Herd turns in McPheat's shot (69) and Hooper completed the scoring (75) by beating two defenders before cracking home a terrific right-foot shot.

April 23, 1962 v Rotherham United (h), won 4-0
The goal of the game came from Hooper who ran 50 yards before hitting a great strike on eight minutes. Hurley netted the second from a corner from Overfield. Three minutes later, just over the hour mark, McPheat makes it three. The fourth came from Clough (71) and ran Hooper close for the goal of the game. Morgan crosses after some clever work from Herd. Clough, pulling the ball down from practically shoulder-height with the inside of his right-foot, turned smartly to beat Ironside.

April 24, 1962 v Rotherham United (a), won 3-0
How times have changed. Two games in two days and three goals for Clough, who is driving the promotion train at full speed. McPheat crosses for Clough who whips round to crack the ball into the roof of the net. Anderson sets up Hurley for the second and the third came when Irwin's free-kick ran loose to Clough, who dashed in to crack the ball home. Rotherham are glad to see the back of him. Sunderland have taken 15 points from their last eight games. They have scored 19 and conceded only two. They are second behind champions Liverpool and it's now between Leyton Orient and Sunderland for the second promotion place.

April 28, 1962 v Swansea Town (a), drew 1-1
Disaster for Sunderland who lose out to Leyton Orient on the final day of the season. O's won 2-0 in East London to Bury while Sunderland cannot translate their dominance at the Vetch Field into goals. Three thousand travelling fans witnessed abject misery. Clough played his part when cleverly beating two men to score past King after 20 minutes. Swansea's goal from Reynolds (64) came as a surprise and losing McNab to injury took some of the thrust out of Sunderland.

Brian Clough's goals total for the season: League 29 League Cup 5

1962-63

August 18, 1962 v Middlesbrough (h), won 3-1
A crowd of well over 50,000 saw this game and 19-year-old outside-left, Clarke, make his debut. Clough scores past Appleby from close range for

the first on 36 minutes. Anderson's free-kick was turned in by Hurley (66) and four minutes later Sunderland stormed through again on the right. Herd and Hooper combine brilliantly to set up Clough, who cracks home the third. Burbeck replied (78).

August 28, 1962 v Charlton Athletic (a), drew 2-2

McNab scored the first and then a powerful run down the left from Fogarty beat Sewell and found Clough. He beat two defenders before scoring past Hinton. Kinsey pulls one back for Charlton (60) and the comeback is complete from Kinsey's second, this time a header (70).

September 1, 1962 v Swansea Town (h), won 3-1

Right result – wrong season, as Sunderland run out comfortable winners. Hurley and Fogarty are released for international duty with Republic of Ireland. Morgans beat Montgomery after 13 minutes but Clough restores parity (32) after Herd's shot was charged down and Clough struck from close range. Just before half-time Clough scored again after Davison's corner wasn't cleared and his first-time shot ended in the net. Anderson nabbed the third from a quick throw-in and a cross from Irwin.

September 5, 1962 v Rotherham United (h), won 2-0

Yet again Clough breaches Rotherham's defence after picking up a ball from Irwin, swivelling smartly and beating Ironside in the Rotherham goal. Some neat work between Clough and Fogarty gave the latter the opportunity to race clear and score the second goal. For the record, Rotherham did manage to keep Clough at bay a week later when winning 4-2 in the League Cup at Milmoor.

September 15, 1962 v Luton Town (h), won 3-1

When Montgomery could only parry Walden's cross for Turner to score on 53 minutes, it looked unlikely Sunderland would get anything from the game. However, Luton's goal was a beginning rather than an end and goals from Clough (58 and 78) and Fogarty (75) secured the victory. Clough timed his run perfectly to beat Baynham for the equaliser after a header from Anderson had put him through. Sunderland went ahead after excellent work from Mulhall set up Fogarty after Clough's shot had been dropped. Mulhall fed Herd to fire in a cross, which Clough rose to bury for the third.

September 22, 1962 v Southampton (a), won 4-2

Clough opened the scoring (31 mins) after picking up a cross from Kiernan and, with a defender on either side, turned smartly and beat

Reynolds with a low drive. Kirby equalised 10 minutes later before Clough stepped up a gear. A quick free-kick from Fogarty found Davison whose quick cross was turned into the goal by Clough (52). Clough then had a third disallowed for offside before rising above all others to turn home a Davison cross (65). Mulhall (75) scored a deserved goal after being put clear by Herd. Williams restored some respectability (83) but the day – and the ball – belonged to Clough.

October 6, 1962 v Derby County (h), won 3-0
Sunderland are described as making the Rams look like sheep in this convincing win. Mulhall was under pressure from Barrowcliffe and laid it off to Clough, who scored from close range. Two minutes later, McNab's cross was turned in by Young for an own goal. Anderson ran through the middle and set Clough clear who made no mistake for the third.

October 13, 1962 v Newcastle United (a), drew 1-1
A game dominated by the two defences was watched by 62,170. On 30 minutes the Herd-Davison-Clough triumvirate yields another goal but Newcastle equalise just before half-time through Kerray.

October 20, 1962 v Walsall (h), won 5-0
This could have been double-figures. Wave after wave of attacks are engineered and the contribution of Herd is substantial. Davison is the first to beat Boswell on 10 minutes. He also rounds off the rout (87). In between, Anderson (44), Clough (54), and Mulhall (74) help themselves to a headline or two. Clough's goal was the result of a Mulhall corner at which he rose with a well placed header.

October 27, 1962 v Norwich City (a), lost 2-4
Clough brings Sunderland level after a one-two with Fogarty is finished off by beating Kennon from close range. Fogarty puts Sunderland ahead before half-time but the Canaries pulverise the Rokerites in the second half, netting three without reply. Hill's hat-trick inflicts most damage.

November 3, 1962 v Grimsby Town (h), won 6-2
Grimsby's net bulges with Sunderland rockets as Clough registers another hat-trick. Davison scored two in the first 15 minutes while Herd added the sixth (70). Clough's first came after being put through by Herd to beat White in the Grimsby goal. His second came courtesy of Mulhall who resisted four fierce tackles before setting up Clough to score on the turn. His third was scored after firing home from Davison's centre.

THE LIFE OF **BRIAN**

November 10, 1962 v Plymouth Argyle (a), drew 1-1

Clough saves the day with a last-minute equaliser to spoil Plymouth's party. Montgomery had dropped Corbett's cross and Lill hit the back of the net (61). However, a superb pass from Crossan unleashed Clough who beat McLaren with a low drive.

December 1, 1962 v Cardiff City (h), won 2-1

Allchurch tried to get Cardiff back into the game with a strike on 60 minutes but Sunderland's two goals proved to be enough. Davison had put them ahead in the first-half and then threaded a pass through to Clough (52) who had an even chance against the Bluebirds keeper, Vearncombe. Clough was always the favourite in such situations and this was no exception.

December 8, 1962 v Huddersfield Town (a), won 3-0

A vital win against promotion rivals at Leeds Road, where Sunderland climb to second – behind Chelsea – after an easy win. McNab puts Clough through on 46 minutes and he runs on to beat Wood with a tremendous shot. Three minutes later Crossan puts away Herd whose pass is collected by Clough, who beats Wood with another great shot.

December 15, 1962 v Middlesbrough (a), drew 3-3

Goals from Mulhall (19), Clough (23), and Herd (25) put Sunderland into an early 3-0 lead. But Horner, Kaye and Orrit somehow managed to make it all square by half-time. Clough's goal came when he ran onto a lobbed pass to beat Emerson with ease. Sunderland were lucky to hold on to a point after McNab's injury.

December 22, 1962 v Leeds United (h), won 2-1

Brian Clough's 250th league goal. The idea that he will score just one more in his career is anathema to all logical thinking. He has scored 24 league goals before Christmas, which is nothing short of exceptional. He also has four League Cup goals, including two in the 3-2 victory over Blackburn which helped Sunderland to the semi-finals.

December 26, 1962 v Bury (h) lost 0-1

Treacherous weather conditions provided the backdrop to Sunderland's worse news for years. Their ace striker, Brian Clough, is stretchered off in the 27th minute with an injury that effectively ends his playing career. The prognosis was torn ligaments in the right knee, which will leave him in plaster for months. Clough was set for an all-time league and cup scoring record in his most prolific season to date. Sunderland look to Nicky

Sharkey, a 19-year old prospect, to carry on Clough's mantle.

Clough scored one more goal in his career. It came against Leeds United and it was the only occasion in which he scored in the top division.

It brought the curtain down on a playing career that spanned 274 games and yielded an astonishing 251 league goals.

Cup Goals

September 25, 1961 v Bolton Wanderers (LC 1 replay) (h), won 1-0

After the sides had drawn 1-1 at Burnden Park, Fogarty sends Hooper flying down the wing and breaks clear of Farrimond, before hitting a tremendous shot on the run. Clough was already racing through the middle and touches home past Hopkinson. Clough has one disallowed seven minutes from the end.

October 4, 1961 v Walsall (LC 2) (h), won 5-2

Another hat-trick at Roker Park. The first came from a header after a great effort from Hurley after 43 minutes. On 67, Clough and McPheat combine well before Clough scores with a 20-yard strike. Three minutes from time, Herd passes to Clough, who beats Ball from close range. McNab and a Hill own goal complete the rout. Taylor scored both for Walsall.

The end...Brian receives attention at Roker Park after his fateful Boxing Day injury.

February 7, 1962 v Norwich City (LC 5) (h), lost 1-4

The only bright spot for Sunderland in this game came on 70 minutes when Anderson centred from the right and Clough met the ball at waist-height to volley it wide of Kennon.

September 24, 1962 v Oldham Athletic (LC 2) (h), won 7-1

After taking the lead, Oldham succumbed to a Sunderland onslaught. Mulhall equalised, Fogarty added a second, and Kiernan a third after a deflection off Williams. On the hour Clough got on the scoresheet when converting Fogarty's blocked shot. After Kiernan grabbed his second from a pass by Mulhall, Clough added to Oldham's misery by slamming the sixth past Bollands. Fogarty deservedly scored a second and Sunderland's seventh.

December 5, 1962 v Blackburn Rovers (LC 5) (h), won 3-2

A terrific night at Roker Park sees Sunderland progress to the semi-final of the League Cup for the first time. Sadly, events on Boxing Day mean that Clough will not be part of it. This was Clough's night, scoring twice against a team from the top flight. His first goal was laid on by Herd after 11 minutes but he still beat two defenders before scoring past Else – a terrific strike which put Sunderland level. He then had a shot saved by Else but McNab was on hand to make it 2-1. On 83 minutes, Sunderland made it safe after good work from Fogarty set up an easy goal for Clough. A late own goal ensured the jitters were part of a thrilling cup night.

For the record, Clough-less Sunderland lost 3-1 to Aston Villa at Roker Park in the first leg of the semi-final on January 12, 1963. Due to the worst winter weather for many years, which resulted in a massive fixture backlog, the second leg – which ended goalless – was not played until April 22.

Chapter 4
Hartlepools United
The Boss

Hartlepools won't be at the bottom of the fourth division for much longer. They have the players to climb up. If you want to see some stuff from Saturday onwards get yourself down to a little place called Harlepools. It won't be a little place for very long.
Brian Clough at dinner on the night of his testimonial at Sunderland

To describe Hartlepools' ground as a tip would be giving a bonus to a tip.
Brian Clough in retirement

I know we will get better and we are not going to beat everything right away. The job we have to do will take time and patience but I am confident we can do it.
Brian Clough after the FA Cup victory over Workington, November 1965

We really were rock bottom but got a spirit together. We avoided re-election, which was the norm for Hartlepools before I went there. We got seventh from bottom, which was the equivalent of winning the Premiership
Brian Clough in retirement

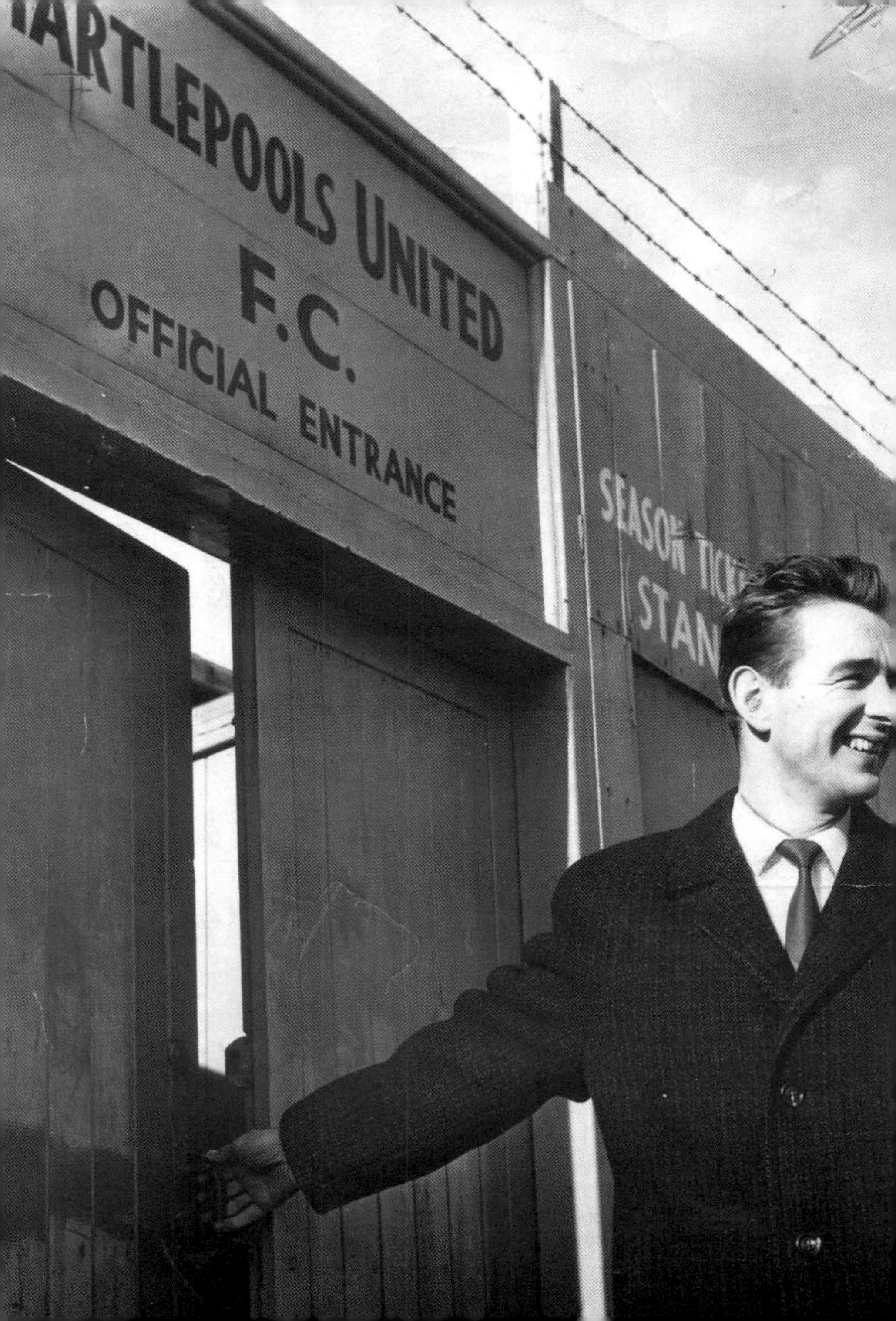
ARTLEPOOLS UNITED
F.C.
OFFICIAL ENTRANCE
SEASON TICK
STAN

Brian Clough's first taste of football management can be viewed now as a blueprint for what was in store throughout the remainder of his eventful career. It stood him in very good stead.

Limited resources, a difficult chairman and raising the game and attitude of average players were aspects of the Hartlepool experience he would, in small or large measure, encounter at Derby County, Brighton & Hove Albion, Leeds United and Nottingham Forest.

Although his time at Hartlepool between 1965 and 1967 (when they were still known as Hartlepools United before the 's' was dropped in 1968) did not yield the same degree of success he achieved at Derby or Forest, in relative terms Brian Clough – ably assisted by Peter Taylor – brought a renaissance to this little north-eastern outpost which has never been forgotten.

Just a cursory look at the final league positions, before and during the Clough period, speaks volumes. Before his arrival the club had finished rock bottom, or one off the basement position, in five of the previous six seasons. In the two seasons in which Clough was in charge, Hartlepool finished seventh from bottom and eighth from top.

The season after he left they were promoted while under the management of Angus McLean, although it is fair to say that several of Clough's players remained on the staff.

The 35 league victories masterminded by Clough and Taylor are set out below . . .

October 30, 1965 v Bradford Park Avenue (a), won 3-1

Hartlepool greet Brian Clough with a win. Cliff Wright put 'Pools' ahead and on 35 minutes Mulvaney makes it two. Ellan replies for Bradford but Mulvaney's second, six minutes from time, secured the win in the mud.

November 6, 1965 v Crewe Alexandra (h), won 4-1

Prior to the game, Clough says: "All I want to do is win on Saturday and we shall". The television cameras are present for Clough and Peter Taylor's first game in charge at home. They make much of Clough being the Godfather of Taylor's two children. After 15 minutes, Wright opens the scoring, only for Crewe's Cane to equalise on 65. Pythian restores the lead two minutes later and Wright (88) claims a second.

January 8, 1966 v Port Vale (h), won 2-0

The goals came from Thomson on 60 minutes and Phythian (87).

Brian Grant enjoyed a good debut while Clough's other signing, goalkeeper Les Green, is starting to settle in. Green would later be reunited with

THE LIFE OF **BRIAN**

Cloughie at Derby County in 1968.

Clough says: "I will need cash if we are going to survive. I don't want a licence to print money, I just need a few thousand to buy the three or four players I want. I don't even need the amount Alvan Williams (previous manager) was given to spend on players".

February 5, 1966 v Wrexham (h), won 4-2
Wright slips a pass to Pythian who turns and scores on three minutes. Wrexham then take the lead before Pythian (58) helps himself to a second, He also lays off the ball to Fogarty (63) who ran on to score his first goal of the season. Thompson (89) rounds off the scoring with a close-range effort.

February 26, 1966 v Aldershot (h), won 3-0
Hartlepools start the game placed 92nd in the Football League. Clough has added Gill to his two previous signings, Green and Grant, and is clearly addressing the defensive shortcomings as a priority. Pythian, Fogarty and Thompson get the goals in this easy victory.

March 5, 1966 v Luton Town (h), won 2-0
Phythian sweeps in to score on 14 minutes after Luton fail to clear. Eight minutes after the break Wright hammers home Stornton's free-kick.

March 25, 1966 v Chesterfield (a), won 3-1
Mulvaney scored on 23 minutes and after Whitehead (54) had equalised, Phythian scored a fine headed goal 20 minutes later. Parry scored his first league goal after converting Phythian's pass.

Clough has added outside-right, John Bates, from Consett, to the squad but fails in his attempt to sign his former Middlesbrough chums, Billy Day and Edwin Holliday.

Clough says: "If we can get the players we want, and I think we can, promotion next year is by no means out of the question. There isn't a lot of difference between the top and the bottom of the fourth division. Next season I want to see 10,000 in this ground for every home match".

There is an incident involving Stan Stornton, who complained about being dropped and was suspended for two weeks. He says: "I am going to ask the club to release me from my contract. I was happy here last year but now I want to get away as quickly as possible".

April 8, 1966 v Stockport County (h), won 2-1
This is the first win in a very successful Easter campaign

Clough: "Ken Simpkins wants to take weight off and the only effective way of doing this is by dieting. You can do all the training you like but you will put it all back on by eating the wrong food".

April 9, 1966 v Notts County (h), won 2-0
Wright pulled the ball back for Fogarty to scored the first on 36 minutes. Thompson (56) crashes home Thompson's cross to make it 2-0.

April 11, 1966 v Stockport County (a), won 2-1
Hartlepools have taken the maximum six points from the Easter programme.

Clough: "Never change a winning team? Nonsense. That is the coward's way out. If I had not changed the team that beat Stockport on Friday we would have been beaten by Notts County on the Saturday. I haven't got a lot of players, and choice is limited, but this does not stop me picking my side to counter a particular situation".

April 23, 1966 v Chester City, won 2-0
Pythian exchanges a one-two with Fogarty to open the scoring on 36 minutes. In the second half Bates crossed low into the area and Fogarty (69) back-heeled it home from two yards.

May 7, 1966 Lincoln City (h), won 3-1
Thompson sets up Mulvaney who hits a great strike to open the scoring. For Pools' second, a Mulvaney shot is pushed out and Fogarty (35) follows up to score. After Lincoln had got one back, Mulvaney made sure of both points with a close-range effort.

May 9, 1966 v Barrow (h), won 3-0
Ashworth put Pools ahead after 36 minutes when he ran in to head home Hamilton's corner. Cliff Wright (74) made it two by converting Phythian's pass. With nine minutes left, Mulvaney makes sure after Drysdale headed on.

1966-67

August 27, 1966 v Wrexham (h), won 2-1
Post-World Cup euphoria is transmitted to Victoria Park, where Fogarty
sets up Livingstone to score from 10 yards. On 54 minutes, McCloughlin
equalised for Wrexham after Simpkins had mis-punched. On the hour
Pythian benefits from a defensive mistake and goes through to score from
12 yards.

September 5, 1966 v Barrow (h), won 2-1
John McGovern makes a winning debut at home to unbeaten Barrow. The
winner was scored 10 minutes from time after McGovern's cross was put
in by Livingstone. Earlier Hartlepools had levelled on 18 minutes when
Fogarty had converted a penalty.

September 24, 1966 v Exeter City (h), won 3-1
Mulvaney set up Phythian for a goal after just one minute following good
build-up by McGovern on the right. Smith (68) equalised for Exeter but
Phythian (73) shoots home from 12 yards. On 81 minutes, Mulvaney
collects Somers' cross from the left to go on and score.

September 26, 1966 v Barrow (a), won 3-2
Hartlepools come from two down after 25 minutes to score three in seven
minutes and cause a shock defeat of Barrow. A header from Mulvaney, a
tap-in from Phythian and a second for him, when he shot home from
Somers' free-kick, do the damage. Pools are the only side in the division to
beat Barrow and now they have completed the double over them.

October 15, 1966 v Lincoln City (h), won 5-0
This is Clough's biggest margin of victory since his arrival almost one year
ago. The goals were scored by Phythian, Mulvaney (2) and a penalty each
for Fogarty and Wright

October 17, 1966 v Newport County (a), won 2-0
Phythian continues his fine start to the season with the opener on 38
minutes from the six-yard box. The match was put beyond doubt by
Sheridan, who scored his first goal for the club after 68 minutes, a 25 yard
effort after good work from Somers.

A letter in the *Northern Daily Mail* is full of praise for Brian Clough.
It reads: "Mr Clough is doing a wonderful job with the team considering he
has spent next to nothing and he is providing the best football I have seen

here in over 40 years. However, I do not agree with the speculation surrounding the sale of Fogarty".

October 29, 1966 v Stockport County (h), won 1-0

The one-nil defeat of Stockport, courtesy of yet another goal from Phythian, is followed by a determined assertion from Clough:
"If I had the money to buy the one or two players I want, I would guarantee promotion. That is how confident I am of succeeding".

December 3, 1966 v Bradford Park Avenue (a), won 2-1

Clough dropped three for this game – keeper Simpkins was replaced by Green; John Gill, signed from Mansfield for £2,500, is dropped for Bobby MacLeod, and inside-right Terry Bell made way for Tony Parry, who is in for his first game of the season. Strikes from Wrighton (53) and a Taylor own goal (68) make it 2-0 in the second half before Waddell gets one back for Bradford.

December 10, 1966 v Port Vale (h), won 2-1

Goals came from Mulvaney and the prolific Phythian

Clough: "We have done a lot here with no cash at all but it's both flattering and frightening that people think we have a magic wand and can do even better. We can't, and it is frustrating, too, because we are so close to what we are trying to achieve.
"With the present team I think our chances of getting promoted are fairly remote. The players are doing as well as they can but I think they are a little short of what is needed to go up. However, the difference between us and the top teams is only slight and it would not take a lot to rectify it".

December 17, 1966 v Aldershot (h), won 3-2

Mulvaney scored in the first 30 seconds to get Hartlepool off to a flier and further goals from Wright and a second from Mulvaney eight minutes from time finally see off a determined Aldershot.

Clough: "We are in the right position and while we have done well, we need to build further to make it all worthwhile".

December 27, 1966 v Brentford (a), won 2-1

Hartlepool go up to fourth after this win, behind Stockport, Southport and Barrow. Brentford took the lead through Docherty on 57 minutes but 20 minutes later Phythian followed up from Wright to equalise. The winner was also scored by Phythian – his 17th of the season.

January 21, 1967 v Bradford (h), won 1-0
Hartlepools have invested £15,000 in floodlights but a comical piece in the local press suggests that "it will take more than lights to pull the locals away from the social clubs to watch a football match".
The goal came in the 77th minute, when Phythian scored from close in.

January 30, 1967 v Chester City (h), won 3-2
McGovern was instrumental in this victory and he set up Phythian for a class goal, after a 25-yard strike. He also supplied the cross for Mulvaney to net the third.

February 11, 1967 v Crewe Alexandra (a), won 2-1
Simpkins plays a blinder to keep Crewe at bay. Mulvaney scored the first from an acute angle while Wright despatched the second.

February 25, 1967 v York City (h), won 4-2
Albert Broadbent, bought from Bradford PA for £3,000, makes his debut. He replaced Terry Bell.

Clough: "I have bought Albert for one reason and one reason only – to provide the missing link in midfield. He is not here to score goals or defend but simply to create for others. Some people may question why I have paid so much for a 31-year-old but if a player is 21 or 41, it doesn't matter so long as he does a job for you. We have a young side and Albert's experience will do them no harm at all".

March 11, 1967 v Barnsley (a), won 2-1
Phythian scores again on 22 minutes before Earnshaw equalises. The remarkable season Phythian is enjoying continues on 56 minutes when he grabs the winner.

March 18, 1967 v Chesterfield (h), won 3-2
Two more from Phythian and one from Mulvaney put Hartlepools three up after 35 minutes.

March 24, 1967 v Luton Town (h), won 2-1
Phythian's 25th goal comes from the penalty spot. French beats Green from 25 yards for the equaliser but Mulvaney scores the winner.

March 27, 1967 v Luton Town (a), won 2-0

The club's Easter coach travel was supplied by Gold Case Travel Ltd and they undertook the trip to Luton free of charge. The Bourn Hotel and another coach company, Richardsons, also helped towards the club's expenses. Clough describe all contributions as "lovely gestures".

Parry scores his first league goal of the season while the emerging McGovern nets a great effort from 25 yards.

April 1, 1967 v Rochdale (h), won 2-1

Clough offers a big 'thank you' to both Middlesbrough and Sunderland who are helping out by treating injury-hit Pools' players and providing facilities to the Victoria Road ground. Somers and Broadbent cancel out Rochdale's opener late on.

April 15, 1967 v Notts County (h), won 2-1

Clough: "I know it is starting to look as though we need a miracle to get promotion – the way the other results are going at the top anything could happen. While we still have a chance we will be going ahead full steam".

Mulvaney cancels out County's opener from Brace and then nets again to clinch victory on 68 minutes. Green is made a free agent and is finished with Hartlepools.

Even the kids couldn't wait to get a piece of Cloughie as the young manager made his mark.

THE LIFE OF **BRIAN**

April 29, 1967 v Bradford Park Avenue (h), won 2-0
McGovern is out for rest of the season after injuring himself in the defeat at Halifax. John Joyce, 17, made his league debut in Clough's final victory for Hartlepools United.
This was described as a "Somers Day" in the press after he scored one of the goals. The other went to Ernie Phythian who shared 44 goals with Mulvaney over the season. Phythian equalled the club's post-war record of 26 goals in a season with a great shot from 15 yards.

Cup Run

v Workington Town (h), won 3-1 (FAC 1)
The greatest success of Brian Clough's era was the progress of Willie McPheat, who scored two vital goals.

v Wrexham (h), won 2–0 (FAC 2)
Wright (56 minutes) and Mulvaney (79) put Pools into the third round. Two consecutive victories in the FA Cup haven't happened for many a long year. The overnight frost forms the wintry backdrop to the tie.
Clough: "I would really like another small club at home but that is a bit too much to hope for."

After Hartlepools draw Huddersfield Town, away, in the third round, Clough said: "Don't get the idea we are depressed in any way. We'll be going into this one like we go into any other. We aim to win".

January 24, 1966 v Huddersfield Town (a), (FAC 3), lost 1-3
The game is shrouded in controversy when Huddersfield are awarded a goal even though the ball had not completely crossed the line. Pools keeper Kenny Simpkins has always maintained it wasn't a legitimate goal.
Att: 24,505 – the largest crowd to watch Hartlepools since 1952 (v Burnley, 38,608)

Chapter 5
Derby County
Path to the Championship

I came from Burton Albion 18 months ago to be with Brian Clough and I intend to stay with Brian Clough. He's fulfilled all that I thought of him when I came from Burton and I intend to go with Brian Clough to the top of the tree, and we'll start at Derby.
Peter Taylor in 1967

Brian absolutely breezed into the place and sorted it out from top to bottom. The first thing he did was walk down the corridor asking for the removal of all the old sepia prints depicting County legends back to the Steve Bloomer era. It was a symbolic break with the past and the obsession with the cup-winning side of the 40s. The message was simple: 'We're looking back no more, we're looking forward'.
Neil Hallam, journalist

I wanted everybody to feel how I felt last night. It was an unforgettable feeling and I only wish everybody in the world could have shared it with me.
Brian Clough on Derby County's first league championship

There is no doubt that Derby County would have been the team of the 70s had Brian Clough and Peter Taylor not walked out in such dramatic fashion in 1973.

In five years they had transformed the football landscape and took Derby up, over, and beyond even the most fantastic and elaborate of dreams. The thousands of Derby fans fortunate enough to experience it have marvellous memories to cherish forever. Derby fans who didn't have heard the tales so many times that the afterglow of Clough and Taylor will never be distinguished. They were simply the best that Derby County has ever seen and the following spotlight on the Rams' First Division championship-winning season and greatest-ever European Cup campaign will hopefully preserve a little more of that Clough magic.

On the eve of the campaign there was a prophetic comment in *The Sun* from Peter Batt. "Whatever happens this season, Brian Clough's obvious potential must blossom into overwhelming success sometime within the next 10 years. He is an intelligent, articulate radical."

And so after the second division title win of 1969 and those never-to-be-forgotten cup-ties of the late 60s, the scene was set for the greatest journey Derby County fans had ever witnessed . . .

August 14, 1971 v Manchester United (h), drew 2-2

Derby look set to be brushed aside by United who adjust quicker to the boggy conditions and go in at the break 2-0 down courtesy of Kidd and Gowling. Clough's half-time briefing does the trick as the Rams pile on the pressure and take a point from a very exciting encounter. Hector and Wignall score the goals in a game Derby should have won but for their slow start.

Derby County: Boulton; Webster, Robson, McGovern, Hennessey, Todd, Gemmill, Wignall, O'Hare, Hector, Hinton. Sub: Durban.

Manchester United: Stepney; O'Neill, Dunne, Gowling, James, Sadler, Morgan, Kidd, Charlton, Law, Best. Sub: Aston.

Referee: Mr. D. Pugh (Chester)

Post-match Comments:

Brian Clough: "If you play like that again you will get me the sack".

Other Comments: The Wignall-O'Hare-Hector spearhead suffered because the supply line wasn't there and Gemmill and McGovern must take the blame.

August 18, 1971 v West Ham United (h), won 2-0

Derby race out of the traps this time and are two up after eight minutes.

There is confusion over the first scorer, with O'Hare being credited by most but a Bobby Moore own goal seemed more likely.
Derby County: Boulton; Webster, Robson, McGovern, Hennessey, Todd, Gemmill, Wignall, O'Hare, Hector, Hinton. Sub: Durban.
West Ham United: Ferguson; McDowell, Lampard, Bonds, Stephenson, Moore, Ayris (Howe 71), Best, Hurst, Taylor, Robson.
Referee: Mr. J. Hunting (Leicester)

Post-match Comments:
Brian Clough: "West Ham are a good footballing side but we made hard work of it today. We will play better than this".

August 21, 1971 v Leicester City (a), won 2-0
Leicester lose for the first time since January and Derby are heralded for their stylish superiority. Shilton keeps the scoreline respectable for Foxes. Hector (63) and a Hinton penalty three minutes later take the spoils.
Leicester City: Shilton; Whitworth, Nish, Kellard, Sjoberg, Cross, Farrington, Brown, Fern, Sammels, Glover. Sub: Carlin.
Derby County: Boulton; Webster, Robson, McGovern, Hennessey, Todd, Gemmill, Wignall, O'Hare, Hector, Hinton. Sub: McFarland.
Referee: Mr. R. C. Challis (Tonbridge)

Post-match Comments:
Brian Clough is in the Bill Shankly class when it comes to praising his side. But he was unusually modest and refused to be drawn on the thoughts provoked by his side's stunning display – Derby for the league championship?

August 24, 1971 v Coventry City (a), drew 2-2
Derby do not perform well and Roy McFarland makes two mistakes to help Coventry grab both their goals. The saving grace comes in the shape of a Wignall header, neatly glanced in with only five minutes left on the clock.

Post-match Comments:
Brian Clough: "We deserved nothing and will win nothing if continuing to play like that. It was unfortunate for Roy because he has been absolutely brilliant for us."
Derby County: Boulton; Todd, Robson; Hennessey, McFarland, McGovern, Gemmill, Durban, O'Hare, Hector, Hinton. Sub: Webster.

August 28, 1971 v Southampton, (h), drew 2-2

Before the game Brian Clough sends out the warning: "Start kicking and you'll end up in the book!" as it is suggested that the best way to stop Derby is through sheer force. Derby out-play Southampton for over an hour as McGovern and Hector establish a comfortable lead. But then Rams concede twice in the final 20 minutes, with Stokes and Gabriel netting for Saints.

Derby County: Boulton; Todd, Robson; Hennessey, McFarland, McGovern, Gemmill, Durban, O'Hare, Hector, Hinton. Sub: Webster.

Southampton: Martin; Kirkup, Fry; Fisher, McGrath, Gabriel; Paine, Channon, Stokes, O'Neil, Jenkins. Sub: Walker.

Referee: Mr. N. C. Burtenshaw (Great Yarmouth)

August 31, 1971 v Ipswich Town (a), drew 0-0

A good game as Derby maintain their unbeaten start to the season. Only Sheffield United can boast a similar record. Wignall did score what seemed to be a perfectly good goal but the effort was ruled out.

Ipswich Town: Best; Hammond, Harper; Morris, Bell, Jefferson, Roberts, Mills Clarke, Hamilton, Miller. Sub: Lambert.

Derby County: Boulton; Todd, Robson, Hennessey, McFarland, McGovern, Gemmill, Durban, Wignall, Hector, Hinton. Sub: Webster.

Referee: Mr. K. Walker (Ashford)

Post-match comments:

Brian Clough: "We haven't put in a consistent 90 minutes all season and we are still amongst the leaders. There is better to come, so look out!"

September 4, 1971 v Everton (a), won 2-0

The scoreline disguises a drubbing because Derby win with ease. Everton are reduced to 10 men but it would not have made any difference had they retained their full complement. Clough leaves out Hennessy and O'Hare while Hector was at his most brilliant and scored a good goal on 13 minutes. Wignall registers his fourth goal in five games on 72 minutes.

Everton: West; Scott, Newton (K), Kendall, Kenyon, Darracott, Husband, Ball, Johnson, Hurst, Morrissey. Kendall substituted for Royle in the 27th minute.

Derby County: Boulton; Webster, Robson, Todd, McFarland, McGovern, Gemmill, Durban, Wignall, Hector, Hinton, Sub: O'Hare.

Referee: Mr. A. Oliver (Leigh-on-Sea)

Post-match Comments:

Brian Clough: "O'Hare's ankle is not quite right and Hennessey has a bruised thigh but all credit to Ron Webster who had a fine game.

Other Comments: I am thinking of becoming player-manager again. Harry Catterick (Everton manager).

September 11, 1971 v Stoke City (h), won 4-0

Gordon Banks takes a spanking as a rampant Derby, fresh from a 0-0 draw with Leeds United in the League Cup, turn on the style. Todd takes all the headlines and thumps home the first after 29 minutes. Almost immediately O'Hare gets on the end of a Hinton cross to head home the second. The second half saw good approach work from Wignall, which was converted for the third goal by Hinton. Right on time, the consistent Gemmill wrong-footed Banks for the fourth.

Derby County: Boulton; Webster, Robson, Todd, McFarland, Gemmill, Durban, Wignall, O'Hare, Hector, Hinton. Sub: McGovern.

Stoke City: Banks; Marsh, Pejic, Bernard (Stevenson 45), Smith, Lees, Mahoney, Greenhoff, Ritchie, Dobing, Haslegrave.

Referee: Mr. E. D. Wallace (Swindon)

Post-match Comments:
Brian Clough: "We started well and got stronger. There is a long way to go but I am a happy man today".

Other Comments:
When Brian Clough paid £170,000 for Colin Todd, a string of more experienced managers shook their heads and announced: "It's too much for a player that doesn't win matches".

"What a player! Colin Todd is doing for Derby what Bobby Moore does for England – and doing it better". Tony Waddington (Stoke City manager)

September 18, 1971 v Chelsea (a), drew 1-1

Derby throw away a point and could have lost both but for the bar rejected Osgood's late header. Once again Todd is voted man-of-the-match and McFarland, who is back to full strength, cracked home the opener on 32 minutes. Baldwin (67) equalises with a classy strike.

Chelsea: Bonetti; Boyle, Harris, Hollins, Webb, Hinton (M), Cooke, Baldwin, Osgood, Hudson, Houseman. Sub: Garland.

Derby County: Boulton; Webster, Robson, Todd, McFarland, McGovern, Gemmill, Wignall, O'Hare, Hector, Hinton. Sub: Hennessey.

Referee: Mr. R. Nicholson (Manchester)

Post-match Comments:
Brian Clough: "Again we have let a team back into a game which should have been won and filed away for the historians".

September 25, 1971 v West Bromwich Albion (h), drew 0-0
Derby won the corner count 21-to-zero, which sums up the level of frustration inside the Baseball Ground. West Brom manager, Don Howe, has been advocating attacking football but his team are clearly not listening to him. Such a drab contribution should have been punished by Derby.
Derby County: Boulton; Webster, Robson; Todd, McFarland, Gemmill; Durban (McGovern 47), Wignall, O'Hare, Hector, Hinton.
West Bromwich Albion: Cumbes; Hughes, Wilson; Cantello, Wile, Kaye; McVitie, Brown, Gould, Hope, Harford. Sub: Suggett.
Referee: Mr. D. Nippard (Bournemouth)

Post-match Comments:
Brian Clough: "It was a dull game but we should have won and missed the chances we had created with skill and hard work.

Other Comments: "It wasn't pretty but we'll take our point and not many visiting teams to the Baseball Ground will say the same this season. (Don Howe, West Bromwich Albion manager)

October 2, 1971 v Newcastle United (a), won 1-0
Once again Derby exhibit their excellence with a cool command of a game they should have won more emphatically. They showed character after exiting the League Cup at Leeds United in the week and are the only unbeaten team in the league after Sheffield United's defeat against Manchester United. Hinton claimed the goal and the points for Derby. Todd is described in the press as "Standing out like a jewel".
Newcastle United: McFaul, Craig, Ellison, Gibb, Howard, Clark, Barrowclough, Tudor, Macdonald, Nattrass, Hibbitt. Sub: Dyson.
Derby County: Boulton, Webster, Robson, Hennessey, McFarland, Todd, McGovern, Durban, O'Hare, Hector, Hinton, Sub: Gemmill.

Post-match Comments:
Brian Clough: "What amazes me is that Newcastle should have this lad (Todd) on their doorstep for so long and not do anything about it. There were plenty to say I had made a mistake when I bought him but where are they now? Todd was cheap at the price."

Other Comments:
The gay canary and blue of Derby County's second strip provided a fitting backcloth for Brian Clough's expensive diamond, Colin Todd. The setting was perfect.

It was only Newcastle's defence that restricted embarrassingly superior Derby to a Alan Hinton goal hooked in after 61 minutes.

October 9, 1971 v Tottenham Hotspur (h), drew 2-2

Todd scores a dynamite blast from 20 yards to equalise Spurs' opener from Chivers on 54 minutes. The goal is all the more remarkable in that he ran half the length of the pitch to collect a pass from Hinton before spanking the ball home. It looked like McFarland had won it for Derby six minutes from time when he headed home from Hector's corner. Pearce equalised two minutes from time with a controversial goal which saw Boulton harshly treated. The press are calling for Todd to play for Ramsey's England.

Derby County: Boulton; Webster, Robson; Todd, McFarland, McGovern; Gemmill, Durban, O'Hare, Hector, Hinton. Wignall substituted for Webster in the 24th minute.

Tottenham Hotspur: Jennings; Evans, Knowles; Mullery, Collins, Real; Pearce, Perryman, Chivers, Peters, Gilzean. Pratt substituted for Knowles in the 52nd minute.

Referee: Mr. C. I. Smith (Manchester)

Attendance: 35,744

Post-match Comments:
Brian Clough: "There is no point talking about championships when you cannot hold down a lead".

Other Comments: On a pitch which boasted 11 internationals, Colin Todd was head and shoulders above the lot of them.

Gilzean was miles offside when Chivers scored the first and our keeper had the ball knocked out of his hands before Pearce got their second. **Alan Hinton (Derby County winger)**

October 16, 1971 v Manchester United (a), lost 0-1

George Best ends Derby's unbeaten start to the season. Derby appear to lack belief in their ability despite being amongst the league leaders. Kidd and Gowling both hit the bar. The performance of Todd and Hennessey provide the biggest consolation to Derby. Rams marched out with their unbeaten record waving like a banner. But 90 mocking minutes later it had been trampled on by as magical a Manchester United performance you could hope to see. If United had won by six no Derby player could have complained.

Manchester United: Stepney, O'Neil, Dunne, Gowling, James, Sadler, Morgan, Kidd, Charlton, Law, Best. Sub: Aston.

Derby County: Boulton, Todd, Robson, Hennessey, McFarland, McGovern, Gemmill, Durban, O'Hare, Hector, Hinton. Sub: Wignall.

Referee: Mr. P. Partridge.

Post-match Comments:
Brian Clough: "United deserved to win".

October 23, 1971 v Arsenal (h), won 2-1

Derby's midfield trio of Durban, McGovern and Gemmill soak up the praise after this very one-sided affair. O'Hare scores the first after a flowing move involving the pacy Gemmill. Completely against the run of play, Graham converts Armstrong's corner kick. It looked like another case of *déjà vu* for the Rams but a controversial penalty converted by Hinton ensured justice was done.

Derby County: Boulton, Webster (Powell 68), Robson, Todd, McFarland, McGovern, Gemmill, Durban, O'Hare, Hector, Hinton.

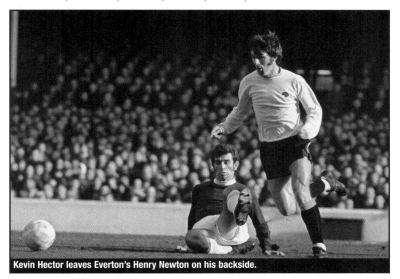
Kevin Hector leaves Everton's Henry Newton on his backside.

THE LIFE OF BRIAN

Arsenal: Wilson, Rice, Nelson, Kelly (Simpson 75), McLintock, Roberts, Armstrong, George, Radford, Kennedy, Graham.
Referee: Mr. W. J. Hall (Preston)

Post-match Comments:
Brian Clough: "They can have no complaints. We deserved it over the 90 minutes, so I don't care about the penalty".

Other Comments:
Derby spun Arsenal in circles with a victory so comprehensive that the Hector penalty incident should never have been allowed to remain a point of contention. Arsenal, double champions and winners of their previous seven matches, didn't create a chance. George Graham's goal was given to them by a goalkeeping blunder.

October 30, 1971 v Nottingham Forest (a), won 2-0
Hard graft, rather than panache, earned this victory at the City Ground, which is something of a happy hunting ground for Derby. McGovern is back to his dominant best, O'Hare gives a good account, although most of the Derby team lack their usual spark and a clean sheet and a penalty save says a lot about Boulton's form this season. Hinton scored his penalty and Robson cracked home a goal from 20 yards.
Nottingham Forest: Hulme, O'Kane, Fraser; Chapman, Hindley, Richardson; Lyons, McKenzie, Buckley, Robertson, More. Sub: McIntosh.
Derby County: Boulton, Webster, Robson, Powell, McFarland, Todd, McGovern, Gemmill, O'Hare, Hector, Hinton. Sub: Durban.
Referee: Mr. D. Smith (Stonehouse, Gloucestershire)

A few days after this game, on November 3, former Manchester United manager Matt Busby had this to say on Brian Clough:
"Derby have already served notice that they are going to be a force in the game. Here is a side bristling with confidence and character – a bit like their manager, Brian Clough, I suppose. Clough may not be everyone's cup of tea but he's doing a tremendous job at Derby. He has proved himself a shrewd judge of players – finding bargains like Roy McFarland and John O'Hare and transforming them into international players. Clough has also shown he is not afraid to back his judgment with a hefty chequebook, as he did to get Colin Todd".

November 6, 1971 v Crystal Palace (h), won 3-0
Derby stroll through this game and some fans growl for more. The team is

very compact and settling down to offer a good blend of skill, hard work and consistency. They closed a point on leaders Manchester United. Bell sparked the panic amongst Crystal Palace with an own goal in the first half while Wignall headed home Hinton's corner early in the second. Hector added a third with just a couple of minutes left.

Derby County: Boulton, Webster, Robson, Todd, Hennessey, McGovern, Durban, Wignall, O'Hare, Hector, Hinton. Sub: Powell.

Crystal Palace: Jackson; Payne, Wall, Goodwin, Bell, Blyth, Tambling, Craven, Hughes, Wallace, Taylor. Sub: Pinkney.

Referee: Mr. E. Jolly (Manchester)

Post-match Comments:

Brian Clough: "We had enough chances to win half a dozen matches. It is too early to be talking about championships. I am happy with the two points."

When it comes to inflicting slow torture on their fans, Derby County have all other clubs beaten hands down. Their inability to find a striker to add the killer punch to their championship approach work could prove costly.

November 13, 1971 v Wolverhampton Wanderers (a), lost 1-2

Derby lack consistency and after being gifted a goal, which had been headed into an empty net by O'Hare, contrived to exchange it for a defeat. Wolves scored through Richards before half-time and although Derby looked livelier in the second half, Boulton couldn't hold a Hibbitt shot and Richards was on hand to seal a Wolves victory.

Wolverhampton Wanderers: Parkes, Shaw, Parkin, Bailey, Munro, McAlle, McCalliog, Hibbitt, Richards, Dougan, Wagstaffe. Sub: Daley.

Derby County: Boulton, Webster, Robson, Todd, McFarland, Hennessey, McGovern, Gemmill, O'Hare, Hector, Hinton. Sub: Durban.

Referee: Mr. D. Laing (Preston)

Post-match Comments:

Brian Clough: "Wolves raised their game. Everyone wants to beat Derby".

Other Comments: "This win should give us confidence and help us recover the form we showed last season. **Bill McGarry (Wolves manager)**

November 20, 1971 v Sheffield United (h), won 3-0

Derby's skilful, penetrating, classy football returns as Sheffield are swept aside. The Blades had conceded five against West Ham in the week and are

clearly faltering with their form at present. Derby got off to a flier with Hector scoring after two minutes. The other goals were both penalties. Hinton despatched one with a blast and the other with measured placement.
Derby County: Boulton; Webster, Robson, Todd, McFarland, Hennessey, McGovern, Gemmill, O'Hare, Hector, Hinton. Sub: Durban.
Sheffield United: Hope; Badger, Hemsley, Flynn, Colquhoun, Hockey, Woodward, Salmons, Reece, Currie, Scullion. Sub: Dearden.
Referee: Mr. V. J. Batty (Helsby)

Post-match Comments:
Brian Clough: "The Blades deserved what they got".

Other Comments:
Derby mastered the match in midfield. The running of Archie Gemmill and the distribution of John McGovern were a class higher than anything United could offer.

November 27, 1971 v Huddersfield Town (a), lost 1-2
This is Derby's third defeat in their last four away games in the league. Despite an awesome display in the first half, it is goals that win games and in the rain at Leeds Road, Derby just couldn't convert their superiority into victory. Worthington put Huddersfield ahead and Lawson dived to head past Boulton to put The Terriers two up. Despite a coolly despatched goal from McGovern, Derby could not convert any of Hinton's well worked crosses.
Huddersfield Town: Lawson (D), Clarke, Hutt, Jones, Ellam, Cherry, Mahoney, Smith (S), Worthington, Lawson (J), Chapman. Sub: Smith (D).
Derby County: Boulton, Webster, Robson, Todd, McFarland, Hennessey, McGovern, Gemmill, O'Hare, Hector, Hinton. Sub: Durban.
Referee: Mr. G. W. Hill (Kirby Muxloe)

Post-match Comments:
Brian Clough: "I just don't know how we lost. I just don't know. After the way we played in the first half and the last 15 minutes, how could we lose?"

Other Comments:
It is not often that Brian Clough is lost for words, so Leeds Road, Huddersfield, 1971 warrants a mention in somebody's book of records.

December 4, 1971 v Manchester City (h), won 3-1
A great attacking display from two talented sides and Derby have to be at

their best to secure the points and move back to second in the league table. Robson quells the tide of class displayed by Summerbee. Hinton scored from the spot after McGovern's weaving run had been upended in the box. In a devastating couple of first half minutes Derby broke into a 3-0 lead. Hinton was the supplier for Webster's first goal under Clough and Durban's first of the season. But for Corrigan in the City goal, Derby could have slaughtered Joe Mercer's side. A Lee penalty reduced the arrears in what was a very physical game.

Derby County: Boulton, Webster, Robson, Todd, McFarland, McGovern, Durban, Gemmill, O'Hare, Hector, Hinton. Sub: Hennessey.

Manchester City: Corrigan; Book, Donachie, Doyle, Booth, Oakes, Summerbee, Bell, Davies, Lee, Mellor. Sub: Towers.

Referee: Mr. W. Johnson (Kendal)

Post-match Comments:

Brian Clough: "It was ugly at times and my players know that is not the Derby way".

Other Comments: Derby were well worth their win and one had to admire the brilliance of Todd, McFarland, Webster and Durban who took on Bell in midfield – and beat him. **Kenneth Wolstenholme (BBC *Match of the Day* commentator)**

December 11, 1971 v Liverpool (a), lost 2-3

Once again bad defensive mistakes result in defeat for Derby. A goal from O'Hare in the first half was sandwiched by two from Whitham. O'Hare grabbed his second after the break but Derby succumbed to Whitham again in the 53rd minute when he converted Heighway's cross for his hat-trick.

Liverpool: Clemence, Lawler, Lindsay, Smith, Ross, Hughes, Keegan, Hall, Heighway, Whitham, Callaghan. Sub: Boersma.

Derby County: Boulton, Todd (Walker 60), Webster, Hennessey, McFarland, McGovern, Durban, Gemmill, O'Hare, Hector, Hinton.

Referee: Mr. C. Howell (North Shields)

Post-match Comments:

Brian Clough: "One of the few good things about coming to Anfield is meeting this fellow again," said with a broad smile after popping his head out of the Derby dressing room and coming face-to-face with Reds' boss Bill Shankly.

"Two goals away from home with my defence should have been enough".

THE LIFE OF **BRIAN**

Other Comments:
"We should have beaten you 5-2, Brian".
Bill Shankly, Liverpool manager

Derby's lack of reserve strength was cruelly exposed. When they lost
Colin Todd with a broken nose, their defence was in complete disarray.
Mike Ellis, journalist

December 18, 1971 v Everton (h), won 2-0
A moment of brilliance from Hinton illuminated the Baseball Ground on
this day and the minds of thousands for many days to come. He had already
opened the scoring courtesy of a mistake from West on 49 minutes. It is
accepted as the best goal scored at Derby for a very long time indeed.
Derby County: Boulton, Webster, Robson, Hennessey, McFarland,
McGovern, Durban, Gemmill, O'Hare, Hector, Hinton. Sub: Butlin.
Everton: West, Wright, McLaughlin, Kendall, Kenyon, Newton (H),
Husband, Ball, Royle, Hurst, Whittle. Sub: Scott.
Referee: Mr. B. H. Daniels (Rainham)

Post-match Comments:
Brian Clough: "It is not often I jump from my seat but Alan's goal was
something special. For 20 minutes in the first half, O'Hare had touched
new peaks".

Other Comments:
"Alan Hinton's wonder goal confirmed Derby's superior craft, graft and
striking power". **John Sadler, journalist**

December 27, 1971 v Leeds United (a), lost 0-3
Goals from Gray and two from Lorimer remind Derby they still have a long
way to go. Leeds are ugly and beautiful at the same time, and bruise and
goals provide the evidence.
Leeds United: Sprake, Madeley, Cooper, Bremner, Charlton, Hunter,
Lorimer, Clarke, Jones, Giles, Gray. Sub: Jordan.
Derby County: Boulton, Webster, Robson, Bailey, McFarland, Hennessey,
McGovern, Gemmill, O'Hare, Hector, Hinton. Sub: Durban.
Referee: Mr. A. E. Morrissey (Bramhall, Cheshire)

Post-match Comments:
Brian Clough: "They played us off the park. We are being out-fought and

the simple truth could be that we are not big and strong enough to dish it out when it is needed, especially away from home".

"If we don't do something soon we are going to end up an ordinary middle-of-the-table team with no chance of Europe".

Other Comments:
"The man who might possibly have stopped the landslide, defensive ace Colin Todd, could only watch from the sidelines having suffered a broken nose recently".

January 1, 1972 v Chelsea (h), won 1-0
Derby, who are unbeaten at home, have England under-23 international Colin Todd back after breaking his nose three weeks ago. Rams look edgy and are relieved when Gemmill lets fly with six minutes to go. The ball took a deflection on its way in.
Derby County: Boulton, Webster, Robson, Todd, McFarland, McGovern, Durban, Gemmill O'Hare, Hector, Hinton. Sub: Hennessey.
Chelsea: Sherwood; Mulligan, Harris, Hollins, Dempsey, Webb, Garland, Kember (Cooke 87), Osgood, Hudson, Houseman.
Referee: Mr. T. W. Dawes (Bury St Edmunds)

Post-match Comments:
Brian Clough: "Now I know you can never win the championship until all the players show the toughness you see from other top clubs".

Other Comments:
"There is no question Steve (Sherwood) would have saved it very easily if I hadn't stuck my head in the way. I thought throughout the game he was tremendous

Archie Gemmill let fly against Chelsea.

for a lad playing his first league game".
David Webb, Chelsea

One thing was clear. Derby are looking less and less like a team capable
of winning the First Division title.

January 8, 1972 v Southampton (a), won 2-1
With Clough on a scouting mission, it was left to his assistant, Peter Taylor,
to oversee an injury-time goal from Durban sink Southampton.
Southampton: Martin, McCarthy, Fry, Stokes, Gabriel, Byrne, Paine,
Channon, Davies, O'Brien, Jenkins. Sub: Kirkup.
Derby County: Boulton, Webster, Robson, Durban, McFarland, Todd,
McGovern, Gemmill, O'Hare, Hector, Hinton. Sub: Hennessey.
Referee: Mr. A. P. Oliver (Leigh-on-Sea)

Post-match Comments:
Peter Taylor: "As an attacking force Southampton just weren't in it.
Their aerial threat never bothered us at all. We were on top the whole 90
minutes. Boulton would have saved O'Brien's goal if the ball had not hit
O'Hare and been diverted".

Other Comments:
"We murdered them in the first half".
Ron Davies, Southampton

January 22, 1972 v West Ham United (a), drew 3-3
Lampard equalised Hinton's opener and 'Pop' Robson put the home side
into the lead. Hinton set up Durban for an equaliser but Brooking seemed
to have won it on 80 minutes. Hinton had different ideas, though, and set
up Hector to earn a draw.
West Ham United: Ferguson, McDowall, Lampard, Bonds, Taylor, Moore,
Redknapp, Best, Hurst, Brooking, Robson. Sub: Eustace.
Derby County: Boulton, Webster, Robson, Durban, McFarland, Todd,
McGovern, Gemmill, O'Hare, Hector, Hinton. Sub: Hennessey.
Referee: Mr. J. E. Thacker (Scarborough)

Post-match Comments:
Peter Taylor: "This was purely for the fans and not the managers. We
made too many errors in defence and for too long we lost a grip in
midfield. We should never have given away three goals".

January 29, 1972 v Coventry City (h), won 1-0

Another clean sheet and a lightning start to the second half when Robson netted after just 16 seconds. Coventry were poor but difficult to break down.

Derby County: Boulton; Webster, Robson, Durban, McFarland, Todd, McGovern, Gemmill, O'Hare, Hector, Hinton. Sub: Hennessey.

Coventry City: Glazier; Smith, Cattlin, Machin (McGuire 60), Blockley, Parker, Young, Carr, Chilton, Rafferty, Mortimer.

Referee: Mr. H. New (Bristol)

Attendance: 29,385

Post-match Comments:

Brian Clough: "Colin (Todd) showed us all that he is now ready to step into the England side".

Other Comments:

"Derby have only conceded a Francis Lee penalty at home in the past three months".

February 12, 1972 v Arsenal (a), lost 0-2

Having thumped Notts County, 6-0, the previous week in the FA Cup, Derby could not find the net against Arsenal who exacted sweet revenge for their defeat at the Baseball Ground. Defending champions, the Gunners are now firing on all cylinders again and move within a point of Derby at the top. But for the heroics of Boulton it would have been a lot worse. Goals by George and Graham (penalty) won the game.

Arsenal: Wilson, Rice, Nelson, Kelly, McLintock, Simpson, Armstrong, Ball, George, Kennedy, Graham. Sub: Radford.

Derby County: Boulton, Webster, Robson, Durban, McFarland, Todd, McGovern, Gemmill, O'Hare, Hector, Hinton. Sub: Hennessey.

Referee: Mr. K. Burns (Stourbridge)

Post-match Comments:

Brian Clough: "The diving header from Charlie George was a marvellous goal. He deserved to be on the winning side with a goal like that".

Other Comments:

The lack of total commitment by one or two Derby players looked all the more criminal by comparison. Men like Hector, Gemmill and Roy McFarland could never be included in this criticism.

THE LIFE OF **BRIAN**

February 19, 1972 v Nottingham Forest (h), won 4-0

Ten goals against the two Nottingham teams in the past two weeks keep the Derby end of the A52 very happy indeed. The three H's – Hinton (2), O'Hare and Hector – grabbed the goals.

Derby County: Boulton, Webster, Robson, Durban, McFarland, Todd, McGovern, Gemmill, O'Hare, Hector, Hinton. Sub: Hennessey.

Nottingham Forest: Barron, Gemmell, Winfield, Chapman, Hindley, Cottam, Lyons, O'Neill, Cormack, Richardson, Moore. Sub: McIntosh.

Referee: Mr R Matthewson (Manchester).

Post-match Comments:
Brian Clough: "We murdered them".

Other Comments:
Derby fans had waited for the day when their team would thrash Forest out of sight. When it came it was almost too embarrassing to be a pleasure.

Apparently there were grumbles from the Forest dressing room about the boggy Baseball Ground pitch but they needn't worry too much, because they won't have to play on it next season.

March 4, 1972 v Wolverhampton Wanderers (h), won 2-1

This was a great result on a cold, wet afternoon when Wolves looked like achieving the double over the Rams. Prior to the game Ian Storey-Moore is unveiled as Derby's new signing but the story has a bizarre twist when Moore signs for Manchester United instead. Boulton brings down Dougan for a penalty which McCalliog converts. Munro upends Hector in a harmless part of the area and the referee awards another penalty. Hinton made no mistake, as usual. McFarland forces home Hinton's cross for the winner and it was the least the captain deserved after another brilliant performance. Wolves apply pressure but failed to find an equaliser.

Derby County: Boulton; Webster, Robson, Durban, McFarland, Todd, McGovern, Gemmill, O'Hare, Hector, Hinton. Sub: Walker.

Wolverhampton Wanderers: Parkes, Shaw, Taylor, Hegan, Munro, McAlle, McCalliog, Hibbitt, Richards, Dougan, Wagstaffe. Sub: Daley.

Referee: Mr. R. C. Challis (Tonbridge)

Post-match Comments:
Brian Clough: "I am sorry he (Ian Storey-Moore) has changed his mind. I wish him well with Manchester United".

Other Comments:
"They fought hard for each other and there's a lot of unselfish running in the team. I am looking forward to playing with them". **Ian Storey-Moore after Clough thought he had signed him from Forest for £200,000.**

In a bizarre twist, Ian Moore eventually signed for Manchester United. Clough was alleged to have blown the deal by parading Moore at the Baseball Ground, claiming: "He's ours".
"It was a gimmick which has blown up in his face".
Ken Smales, Nottingham Forest manager.

March 11, 1972 v Tottenham Hotspur (a), won 1-0
This drab encounter took an unexpected twist with four minutes to go when England and Jennings fail to communicate and Hector is pulled down. Hinton converts his 10th goal of the season and Derby remain in touch with Manchester United and Leeds at the top.
Tottenham Hotspur: Jennings, Evans, Knowles, Holder, England, Beal, Gilzean, Perryman, Chivers, Peters, Morgan. Sub: Pearce.
Derby County: Boulton, Webster, Robson, Hennessey, McFarland, Todd, McGovern, Gemmill, O'Hare, Hector, Hinton. Sub: Daniel.
Referee: Mr. A. E. Morrissey (Bramhall)
Attendance: 36,310

Post-match comments
Brian Clough: "This was an important win for us. We have lost our fluency at the moment but it will return".

Other Comments
"One three-letter word describes Spurs here today – BAD. And a five-letter word will do for Derby – WORSE!"

"Earlier in the season the Rams were a delight to watch. They attacked opponents both at home and away with gay abandon. Now a cautious efficiency has spread through the team".

March 18, 1972 v Leicester City (h), won 3-0
Having been knocked out of the FA Cup in midweek by Arsenal this was an important with for Derby, who must now throw all their energy and effort into winning the title. Wallington replaced Shilton in goal and was helpless when Robson put O'Hare through to chip the opener. Durban scored from a corner in the second half and Hector claimed the third to put Derby

THE LIFE OF **BRIAN**

second in the league, while Leeds were winning through to the FA Cup semi-finals. Derby have lost only once this year in the league.
Derby County: Boulton, Webster, Robson, Durban, McFarland, Todd, McGovern, Hennessey (Webster 63), O'Hare, Hector, Gemmill.
Leicester City: Wallington; Whitworth, Nish, Cross, Manley, Woollett, Fern (Lee 68), Sammels, Weller, Birchenall, Glover.
Referee: Mr. V. James (York)

Post-match comments:
Brian Clough: "We must keep fighting hard. It is all we can do. It is all we know how to do".

Other comments:
This was Derby's 10th successive home win – and they earned 10 out of 10 for a performance which proved they intend to contest the First Division title race to the bitter end.

March 22, 1972 v Ipswich Town (h), won 1-0
The press hail "Hercules Hector" as he makes another colossal contribution. Hinton hobbles off again with a recurring hamstring problem but Derby's defence has all the hallmarks of a championship-winning outfit. Clough has always said that great teams are built on clean sheets and the whole of Derby – from schoolkids to granddads – are absolutely hooked on the fortunes of their club. They now sit just three points behind Manchester City with a game in hand. Hector scored the only goal on 15 minutes.
Derby County: Boulton; Webster, Robson, Durban, McFarland, Todd, McGovern, Gemmill, O'Hare, Hector, Hinton. Walker substituted for Hinton in the 23rd minute.
Ipswich Town: Best: Mills, Harpur, Morris, Hunter, Jefferson, Robertson, Miller, Mills, Belfitt, Whymark. Lambert substituted for Belfitt in the 75th minute.
Referee: Mr. E. D. Wallace (Swindon)

Post-match Comments:
Brian Clough: "The pitch hasn't helped us tonight but we beat a very good Ipswich side who coped better with the conditions than we did".

March 25, 1972 v Stoke City (a), drew 1-1
Having fallen behind to a Greenhoff penalty early in the second half, Derby rally well but just cannot carve out a winner. Durban continued his

rich vein of form by netting the equaliser a few minutes later. It was a game Derby should have won as Stoke has its mind set on Wembley and a League Cup final against Chelsea (which they won). The referee controversially ruled out a late Hector effort.

Stoke City: Banks, Marsh, Jump, Bernard, Smith, Bloor, Conroy, Greenhoff, Ritchie, Dobing, Burrows. Sub: Mahoney.

Derby County: Boulton; Webster, Robson, Durban, McFarland, Todd, McGovern, Gemmill, O'Hare, Hector, Walker. Sub: Hennessey.

Referee: Mr. R. B. Kirkpatrick (Leicester)

Post-match Comments:

Brian Clough: "I've said it all along, that I don't think we are quite ready to win the championship".

Other Comments:

"Derby were left bickering about a last-minute decision by referee, Roger Kirkpatrick, who penalised Kevin Hector when Gordon Banks dropped the ball in the net. 'Ask the referee if he saw anything', Clough told me, so I did. 'Ask that expert if he was watching the game because if he was he knows the answer to that question', came the emphatic response. 'And another thing. I'm not only a good referee but I can also beat *him* at talking facts'."

March 28, 1972 v Crystal Palace (a), won 1-0

Gemmill misses a penalty after 18 minutes and it seems set to be one of those nights for Derby. However, Manchester City and Leeds United still have Derby for company after Hennessey's shot, initially blocked by Jackson, was tapped home by Webster. Next up are Leeds and the most important game of the season to date.

Crystal Palace: Jackson, Payne, Goodwin, Kellard, McCormick, Bell, Craven, Queen, Wallace, Taylor, Tambling (Wall 45).

Derby County: Boulton, Webster, Robson, Durban, McFarland, Todd, Hennessey, Gemmill, O'Hare, Hector, Walker. Sub: Daniel.

Referee: Mr. C. H. Nicholls (Plymouth)

Post-match Comments:

Brian Clough: "We acquitted ourselves well, as we have key men missing. The big test will be Leeds, of course".

Other Comments:

"What a scrap! Defiant Derby County and an unrelenting Liverpool last

night served notice on Manchester City and Leeds United that the chase
for the championship is far from being a two-horse race. **Bob Driscoll,
journalist**

Derby without Alan Hinton are like a one armed boxer.
Bob Driscoll, journalist

April 1, 1972 v Leeds United (h), won 2-0

Derby are devastating and sweep Leeds aside on a memorable night at the
Baseball Ground. It is far easier than anyone thought and a 5-0 scoreline
could easily have been the outcome. It was as complete a Derby
performance as you are ever likely to see. O'Hare scores the first to mark
his 200th game for Rams and Hunter cannot help but turn the ball into his
own net for 2-0.

Derby County: Boulton, Webster, Robson, Durban, McFarland, Todd,
McGovern, Gemmill, O'Hare, Hector, Walker. Sub: Hennessey.

Leeds United: Sprake, Reaney, Cooper, Bremner, Charlton, Hunter,
Lorimer, Clarke, Madeley, Giles, Gray. Sub: Bates.

Referee: Mr. D. W. Smith (Stonehouse)

Post-match Comments:
Brian Clough: "We played the Derby way and won. In football terms
nothing could make me happier".

Other Comments:
"Derby were full value for their win. They all played magnificently. I said
at the start of the season they would win the title if we didn't. I still think
so".
Don Revie, Leeds United manager

Players of the calibre of Clarke, Gray and Lorimer were anonymous,
which speaks volumes for the Derby defence.
Kenneth Wolstenholme, BBC *Match of the Day* commentator

April 3, 1972 v Newcastle United (h), lost 0-1

The game after the big game is lost and Derby rue missed opportunities.
McFarland has to leave the field to receive four stitches in a head wound
and it was he who conceded the free-kick from which Newcastle scored.
McDonald's shot was well saved by Boulton but eventually the ball broke
to Cassidy, who scored from close range.

Derby County: Boulton, Webster, Robson, Durban, McFarland, Todd,

McGovern, Gemmill, O'Hare, Hector, Hinton. Sub: Hennessey.
Newcastle United: McFaul, Craig, Clark, Gibb (Cassidy 31), Howard, Moncur, Barrowclough, Green, Macdonald, Tudor, Reid.
Referee: Mr. R. Tinkler (Boston)

Post-match Comments:
Brian Clough: "We couldn't break them down and full marks for Bobby Moncur. He stopped us on his own".

Other Comments:
The First Division championship scramble was blown wide open again yesterday with one swing of Tommy Cassidy's right leg. It ended Derby's magnificent run of 26 games without defeat.

April 5, 1972 v West Bromwich Albion (a), drew 0-0
Derby are still top even after this very dull encounter which offered little in the way of spark or goals. Astle is well marked by McFarland.
West Bromwich Albion: Osborne, Nisbet, Wilson, Suggett, Wile, Robertson, Hope, Tony Brown, Astle, Alistair Brown, Hartford. Sub: Gould.
Derby County: Boulton; Webster, Robson, Durban, McFarland, Todd, McGovern, Gemmill, O'Hare, Hector, Hinton. Sub: Hennessey.
Referee: Mr. R. C. Challis (Tonbridge)

Post-match Comments:
Brian Clough: "We'll keep plugging on but there were a lot of tired legs out there today".

Other Comments:
Derby are still top but what a bore!

April 8, 1972 v Sheffield United (a), won 4-0
Derby are at their most clinical as they slice through the Blades time and time again. Gemmill and Durban helped Derby into a 2-0 lead on a blustery afternoon while Hector established a landmark with his 200th league goal. O'Hare completed the whitewash with a goal eight minutes from time.
Sheffield United: Hope, Badger, Hemsley, Mackenzie, Colquhoun, Salmons, Woodward, Scullion, Dearden, Holmes, Ford. Sub: Flynn
Derby County: Boulton, Webster, Robson, Durban, McFarland, Todd, McGovern, Gemmill, O'Hare, Hector, Hinton. Sub: Hennessey.
Referee: Mr. J. K. Taylor (Wolverhampton)

Roy McFarland scored against Huddersfield.

Post-match Comments:
Brian Clough: "We're delighted to score four but it should have been seven and we earned every one".

Other Comments:
Derby were exhilarating and a treat to watch. Their control, passing, and non-stop running defined Clough and Taylor's philosophy that skill, properly applied, will win matches.

April 15, 1972 v Huddersfield Town (h), won 3-0
Derby stay top with only two games remaining – and what games they are; against Manchester City and Liverpool, both of whom are title challengers. The result all but resigns Huddersfield to relegation. McFarland, Hector and O'Hare helped master the Terriers in an unconvincing display.

Derby County: Boulton; Webster, Robson, Durban, McFarland, Todd, McGovern, Gemmill. O'Hare, Hector, Hinton. Sub: Hennessey.

Huddersfield Town: Lawson (D.), Clarke, Hutt, Smith, Ellam, Cherry, Hoy, Jones, Worthington, Lawson (J.), Chapman. Sub: Lyon

Referee: Mr. J. M. Yates (Redditch)

Post-match Comments:
Brian Clough: "It is unbelievable. You can play as badly as that, win by three goals and stay top of the league. We were rubbish. We should have hammered them out of sight but we just didn't turn it on".

Peter Taylor: "I have never seen us look so slack and lethargic in every position. We didn't have one really sharp player today".

Other Comments:
This game ensures the Rams of European football next season

April 22, 1972 v Manchester City (a), lost 0-2
Marsh has one of the games of his life as he makes all the difference in a super-charged affair at Maine Road. His goal in the 25th minute was sheer mastery and he won the penalty for the second just as Derby seemed set to claw an equaliser. Hennessey came on for Webster (knee injury).
Manchester City: Corrigan, Book, Donachie, Doyle, Booth, Jeffries, Lee, Bell, Summerbee, Marsh, Towers. Sub: Hill.
Derby County: Boulton, Webster (Hennessey 35), Robson, Durban, McFarland, Todd, McGovern, Gemmill, O'Hare, Hector, Hinton.
Referee: Mr. N. Burtenshaw (Great Yarmouth)

Post-match Comments:
Brian Clough on Rodney Marsh:
"Not a bad player".

Brian Clough on the championship:
"We haven't a chance of the title".

Other Comments:
City coach Malcolm Allison said afterwards that Derby would still win the title. "I have fancied them since Easter and I see no reason to change my mind now. I think they will beat Liverpool in their final match and that will be enough".

May 1, 1972 v Liverpool (h), won 1-0
Derby have given themselves a chance to win the title but they must hope that Leeds lose at home to Wolves and Liverpool do not win at Arsenal. Clough puts 16-year-old Powell in the side in place of the injured Webster. He is simply brilliant. Todd is announced as Footballer of the Year and the whole evening is rounded off with a goal from McGovern who beat Clemence on 62 minutes. The team that Brian Clough said could not win the Football League Championship are closer to the title than any previous Derby County team.
Derby County: Boulton, Powell, Robson, Durban, McFarland, Todd, McGovern, Gemmill, O'Hare, Hector, Hinton. Sub: Hennessey.
Liverpool: Clemence; Lawler, Lindsay, Smith, Lloyd, Hughes, Keegan, Hall, Heighway (McLaughlin 72), Toshack, Callaghan.
Referee: Mr C. Thomas (Treorchy)

THE LIFE OF **BRIAN**

A week later, Leeds United lost at home to Wolves and Liverpool drew against Arsenal at Highbury. Derby County were the First Division champions for the first time in their history.

When Rams were confirmed as title winners, Brian Clough was on holiday in the Scilly Isles, while his team and assistant Peter Taylor were enjoying a well-earned break in Majorca.

Championship Reaction:

Brian Clough
"This is one of the miracles of the century. Our triumph proves there is hope for all the little people in the world.
"A drink? All I'm going to do is hold hands with my wife, Barbara.
"The only message I have for the team is: 'You are Derby County players and you act accordingly' That's all".

Peter Taylor
"It's pandemonium. Everyone at the hotel seems to be Derby supporters. The players are being mobbed by their guests".

Kevin Hector
"We had butterflies – the lot. Our courier said: 'What's wrong with you lot, you look like a load of expectant fathers?' My God, it's true. We've just given birth to the League crown".

Alan Durban
"What a feeling. We are over the moon and there's a big one shining here tonight. What can I say but thanks very much to Arsenal and Wolves".

Colin Boulton
"Tremendous. What a way to spend a holiday. First we are going to finish off the lobster and then the champagne . . . and then more champagne. There's a good chance we'll get drunk!"

Alan Hinton
"There must be two or three hundred people around us. The hotel has stopped. This is the moment that we have been waiting for, especially me after 10 years in the game".

CLOUGHIE Derby

Archie Gemmill
"This is the greatest thing that has ever happened to me in football".

Sam Longson
"I am absolutely overjoyed. Tremendous! We have the finest manager in Europe in Brian Clough. He likes talking but he has the know-how".

...And from the beaten managers...
I don't like to make excuses but we should have had three penalties.
Don Revie (Leeds United)

We fought like tigers. We did enough to win the championship and my players are heartbroken. The only consolation I have is that the best team we played this season have won the championship.
Bill Shankly (Liverpool)

Colin Todd on Brian Clough
It was at Sunderland that Brian Clough the man who acknowledged Todd's ability more than most, first became a major influence on the defender who would become a star for Derby County and England.
Todd says: "He took charge of the juniors at Sunderland for a while and frightened the lot of us. He was strict and he bawled at people even in those days. But he taught me a lot and it was clear he was cut out for management".

Liverpool keeper Ray Clemence left grasping at thin air as John McGovern's shot flies in.

Colin Todd gets the better of West Ham's Trevor Brooking, a Clough target in the early 70s.

Clough on Todd

"He just did enough to make you say he had a chance".

"If this lad had the guile and trickery of President Nixon, he wouldn't only be in the England team. He'd have Alf's job".

"I only wish he would shout more. It would be smashing if he'd swear occasionally. I'd love that".

What a season! The Rams display their silverware at the end of a brilliant 1971-72 season.

Chapter 6
Derby County
The European Nights

The 90 minutes of tomorrow's match comes as a combination of five
years' of hard work and especially the 42 games of last season. We
battled nine months for the right to play in this game and we are hoping
our real fans will be there to see how we tackle this tremendous match.
**Brian Clough on the eve of Derby's first ever game
in the European Cup**

We genuinely thought we could win it but Juventus bought the German
referee and we were out of the European Cup
Brian Clough

The trouble in Turin continued after the match when Brian – insisting on
a translation by the journalist and columnist Brian Glanville, who speaks
perfect Italian – ordered away the local journalists from our dressing
room with the words: "I will not speak to cheating bastards!
Extract from *With Clough by Taylor*

THE LIFE OF **BRIAN**

The thrilling nights of European Cup football under the charge of Brian Clough stand as some of the greatest memories in Derby County's history.

The tie against Benfica is still regarded by many supporters as being the greatest match ever seen at the Baseball Ground.

Clough and Peter Taylor clearly excelled in such an elevated environment and while it is not surprising they brought two European Cups home to the East Midlands, it is heartbreaking to Rams' followers that they dropped them off at the 'wrong' end of the A52!

Derby County's European adventure began all those years ago on a tingling evening in September 1973 . . .

September 13, 1973 v Sarajevo (h), (EC 1, 1st leg), won 2-0

Before the game it is announced that Peter Daniel will replace John Robson, who is only 99 per cent fit, at left-back. Clough said: "It goes without saying that he wouldn't be playing if we didn't think he could make a great job of it".

Peter Taylor on John Robson: "99 per cent fit is not enough".

The first goal came in the 39th minute when the Sarajevo goalkeeper, Janjus, flapped at a free-kick under pressure from Hector and McFarland headed toward goal. The ball seemed to be handled on the line but the ref awarded the goal. For the second, Hector crossed and Gemmill struck home despite the efforts of Janjus.

Derby County: Boulton; Powell, Daniel, Hennessey, McFarland, Todd, McGovern, Gemmill, O'Hare, Hector, Hinton. No substitute used.

"We're over the moon. This was just what we needed. The Yugoslavs were difficult to break down but we did it, and did it well".
Brian Clough

"We can win the European Cup. We have an excellent chance because I think we have a skilful side at Derby".
Brian Clough

"I was thrilled with the way Terry Hennessy played last night. He was absolutely superb and yet he could have been out of the side if Alan Durban had been fully fit".
Brian Clough

"When we go over there for the second leg we will not be be able to

spend 80 minutes in the opposing penalty area. We only managed 75 minutes at West Brom last week".
Brian Clough

September 27, 1973 v Sarajevo (EC 1, 2nd leg) (a), won 2-1
Steve Powell is dropped for the match and Clough said: "He is feeling the accumulative effects of two games in a week and he is barely 17-years-old. It is often hard to remember his age but we must. He is built like a tank but at the moment the tank is empty."
In a bad tempered match, Derby score twice on the counter-attack. McGovern squares Hector's cross to Hinton who beats Janjus after only nine minutes. On 15, McGovern puts O'Hare through to make it 2-0. So the team who cannot find form at home in the league found it in front of 60,000 in the huge concrete bowl of the Kosevo Stadium to put Derby into the last 16 of the competition.
Derby County: Boulton, Daniel, Robson, Hennessey, McFarland, Todd, McGovern, Gemmill, O'Hare, Hector, Hinton.

Headline: "Dashing Derby Beat The Bullies" – *The Sun*

"It was a tragedy it was not televised so that people could have seen what went wrong. Some of their tackling made Frankenstein look like something from Walt Disney. Peter Daniel could have been carried off on a stretcher after 10 seconds".
Peter Taylor

"It was incredible that someone could be sent off two minutes from time for a minor thing like punching Colin Todd on the jaw. That was about their cleanest foul. I would have settled for a broken jaw after five minutes if the rough stuff could have stopped immediately".
Brian Clough

"My word is my bond and my word is that Brian Clough will stay at Derby" – to John Sadler of *The Sun* on the way back from Sarajevo.
Derby County chairman, Sam Longson, on the Clough contract dispute:

"My terms are simple. If someone wants to employ me they take me as I am. If, after five years, they can't take me as I am, then the whole world has gone beserk".
Brian Clough

THE LIFE OF **BRIAN**

On Monday, October 2 the draw is made for the last 16 and Derby are paired with Eusebio's Benfica, the Portuguese champions. Clough was quoted as saying:
"We feel we can beat any side we play. I learned of this draw from a journalist last night and my first thought was how beautiful it was for us from every aspect. If we had to pick one team to play it would be Benfica. Even Ajax and Real Madrid, to me, do not blossom in the mind so much."

October 25, 1973 v Benfica (EC 2, 1st leg) (h), won 3-0

Prior to facing Benfica, Peter Taylor said: "In our favour we have the best player in the world leading us, Roy McFarland. If Roy went and played for Benfica he would be the star of the side'".

Benfica's record going into the game was: played 7, won 7, scored 33.

"The Portuguese will murder you if you let them play the game their own way". **Bobby Charlton:**

The headline in the *Derby Evening Telegraph* read:
Benfica Paralysed By Brilliant Rams

Goals from McFarland, Hector and McGovern provide the city of Derby with their greatest night in football.

"We were absolutely brilliant. We've stuck three past Benfica - what more can I say? At half time, I simply said to the players: 'You are brilliant'."
Brian Clough

"Dynamic Derby last night produced 45 minutes of the finest quality attacking football I have ever seen from an English club in the European Cup".
Frank Clough – The Sun

November 8, 1973 v Benfica (EC 2, 2nd leg) (a), drew 0-0
Derby finish the job in The Estadio Da Luz in front of 75,000.

"There just seemed to be waves of red shirts. Those Belgian submarines they give to NATO wouldn't have stopped Benfica getting through tonight and we defended magnificently".
Brian Clough

March 7, 1973 Spartak Trnava (EC quarter-final, 1st leg) (a), lost 0-1

Pre-match Comments:
"Christ – They've got more caps than some of my lads have had games!"
Brian Clough

Spartak are seven years unbeaten at home in the League. They boast seven full international stars sharing 164 caps. And they have been Czech champions four years out of the last five.

To his informant:
"For God's sake don't tell the team what you have just told me. I brought you in as a spy, not a soul-destroyer!"
Brian Clough

"We are an attacking team, we believe that this is the best way for us to play, the only way for us to play. I suppose you could say that we are not good enough to mount a defensive operation for 90 minutes and I wouldn't disagree with you. But we honestly believe that the best way for us to get a result is to play to our strengths and that means playing the way we do at home – open, attacking football"
Brian Clough

"Not one of us is going just for the ride. I set a great deal of store by the player's state of mind and I am delighted to see them as they are today".
Peter Taylor

Headline: Todd's Boob Foils Derby

"Our chance is gone. I don't think one goal will be enough".
Aton Malatinsky (Spartak manager)

"I do not see Spartak holding out against Derby at the Baseball Ground unless Derby are as pathetic in front of goal again"
Frank Clough – *The Sun*

March 21, 1973 v Spartak Trnava (EC quarter-final, 2nd leg) (h), won 2-0
Pre-match Comments:

THE LIFE OF BRIAN

"We have the best incentive of all. The prospect of attracting the cream of European football to Derby in the semi-finals. We owe that to our supporters".
Peter Taylor

The first goal comes after Hector converts McGovern's low centre into the net. Hector also scores the all-important second after good battling work from Davies.
Derby are in the semi-final draw alongside Ajax, Real Madrid and Juventus.

"I was nervous throughout the 90 minutes. They split our defence more than any defence this season. We must improve by 50 per cent if we are going to win the European Cup".
Brian Clough

"We were not helped by the referee. He was the worst I have ever seen at top level and having refused us the most obvious penalty of all time, he had the audacity to book one of our players for trying to point out where Kevin was tripped".
Peter Taylor

April 11, 1973 v Juventus (EC semi-final, 1st leg) (a), lost 1-3

Pre match Comment:
"We will be in Belgrade for the final"
Peter Taylor

"At this stage of the season the Italian sides start to wane physically. I think Derby can win this tie".
John Charles – Juventus idol after six years with the Turin club.

Two goals from Altafini and another from Causio give the Italians a lot to defend despite a precious away goal for Derby.

April 25, 1973 v Juventus (EC semi-final, 2nd leg) (h), drew 0-0

Pre-match Comments:
"We are stupid enough – or optimistic enough – to believe, genuinely, that we can win"
Brian Clough

"The players are prepared to sell their souls for the club".
Peter Taylor

Headline: Goodbye Europe – A night of misery and disappointment for Derby County.

Roger Davies was sent-off just six minutes after Alan Hinton missed a penalty.
Rarely less than very candid, Brian Clough exceeds even his own usual capacity for controversy by identifying Hinton as the reason behind Derby's semi-final exit.

Clough said: "The man was a disgrace! It was his job to stay on the flanks and leave room for Davies and O'Hare in the middle. Instead he repeatedly wandered into the middle himself and jammed it all up".

"Despite what he said about me, I still think Brian Clough is the best manager in the business. I am not going to let what happened in one match destroy something which has been built up over the years".
Alan Hinton

Alan Hinton – still thinks Cloughie's the best.

Chapter 7
Brighton & Hove Albion
Making Waves by the Seaside

Brian Clough's decision to become manager of our ailing football team is the best thing to happen since Prinny put Brighton on the map!
Brighton & Hove Gazette and Herald, October 1973

Brian Clough was not unhappy at Brighton. In fact he always said they treated him very well. But he missed the big time. Brian is definitely a big time man.
Peter Taylor from *With Clough By Taylor*, 1980

I did not make a mistake going to Brighton. I just went there for the wrong reasons.
Brian Clough

Whenever people recall that I managed Brighton for 32 matches – and won only 12, incidentally – they still believe it was just a convenience, a temporary easy-picking to tide me over until a bigger job came along. They were wrong to think it at the time and they are still wrong to believe it today. I was sincere in my agreement to join Mike Bamber, the pleasantest and finest chairman who ever employed me.
Brian Clough from *Walking on Water*

There are two schools of thought about Brian Clough's eight-month spell at The Goldstone ground. There are those who draw upon one or two statistics to form the opinion that when Clough and Peter Taylor were appointed in October 1973, Brighton were 20th in the old third division. When Clough left eight months later they were 19th and had lost to Walton and Hersham, 4-0, in the FA Cup and 8-2 in the league at home to Bristol Rovers.

On the other hand there are those who view Clough's time at Brighton as the starting point for a revival in the Sussex club's fortunes. After he left for Leeds United in July 1974, Peter Taylor remained and took the club to fourth in the league before Alan Mullery earned the club promotion a year later.

While the first assertion overlooks much of the framework Clough had put in place before being tempted by the lure of then mighty Leeds, the latter view does not go far enough. If Clough had stayed, it is my view that he and Taylor would have earned promotion for the south coast club. Of that there is no doubt.

As it transpired, Clough's unique brand of management was never executed in its entirety, so Brighton fans are left with just 12 victories from the Clough months.

His first game in charge, at home to York City, put 10,000 fans on the gate and the team that day managed a 0-0 draw. The line-up was: Powney, Templeman, Ley, Boyle, Gall, Piper, Bridges, Howell, Beamish, Robertson, O'Sullivan. Sub: Hilton

After the game, Clough said: "They played well enough to have won. I would have liked to have seen them win but York aren't exactly the worst side in the third division, although I've not seen much of it".

This was the starting point for a new challenge and after succeeding Pat Saward, Clough and Taylor brought in a stream of players: Ken Goodeve, Harry Wilson, Ronnie Welch, Peter Grummitt, Paul Fuschillo, Billy McEwan, Steve Govier, Andy Rollins, Ian Mellor and Fred Binney. They cost a combined total of around £200,000, a colossal sum to a club struggling in Division Three. The dynamic duo meant business and at one stage there were also rumours that England's former captain, Bobby Moore, was to join Clough at the Goldstone.

Alas, the glorious potential did not run its course but details of those 12 Clough victories offer evidence of the master plan taking shape well before the master himself had left.

THE LIFE OF BRIAN

Season 1973-1974

November 13, 1973 v Walsall (a), won 1-0
Pat Hilton heads the only goal on 78 minutes.

Clough: "They fought very hard. I was delighted with them. They showed a bit of heart".

December 29, 1973 v Plymouth Argyle (h), won 1-0
Plymouth's 20-year old Paul Mariner, from non-league Chorley, should have added to his 12 league goals. He hit the bar late on and had a fierce drive superbly saved by Grummitt. On 56 minutes, Ken Beamish had diverted the ball over the line for the only goal.

Clough: "I am well pleased with the victory but Plymouth were an attractive side and unlucky not to get a point".

January 12, 1974 v Charlton Athletic (a), won 4-0
The first was scored on 48 minutes when Howell beat Forster in the Charlton goal with a scorching drive. Howell scored his second on 57 minutes with a perfect side foot and completed his hat-trick from the penalty spot (67). Seven minutes later, O'Sullivan hit a great shot which gave Forster had no chance. Prior to the game Clough slapped a gag on his players so Ronnie Howell didn't have the opportunity to speak about his first hat-trick in a career which spanned four clubs. He told the assembled press corps: "It is more than I dare do to talk. Those are the orders we have been given by the boss. I'm sorry". It is the first hat-trick by a Brighton player since Kit Napier in August 1971.

Clough: "We just played well, but there wasn't four goals in it".

Clough, after a meeting with England and Sussex cricketer Tony Greig: "You will see me at the County Ground almost every day next summer. I love cricket far far more than football".

January 20, 1974 v Rochdale (h), won 2-1
This was the first league game to be played on a Sunday at the Goldstone Ground and the 18,885 crowd is the largest league crowd since Seagulls' promotion to the second division in 1971-72. They witness a spirited

Brighton display in which Towner was man-of-the-match. He picked up a ball from Beamish on 35 minutes and smacked home a cracker from 25 yards. Six minutes later, Beamish arrives in good time to belt home O'Sullivan's cross from point blank range. A diving header from Skeete pulled one back for Rochdale.

Clough: "Sunday football is inevitable".

February 23, 1974 v Blackburn Rovers, won 3-0
This is Albion's best performance of the season. Peter Taylor has just signed Paul Fuschillo and Billy McEwan. Taylor said: "This adds to our first team pool and creates more competition for places. There will be more signings. On that you can rely". On 25 minutes, Welch converts a penalty for the first after handball by Waddington. For the second Bridges produces a real piece of class to brush home an O'Sullivan centre. The 33-year-old former Chelsea star Barry Bridges is enjoying a revival under Clough and scores the third for good measure.

February 27, 1974 v Wrexham (h), won 2-1
Brighton show a lot of character to come back from a goal down. On 20 minutes Howell converts a penalty after Beamish was felled. In the 38th minute the old hand, O'Sullivan, lets fly with a 25-yarder that goes in via a post. Fuschillo and McEwan make their debuts.

Clough: "I was delighted with our two strikers".

March 3, 1974 v Aldershot (a), won 1-0
A goal from Beamish moves Albion into 15th position after hovering on the fringe of relegation two months earlier. Howell is given the man-of-the-match award.

Clough: "Superb. But I thought Fuschillo's sending-off was very harsh. We should have won 2-0. All the lads played well and in particular, Steve Piper. Our two strikers had another good day. The best strikers hunt in pairs and this is what is starting to happen with us. Barry Bridges is doing more for us now than he has done in the last 10 years of his professional life. The other week he got two and this time it was Beamish".

March 10, 1974 v Hereford United (h), won 2-1

Albion are caught cold by a 25 yard speculative shot from Dudley Tyler which flashed into the top-right corner. In the 65th minute Wilson drove the ball into the middle, Bridges jumped over it and Beamish hit a low strike for his 10th of the season. With only two minutes left, McEwan set up Piper for the winner – his first-ever league goal. Albion move into the top 10.

Clough: "So, people are talking about the mathematical possibility of us going up". Well listen to me. We couldn't go up if we had Einstein on our side – and he was pretty good at figures".

Clough: "I know some people are surprised that Tony Towner isn't in the side these days. He is a bit of a luxury for us at the moment. I have to have experience. The problem is the midfield, but we are working at it."

Clough: "The whole point of what has gone on out there is that 17,000 people have gone away contented and there will be people going around the town not ashamed to wear an Albion scarf".
On being offered a job to manage in Iran at £400 per week, tax free, Clough said: "I was both delighted and flattered. Of course I am not

Cloughie talks while his assistant, Peter Taylor, and Brighton chairman, Mike Bamber, look on.

going. I am staying at Brighton"
Press Comment: "There isn't room for two Shahs in Iran!"

March 3, 1974 v Port Vale (h), won 2-1
Bridges lets fly from 12 yards to beat Boswell on 16 minutes. McEwan
(25) finds the net with a low shot for the second, while Harris (54) scores
from a fine header for Vale to half the deficit. Fuschillo is man-of-the-
match.

April 3, 1974 v Cambridge United (h), won 4-1
Once again Fuschillo is outstanding. Powney plays with a broken finger.
On 35 minutes Templeman puts Bridges through to open the scoring.
Eight minutes later, Ross scores a penalty for Cambridge but on the
stroke of half-time a 25 yarder from Welch is deflected into the net. On
65 minutes, Beamish finds McEwan to make it 3-1 and the scoring was
rounded off by Howell from the spot after Beamish had been brought
down by Akkers.

Clough: "We never stopped running and working".

Taylor: "I thought it was a great performance from Fuschillo and he
wasn't the only one. John Templeman and Micky Brown had good games
as well. We played some really good football out there and I only hope
the crowd were entertained. As we said before the match, when a player
like Brian Powney doesn't hesitate about playing, that is a spirit you can't
buy".

April 6, 1972 v Walsall (h), won 2-1
After just 10 minutes, Bridges heads home Templeman's cross to draw
level with Beamish on 10 goals. Buckley equalises for Walsall just a
minute later and it wasn't until 61 minutes that Beamish heads
O'Sullivan's corner back to Robertson, who had timed his run perfectly to
head in. Bridges was sent-off and Brighton's disciplinary record leaves
something to be desired, with four players dismissed in nine matches.

Clough: "Players in the lower divisions are inexpert in the art of tackling.
The majority of challenges are too late and this has consequences for the
referee to deal with, and hence the little black book comes out. The
players have too much enthusiasm. They want to do well, which is

understandable, but they lack the right technique. They'll learn, believe me. They will learn".

April 12, 1973 v Southend United (a), won 2-0
Star man for Clough's final victory as manager of Brighton was Beamish. He scored two goals inside four minutes in a second half spell which gave Brighton the points at Roots Hall.

Taylor: "It was a satisfactory result for us. We absorbed them in the first half and took them to the cleaners in the second".

For the record, Clough's final game in charge came against Bristol Rovers at the Eastville Stadium:

April 27, 1974 v Bristol Rovers (a), drew 1-1
Before the game Clough declared: "Rovers won't beat us 8-2 this time". On 18 minutes Beamish puts in a cross which is converted by Robertson from point blank range. With only five minutes left Rovers earn a point from a disputed penalty.

Press comment:
"If Clough and Taylor had not arrived in the nick of time, the last rites might have been performed weeks ago.
Brighton Evening Argus

There was absolutely no hint that Brian Clough would opt out of his five year contract with Brighton so soon. At the end of the season Peter Taylor, who took sole charge, delivered the following message:
"My advice to the fans is to come quickly and buy their season tickets. We are going to break several records at this club and we hope to have a complete sell out of tickets before the season begins. We mean business and now that we have spent money, I expect the public to react accordingly"

But supporting the Seagulls was about to become a more expensive business as the club announced a new, increased scale of admission charges:
West Stand season ticket – Old price £17.10; new £22
South Stand season ticket – Old £11; new £14

West Stand seat – Old £1.10; new £1.25
South Stand seat – Old 65p; new 80p

It was also announced that Brian Clough had scrapped the blue and white stripes of Albion's traditional home kit and changed it to an all-white strip (with blue trim) for the new season.

Not that Cloughie would see his new-look Seagulls. He was on his way to one of the top managerial jobs in the country . . .

Chapter 8
Leeds United
The 44 Days

Name your price. You can have whatever you want to come up here and help me. It's too much for one.
Brian Clough to Peter Taylor

There were two major jobs going at the time, Leeds and Liverpool, where Bill Shankly's reign was ending. I was unlucky enough to be offered the wrong one. If I had gone to Liverpool I would have died there. I would have become as close to that club as the paint on the walls.
Brian Clough

I think it is a very sad day for Leeds and for football
Brian Clough's response to his sacking

Our loss for the second time
Touching sentiment on a Leeds United shirt at the commemorative gates outside The City Ground after the news of Brian's sad passing.

The 44 days spent at Leeds United have gone down in football folklore. The Don Revie era was always going to cast a long shadow over any successor but this was only one of the many contributory factors working against Brian Clough's inimitable style of football when he walked into Elland Road in 1974.

While the great destructive forces of ego, injury, suspension, poor results and just plain bad luck had their part to play, perhaps the most crucial element in the whole drama was rashness – both on Clough's part, in his dealings with the Leeds players at the start of his brief spell in West Yorkshire, and that of Manny Cussins, the Leeds United chairman who cut short Clough's tenure.

This is how Clough's remarkable Leeds story unfolded . . .

The Appointment

Once Ian St John, the Motherwell manager and former Liverpool star, was eliminated from the race along with every other pretender to Revie's throne, all roads led to Majorca where a holidaying Brian Clough, still in charge at Brighton, was making public his desire to take charge of the reigning Football League champions.

Like Revie, who had left Leeds to take over from Sir Alf Ramsey as England manager, Clough hailed from Middlesbrough and regarded his job as keeping the Leeds team at the pinnacle of their profession.

Brian was aware of the anti-Clough talk in the West Riding but it didn't worry him because he implicitly believed he would continue to bring success to a club that had become used to glory. He was not only taking over a championship-winning team, the Peacocks had also been runners-up in the first division championship in three of the previous five seasons, won the FA Cup and reached two other Wembley cup finals. Leeds were also a growing force in Europe.

Clough clearly faced a monumental task in following the revered Revie, and said:"My aim will be to win the friendship and respect of all those who supported Leeds under my predecessor and to attract more recruits".

Before Clough arrived, the recently appointed England manager Revie had a final meeting with his entire former playing and training staff (with the exception of Billy Bremner who was on holiday). He told them: "You ought to give the same support to the next manager".

Players such as left-back Terry Cooper echoed this view when telling the press the team was looking forward to getting down to work with the new manager. They were also pleased that the backroom staff was to remain. Even defender Norman Hunter, the subject of Clough criticism in the past, was quoted as saying: "We'll have to forget the past and pull together for the sake of the club. We will give 100 per cent to Mr. Clough".

Only one Leeds director opposed the appointment but he bowed to the majority view.

There was, understandably, great anger in the Brighton camp and chairman, Mike Bamber, made it clear that he intended to sue for an illegal approach to a manager under contract. It was agreed that a sum of £75,000 would be paid to Brighton in compensation and a friendly between the two clubs was to be arranged to be played at the Goldstone Ground. It was only a temporary smoothing over of an ever-sharpening thorn.

Meanwhile, Clough took the time to send a telegram to Leeds' fiery Scottish international skipper Billy Bremner, saying it was a privilege to be the manager of Leeds and to have the chance to work with such fine players.

Manny Cussins offered Brian the warmest of welcomes when saying: "I am certain we are all going to be very happy with Brian Clough. I think he is an ambitious man, an outspoken man and we have told him to be diplomatic. I think we are all going to be very happy".

However, it was also in evidence that even before his arrival at Elland Road, Clough was being viewed with suspicion. At the civic reception to celebrate the championship triumph of the previous season, he was greeted by boos from the fans.

England striker Allan Clarke ominously voiced his disapproval, saying: "We have not even met Brian Clough yet. If I had just taken over a club I would want to be here with the players, not sunning myself in Majorca".

Day One –Wednesday July 31, 1974

Brian Clough makes his first appearance at Elland Road in the pouring rain. He pledges to make Don Revie's job a little easier when saying: "More Leeds players will be released for England duty in the next 10 years than have been for the last 10. I hope there will be fewer injuries and I am not implying criticism."

Les Cocker, the club's trainer and physiotherapist, decides to accept Revie's invitation to join him as part of the England camp. Clough's response is to say: "It is terrific for him and I congratulate him".

On the forthcoming 1974-75 season, Clough asserts that the League is his priority but he would love to win the European Cup.

On the players, he said: "I don't think it mattered who walked through the door. These players would have got on with the job. It is the way they have been brought up. It is not a problem for me taking over 10 or so internationals, as they are very mature players. I think relationships grow over a period of time. It is a frightening thought that they have not been out

of the top four in the last 10 years. It is a staggering standard to maintain".
On discipline at the club, he thought that it had improved in recent years but was frustrated by the rollover suspensions of Clarke and Hunter who were not eligible for the start of the season.

He stated his intention to apply a code of discipline for players who had been cautioned and said: "Good clubs have such codes. Good players accept those codes".

Clough's contract as Leeds United manager was for four years.

Day Two – Thursday August 1, 1974

Clough's first signing is Jimmy Gordon, a man whom he had known since his time at Middlesbrough. They had been together at Derby for five years and Clough welcomed his arrival by saying: "Jimmy is undoubtedly the most respected trainer-coach in the game, including Les Cocker".

Day Three – Friday, August 2, 1974

Clough announces he is going to give both Terry Cooper and Mick Bates an early chance to regain their regular Leeds United roles after they had suffered serious leg injuries. Both players are named in the side to face Huddersfield Town away at Leeds Road in a testimonial for long-serving Terrier, Steve Smith.

There is press speculation that Leeds and Derby County are favourites to sign out of favour Nottingham Forest striker, Duncan McKenzie. Also, John McGovern is on the transfer list at Derby and is being linked to a reunion with Clough.

Days Four and Five – Saturday/Sunday, August 3/4, 1974

Steve Smith's testimonial finishes Huddersfield 1, Leeds United 2. Clough takes a seat in the stand. The visiting line-up was: Stewart, Reaney, Cooper, Bremner, McQueen, Hunter, Lorimer, Bates, Clarke, Giles and Madeley. Cherry came on for Hunter.

Don Revie is purportedly considering legal advice following comments made by Brian Clough on a TV programme last Friday. Clough said:
"Anyone who saw the programme can make up their own minds. Revie can have 50 transcripts of the broadcast if he wants to".

Clough makes the first overtures to bring John McGovern to Elland Road.

Day Six – Monday, August 5, 1974

It is announced that eight of the first team squad are still yet to sign new contracts for the coming season. Clough claims: "I do not have any disputes on my hands. The last thing I wanted to do when joining Leeds was to talk

THE LIFE OF **BRIAN**

contracts". A directors' statement said that Clough had been given instructions by the board to compete the several outstanding contracts over the next few days.

Day Seven – Tuesday, August 6, 1974

Clough signs Duncan McKenzie for £250,000 from Nottingham Forest. Both Birmingham City and Tottenham Hotspur matched the Leeds offer. Duncan met with all three clubs but was most impressed by Clough and Leeds United.

Eddie Gray, who had played in only one of Leeds United's last 45 games, is named by Clough as part of the 12-strong team playing Aston Villa in a pre-season friendly.

At the club's pre-season get-together, Clough pays his respects to Don Revie. He told the players: "I feel like an intruder at a party which has taken years to arrange. It is a pity that Don Revie and Les Cocker are not here to enjoy it, because they are the men who won the championship with you. It will be my turn next year".

Day Eight – Wednesday August 7, 1974

Aston Villa 1, Leeds United 2. Two goals from Allan Clarke secured victory during Aston Villa's Centenary game at Villa Park. Ray Graydon missed two penalties for the home side.

Clough is being linked with Leicester City's England keeper, Peter Shilton, for £300,000 while the John McGovern speculation continues to gather momentum.

Duncan McKenzie joins the team for a training session and attends the game at Villa Park. On signing, he said: "I had spoken to Birmingham and Spurs before but when Mr Clough came to see me I was very flattered and, naturally, I chose Leeds. I think playing for them will improve my chances of playing for England".

Day Nine – Thursday, August 8, 1974

Eight teams are reported to be interested in Peter Shilton's signature with the front-runners being Arsenal, Leeds and Everton.

Day 10 – Friday, August 9, 1974

Clough makes it clear that Leeds United will not be signing Peter Shilton. "There have been no moves whatsoever. I have made no enquiry and no offer. Although I have contemplated buying Shilton a million times, I have not done so while I have been at Leeds. Nobody is going from this club in exchange deals or any other deals until I have been here a long time.

Brian alongside Billy Bremner and his Leeds team before the ill-fated Charity Shield.

Nobody has asked for a transfer, nobody wants to go and nobody is going. I have two goalkeepers with whom I am delighted".

Days 11 and 12 – Saturday/Sunday, August 10/11, 1974

Leeds and Liverpool disgrace Wembley. The Charity Shield curtain-raiser was settled on penalties, which Liverpool won 6-5, after the game ended 1-1. But the result was very much a minor statistic on a day when Kevin Keegan and Billy Bremner are sent-off for fighting. Managers Bill Shankly and Clough agree that the sendings-off spoiled a good match but the whole affair would cast a long shadow on Clough's time at Elland Road. Crunching tackles from Liverpool hard-man Tommy Smith and Leeds striker Allan Clarke within the first five minutes set the tone for the rest of the game, watched by 67,000.

Day 13 – Monday, August 12, 1974

Perhaps more significant to the fate of Clough was the desire of midfield maestro Johnny Giles to enter management and even though he signs a playing contract for the coming season, his managerial aspirations have a part to play in Clough's imminent demise at the club. All the players, with the exception of Terry Yorath, have now signed contracts. The Welshman was reportedly suffering an illness.

Clough announces there will be no appeal against Billy Bremner's sending-off at Wembley. He is quoted as saying: "Any disciplinary action that might be taken during the season will be private".

Day 14 - Tuesday, August 13, 1974
Leeds play in a testimonial match for Southampton's general manager, Ted Bates. The game ends 1-1 and Duncan McKenzie scores his first goal for Leeds after 18 minutes, in front of 15,000 fans.
Keegan and Bremner are formally charged with bringing the game into disrepute.

Day 15 - Wednesday, August 14, 1974
Clough comes to Billy Bremner's defence when he says: "I am all in favour of cleaning up the game but not on the back of Billy Bremner". He also issues a "hands off" warning to Huddersfield who have voiced their interest in Johnny Giles. Town manager, former Leeds favourite Bobby Collins, visits Elland Road in the hope of securing a deal. Clough commented: "Johnny Giles is absolutely essential to Leeds at the moment but if the situation changes Bobby Collins will be informed. Giles is very much in my plans for the game at Stoke on Saturday".

Day 16 – Thursday, August 15, 1974
Looking forward to the league opener against Stoke City, Clough says: "Attack is my only policy". Clough is without Allan Clarke and Norman Hunter due to suspension. Mick Jones and Terry Yorath are injured and Paul Madeley is fighting to overcome a calf injury. Clough says: "The odds are already stacked against us".

Day 17 – Friday, August 16, 1974
Clough and Bill Shankly meet with Vernon Stokes, chairman of the FA disciplinary committee. Clough said: "We had a long chat with Vernon Stokes who is a man of integrity. Anytime we can get together it must be good for football". It is decided that Leeds and Liverpool are to take strong disciplinary action against their players after the shameful events at Wembley in the Charity Shield.

Days 18 and 19 – Saturday/Sunday, August 17/18, 1974
The league season opens and Leeds are thumped 3-0 by Stoke City. The scoreline belies a competent Leeds display, which deserved so much more. Nevertheless the football world is shocked and the press is starting to sense a few problems brewing in the United camp.

Tony Waddington, Stoke City's manager, said: "It was a marvellous advert for the game and the result could have gone either way". Clough added: "We played well enough to be 3-0 up at half-time. Stoke deserved to win but I felt sorry for the lads. They so badly wanted to win. They played enough football to win three matches".

The Leeds players went into the match without their usual bingo session, which had become such a feature under Don Revie.

The line-up was: Harvey, Reaney, Cooper, Bremner, McQueen, Cherry, Lorimer, Madeley, Jordan, Giles, McKenzie

It is the last game Bremner will play under Clough.

Day 20 – Monday, August 19, 1974

John McGovern, 24, and John O'Hare, 27, rejoin Clough from Derby County for £130,000. In a lightning deal both could go straight into the team to play QPR on Wednesday. Clough said: "I could not let the down the Leeds United supporters and the type of quality player they are accustomed to seeing". The signings go some way to addressing the serious issues of suspensions, injury and illness, which have resulted in a depleted Leeds squad. "I am absolutely delighted to get them, for both the type of players they are and the type of people they are," concluded Clough.

His spending is up to £400,000 in two weeks.

Day 21 – Tuesday, August 20, 1974

Clough reiterates that he does not intend to sell any of his players. "No one goes. There is a job for everyone in the pool".

Leeds appoint Michael Dooley as assistant secretary.

The press continue to analyse Clough's signings and he responds with: "I am very conscience of the fact that Leeds are champions and I cannot afford to bring in any rag, tag and bobtail players here".

Day 22 – Wednesday, August 21, 1974

A 1-0 defeat at Queens Park Rangers increases the pressure at the club. A mistake by David Harvey gifts QPR their goal. Clough arrived to a tremendous reception from the 31,497 crowd. Most of the west stand stood and applauded as he made his way to the dugout.

Clough did not utilise McGovern or O'Hare. He said afterwards: "I was very sorry for David Harvey but it is essential he forgets it. We did not play with confidence and badly missed Bremner, Hunter and Clarke. We created enough chances but could not put them in. We will all be here in the morning working like hell. That is all you can do. It is a bad start by most standards, particularly by Leeds' standards".

THE LIFE OF BRIAN

Day 23 – Thursday. August 22, 1974
Hunter and Clarke are set to return for the home game against Birmingham on Saturday. Not since they returned to the top flight in 1964 has Leeds lost its two opening matches. Clough says: "We are not gloomy. We just have to work harder".

Leeds are drawn away at Huddersfield in the League Cup. Clough's response: "I would have preferred it to be at home".

Day 24 – Friday, August 23, 1974
The FA disciplinary committee reverses its decision to call Allan Clarke before them as a witness. Clough is appeased, as he was livid about Leeds' players being put on trial by television. He even threatened to ban the TV cameras from Elland Road. Vernon Clarke said it did not seem right to investigate a player who had not been cautioned during the match.

Days 25 and 26 – Saturday/Sunday, August 24/25, 1974
A 1-0 home win over Birmingham City brings relief all round.

Clarke scored the goal and Clough said: "No-one in England could have scored it better than the way he did. It was one touch of class above all others".

O'Hare had an impressive debut and Clough said: "He turned on from start to finish all over the pitch. Just wait to see what he is like once he has been here a few weeks".

The crowd was 8,500 down on the corresponding fixture last season. It could be down to any one or a combination of factors – from the bank holiday weekend, violence on the terraces or the dismal results under Clough.

Day 27 – Monday, August 26, 1974
Terry Yorath is due to make his first appearance under Clough in the game at QPR tomorrow. Clough discounts reports of Leeds' interest in Burnley's England international midfield captain, Martin Dobson.

Day 28 – Tuesday, August 27, 1974
This 1-1 draw marked Leeds' best performance so far under Clough, who said: "We came on a ton tonight".

Day 29 – Wednesday, August 28, 1974
Keegan and Bremner are each fined £500 as the FA disciplinary committee executes its clean-up campaign in football. Their suspensions

are also extended to September 30. It brings Bremner's suspension over the past 10 years to 142 days and his fines to £1,000. Leeds chairman Manny Cussins says: "This will not do Leeds United any good but we cannot condone the actions of the players".

Day 30 – Thursday, August 29, 1974
Bremner resumes training with his colleagues, while Clough remains tight-lipped about the FA decision.

Day 31 – Friday, August 30, 1974
In the build-up to the game at Manchester City, Clough is quoted as saying: "He (Asa Hartford) will want to show off against us. Lots of players want to. It is a pity that McKenzie is not opposing him".

The background to the comment is that Hartford almost moved from West Bromwich Albion to Leeds in 1971, until a failed medical revealed the talented midfielder had a 'hole' in his heart and Leeds pulled out of the deal.

McKenzie is set to have a couple of games in the reserves after recovering from a thigh injury.

Days 32 and 33 – Saturday/Sunday, August 31/September 1, 1974
A 2-1 defeat at Maine Road shows that Leeds are still not scoring the goals their efforts deserve. The press are having a field day comparing the three goals this season with the 15 at the same time last campaign under Revie. Clough said: "I am sick of playing well and being on the losing side. How can Allan Clarke score a goal like that and end up on the losing side?"

Over 37,000 were enthralled by this thriller and Clough continued: "The chances keep dropping to the wrong players. I can't crib about a centre-half missing from three yards".

August has not been kind to Clough. September would be worse.

Day 34 – Monday, September 2, 1974
There is a vacancy for the Spurs manager's job and Johnny Giles is known to be interested and will have showdown talks with Clough this week. Manny Cussins states that while the club would miss the genial Irishman's playing ability, they would give fair consideration to anything that would concern his future. He continued: "We have had no contact from Tottenham or anybody else. I think Mr Clough would have told us had Giles been approached".

Day 35 – Tuesday, September 3, 1974

Clough is to give several of his key players some important match practice in a Central League game against Blackburn Rovers at Elland Road tomorrow. Leeds' much-travelled assistant, Maurice Lindley, submits a report on Zurich, Leeds' next opposition in the European Cup, after seeing them win 3-0 away to Geneva.

A report is also due from the specialist on injured Eddie Gray.

Day 36 – Wednesday, September 4, 1974

Former Chairman, Harry Reynolds, 73, passes away. He is highly regarded as the man who put Leeds United on the map. He died shortly before the Central League game against Blackburn in which Joe Jordan scored twice in a 3-0 win.

Meanwhile Brighton & Hove Albion are proceeding with their intention to sue Clough. Seagulls' chairman, Mike Bamber, stated: "All I can say is that we are going full steam ahead with our action".

Day 37 – Thursday, September 5, 1974

Clough states that if Spurs were interested in Giles to replace he would have heard from them. He is reluctant to let Giles or any other players leave.

In the Elland Road dugout alongside trusty ally, Jimmy Gordon. But the smiles didn't last...

Day 38 – Friday, September 6, 1974

Lorimer, Clarke and O'Hare are again selected as the strike-force to face Luton and Clough receives criticism as a result. McKenzie is in the reserves. Clough says prior to the game against Luton: "It is only winning that will prepare us for the European Cup".

Days 39-40 – Saturday/Sunday, September 7/8, 1974

Chaos descends on Elland Road after the 1-1 draw with Luton. All criticism is levied against Clough. The team and manager were jeered by 26,000 as they left the pitch. Even the tannoy played *Who's Sorry Now?* Clough is undeterred: "Our performances as a whole are one yard short of superb. It was down to confidence and that is down to me. I instill or destroy it. I have not been able to instill it as yet. If we had scored a second we would have blossomed. The difference is a matter of inches".

Clarke scored on 26 minutes but Luton equalised six minutes later. It was the lowest attendance at Leeds in over two years.

Clough signing McGovern is another target for fan abuse. The manager said: "The crowd's attitude towards him sickened me. I wouldn't have brought him off if we had been five-one down!"

He added: "I am glad I am the manager of Leeds, and not Luton".

It is reported that Terry Yorath may be the first to leave Elland Road under the Clough regime.

Day 41 – Monday, September 9, 1974

Brian Clough is quoted as saying: "The players back me".

On exiting a board meeting with a big grin on his face, Clough declared: "All we have got to do is get out on the field and start winning".

While the Yorath deal falls through, there is another growing issue for outstanding testimonials for many of the long-standing servants of the club, including Paul Reaney, Johnny Giles and Paul Madeley. Clough saw it as a big problem at a club trying to preach loyalty. He recognised it was not the players' fault and that they should not suffer.

Day 42 – Tuesday, September 10, 1974

In the dressing room before the League Cup tie against Huddersfield Town, the players express their unhappiness with Clough's handling of the team and they ask Manny Cussins and Sam Bolton, a vice-president of the Football League, to hear their case.

Clough is asked to leave the room during a clear-the-air meeting with the players and chairman. It was at this moment that Brian Clough knew he could no longer manage Leeds United.

The game is drawn 1-1, with Peter Lorimer scoring the last goal under Clough. Don Revie was in the crowd.

Clough's final team selection was: Harvey, Reaney, Cherry, Bates, McQueen, Hunter, Lorimer, Clarke, Jordan, Giles, Madeley.

Hours before the game, Cussins met with the players to address any problems they were harbouring. The omens were bad for Clough as the meeting took place on the morning of the funeral of Harry Reynolds, the 'father' of Leeds United. It is widely believed that what transpired in that meeting resulted in Brian Clough's 44-day reign at Leeds United being brought to a premature end. It is thought that Yorath's proposed move to Nottingham Forest was called off due to his prior knowledge of the sensational changes about to unfold at the club.

Day 43 – Wednesday, September 11, 1974
Speculation is rife that Brian Clough has been sacked from Leeds. Press comment suggests Leeds' players have given a vote of 'no confidence' to their manager.

Day 44 – Thursday, September 12, 1974
Chairman, Manny Cussins, stands at the entrance to Elland Road and announces that Brian Clough and Leeds United have parted company. He says: "What has been done has been done for the good of the club. The club and the happiness of the players must come first. Nothing can be successful unless the staff is happy".

When questioned that player-power was the reason behind the removal of Clough, Cussins would only say: "We've been spoiled by Don Revie".

Clough has seen enough and with a substantial financial package ratified prior to the public announcement, he leaves Elland Road for good.

"I have just won the pools," he famously said.

McKenzie, McGovern and O'Hare are not chosen to play in the next game, against Burnley.

Clough's unhappy 44-day reign is over.

Chapter 9
Nottingham Forest
The 42-game Unbeaten Streak

My pinnacle was going 42 league games undefeated, because I was always a league man but it went so unheralded. If anybody else had done what we'd done in such a short spell of time, we wouldn't have only gone down in history, we'd have gone down as the best thing ever. We'd have outdone Penicillin!
Brian Clough

They played us off the park. We never had a kick. They murdered us – particularly in midfield. We never got any rhythm and though it is a bit of a relief that the run is over, we'd have preferred to have won.
Brian Clough – Anfield, December 9, 1978

They treat the ball like they should treat their wives – caressing it, cherishing it. Their speed of thought and movement are incredible and they are the supreme essence of skill. Wenger is one of the great managers. However, with respect, we were Nottingham Forest and they are Arsenal.
Brian Clough – After Arsenal beat the all-time record for league games undefeated with victory over Blackburn Rovers in August 2004, just 26 days before he died.

Aforgettable 0-0 draw was the rather bland beginning to one of the greatest achievements in the history of football. Brian Clough's Nottingham Forest consistently kept defeat at bay for more than a whole year and the post-match comments that follow stand as classic examples of the wit, guile, arrogance, panache and steadfast confidence which often defined the great man's life.

It was thought the monumental feat would never be bettered but it was testament to the lasting respect Brian Clough had for skill and achievement that he had nothing but praise for Arsene Wenger's Arsenal after they had emulated the Forest record, with victory at home to Blackburn Rovers on August 25, 2004. The Gunners went a further seven Premiership matches unbeaten before the new record run was ended by their great rivals, Manchester United, at Old Trafford.

With all due respect to Wenger and his '49 Gun Salute', what Clough and Peter Taylor achieved at Nottingham Forest was far more remarkable by comparison. Whereas as Arsenal, Manchester United and Chelsea are now head and shoulders above the rest of the Premiership in terms of finance and player resources, Forest performed their heroics on a far more level playing field. A huge gulf in football finances, between the haves and the have-nots, did not exist in the late 70s to anything like the extent it does today, where the 'big three' – plus Liverpool and Newcastle United – monopolise the best talent.

In 1977, the unbeaten streak was an impossible notion – unimaginable, unthinkable and unheard of and yet Brian Clough and his men did it. He created a side so irrepressible, unbeatable and insatiable for victory that the world was seeing the absolute answer to every strategy, manoeuvre and grand plan the great game had ever offered; "We played the game as most people think it should be played – quick, neat, decisive and clean".

The game had its very own one-man football think tank. This is how history was made . . .

Season 1977-78

November 26, 1977 v West Bromwich Albion (h), drew 0-0
Having beaten Manchester United, 2-1, at The City Ground two weeks earlier, Forest have failed to score against Leeds in a 1-0 defeat at Elland Road and now against West Bromwich at home. There is little to suggest the team will remain unbeaten for another 41 league matches, until December 9, 1978 . . .
Forest: Shilton, Anderson, Barrett, McGovern, Lloyd, Burns, O'Neill,

Gemmill, Withe, Woodcock, Robertson.
Post match comments:
Brian Clough:
"They earned what they got by the honesty and effort of their players.
We have only scored two goals in our last four games but I don't consider
it a slump, because we played well in all of them".

Other comments:
"There is no point in anyone complaining about us keeping possession –
Forest must accept it because they are top of the league. They never stop
running at you and if you don't work as hard as them to match them all
down the line, you'll be in trouble. But I must say they are as good a team
as we have met all season".
John Wile, West Bromwich Albion captain

"Tony Woodcock gets better every time I see him".
Frank Clough – *The Sun*

Prior to the League Cup tie against Aston Villa on November 29, Brian
Clough was reported as saying the following about striker Peter Withe, who
was enduring a six-week goal drought:
"Get among the goals or else! We are geared to going forward and you
can't afford to have someone going in the opposite direction. If he drops
back any further he'll be getting in Peter Shilton's way. This is placing an
unreasonable burden on other players and we can't carry Peter any longer.
I may drop him against Aston Villa to take some of the pressure off him".

December 3, 1977 v Birmingham City (a), won 2-0
Goals from Martin O'Neill and Woodcock smooth over any rising concerns
of a rocky patch.
Forest: Shilton, Anderson, Barrett, McGovern, Lloyd, Burns, O'Neill,
Gemmill, Withe, Woodcock, Robertson.

Post-match comment:
Brian Clough:
"I was ashamed at half-time. We were in the lead and hadn't even started
to play. We got it together and in the end could have won by another two
or three goals. I just hope we keep on improving".

Other Comments:
"That save explained why anything is possible with Peter Shilton in the

113

THE LIFE OF **BRIAN**

side. The skills that went into the shot and the save were worth the price of admission alone".
Peter Taylor

"The team has been playing up to standard but they don't come up against a side as strong as Forest every week".
Sir Alf Ramsey, Birmingham City manager

"It is hardly surprising that Forest boast the best defensive record in the first division when you consider the goalkeeping skills of Peter Shilton. His stunning 42nd minute save from a close-range Trevor Francis volley amazed Birmingham's biggest crowd of the season".
Hugh Jamieson, journalist
Man of the Match – Larry Lloyd

December 10, 1977 v Coventry City (h), won 2-1
Forest are swept aside by a very impressive Coventry team but goals from O'Neill and McGovern make it two wins out of two. Ian Wallace, a future signing for Clough, scores the Sky Blues' goal.
Forest: Shilton, Anderson, Barrett, McGovern, Lloyd, Burns, O'Neill, Gemmill, Withe, Woodcock and Robertson

Post match comments:
Brian Clough:
"I looked at my watch after 20 minutes and couldn't believe Coventry hadn't scored. They put us under more pressure than any other side, home or away, this season. Gordon Milne can feel proud of his team – but if Coventry played so well, try not to forget we won 2-1".

Although the press went with Archie Gemmill as man-of-the-match, Clough picked out centre-half Larry Lloyd. "He showed tremendous courage and character".

Other comments:
Coventry City boss Gordon Milne, who signed Larry Lloyd for £250,000 from Liverpool and sold him to Clough for just £55,000, agreed with his Forest counterpart: "He was fabulous. He looked every bit a £250,000 player. Forest are certainly not in a false position at the top of the league".

Man of the match – Archie Gemmill

The Forest squad line up prior to the 1978-79 season.

December, 17, 1977 v Manchester United (a), won 4-0

One of the greatest Forest performances of all-time. It was as though 10 years of management had come to fruition on a winter's afternoon at Old Trafford. Woodcock (2), Robertson and a Greenhoff own-goal embarrass United but, given the impressive form of Forest, Dave Sexton's men got off lightly.

Forest: Shilton, Anderson, Barrett, McGovern, Needham, Burns, O'Neill, Gemmill, Withe, Woodcock, Robertson

Pre-match comments:

Prior to the game Brian Clough refused to talk to reporters. The press centred on Forest's new signing, David Needham, a centre-half signed from QPR for £140,000.

"I could not have chosen a harder debut – but I can't wait to get out there. I scored against United for QPR a couple of weeks ago. It would be magic to do it again"

David Needham, in for the injured Larry Lloyd

"He's a great player. Brian Clough and I would have gone for him at Derby but for the world-class form of Roy McFarland".

Peter Taylor on Needham

Post-match Comments:

Brian Clough:
"For years this place has been held up by all as the home of skill but today my team showed them what skill is all about".

"Forest beat us because they were more determined and sharper than we were. Full marks to Forest. They are well worth their place at the top of the league".
Dave Sexton, Manchester United manager

Brian Clough:
"Determination and sharpness are very well but before anything else you have to have skill in your side".

Other Comments:
"At the final whistle, Brian Clough waved an imperious gesture that bordered on contempt at the magnificent mansion called Old Trafford".

"United have been buried in their own back yard"
Barry Davies, BBC Match of the Day commentator

"Forest were simply breathtaking and if they had doubled the score United could have had no complaint. United were reduced to zombies by the arrogance and assurance of the instant control and passing accuracy of the league-leaders. When they defended they had nine at the back. When they attacked they had six up front" – **Press comment**

"That's probably the best away performance of the season – everything went right. It is probably too early to talk about championships but after years of being with a struggling team at Birmingham, I wouldn't swop places with any other player in the country. I'm in a good team and I'm working for the best manager in the game. What more could I want?"
Kenny Burns

"Archie Gemmill overshadowed Lou Macari in midfield, John McGovern eclipsed Sammy McIlroy, Tony Woodcock emphasised his growing stature as an international striker and John Robertson was at his most waspish on the left" – **Press comment**

Man of the match – Archie Gemmill

December 26, 1977 v Liverpool (h), drew 1-1
All the talk continues to be about the punishment exacted on Manchester United. Almost 20,000 more fans show up for this Boxing Day encounter in which Steve Heighway and Archie Gemmill ensure the spoils are shared.
Forest: Shilton, Anderson, Barrett, McGovern, Needham, Burns, O'Neill, Gemmill, Withe, Woodcock, Robertson

December 28, 1977, Newcastle United (a), won 2-0
One of the papers the following morning ran with the headline: "Clough Five Points Clear". It fully captures the omniscient aura Brian Clough exudes. This is very much the era of Clough. Needham scores his first goal for the club while McGovern nets the other. Newcastle would finish the season second from bottom.
Forest: Shilton, Anderson, Barrett, McGovern, Needham, Burns, O'Neill, Gemmill, Withe, Woodcock, Robertson

Post-match Comments:

Brian Clough:
"Obviously it feels good to be five points clear. We might as well be there as anybody else. We were never this far ahead at Derby – but there is still a long way to go.

"It is getting to the stage that when we go away from home we give Peter Shilton the match ball, because he doesn't see enough of it during the game"

Other Comments:
"Brian Clough, the man shunned repeatedly by North-East clubs when making their managerial choices, picked the perfect platform at Newcastle last night to launch his side to the first division championship. Even facing the wind, Forest still managed to look a cut above their opponents" – **Press comment**

December 31, 1977 v Bristol City (a), won 3-1
Five league wins from six and Forest continue to lead the pack. Needham scores again and is further proof of the Taylor/Clough transfer wizardry. Woodcock and O'Neill also get on the scoresheet. Kevin Mabbutt registers for the Robins.
Forest: Shilton, Anderson, Barrett, McGovern, Needham, Burns, O'Neill, Gemmill, Withe, Woodcock and Robertson

THE LIFE OF **BRIAN**

Post-match Comments:
Brian Clough:
"I have been pleased with our attitude over the holiday period and know we are looking forward to playing Everton".

Other comments:
"The gulf in class between Nottingham Forest and the rest is growing with each game" – **Press comment**

January 2, 1978 v Everton (h), drew 1-1
Everton frustrate Forest who lack the sharpness of recent games and are lucky to take a point from this match. A penalty apiece for John Robertson and Trevor Ross for Everton account for the goals.
Forest: Shilton, Anderson, Barrett, McGovern, Needham, Burns, O'Neill, Gemmill, Withe, Woodcock, Robertson

Post-match Comments:

Brian Clough:
"If I had been the Everton manager I would have been very upset if we had gone home empty-handed. But I'm still not too despondent".

Other Comments:
"Brian Clough looked as black as thunder as he strode from the dug-out at the final whistle" – **Press comment**

January 14, 1978 v Derby County (a), drew 0-0
A return to Clough's former club raises the temperature in this game and the outcome keeps both ends of the A52 happy.
Forest: Shilton, Anderson, Barrett, McGovern, Needham, Burns, O'Neill, Gemmill, Withe, Woodcock, Robertson

Post-match Comments:

Brian Clough:
"Not bad for a goalless draw – but hey, it's still hard to get a point at Derby".

Other Comments:

"It was a game crammed with class and entertainment and all superbly controlled by players whose professional discipline was a credit".
John Sadler, reporter

"This was something special. You could feel it all week".
Tommy Docherty, Derby County manager

Man of the match – Peter Shilton

January 21, 1978 v Arsenal (h), won 2-1
Forest have the enviable ability of raising their game for the big matches. Yet again Needham gets on the scoresheet and is joined there by Archie Gemmill. With over three months of the season to go, many pundits and commentators are already tipping Forest for the championship.
Forest: Shilton, Anderson, Barrett, McGovern, Needham, Burns, O'Neill, Gemmill, Withe, Woodcock, Robertson.

Post-match Comments:
Brian Clough:
"We know what we are doing and we are good at it".

Other Comments:
"I think I know Brian's secret. He just goes out and buys a few good players and then makes them work harder than they have ever done before. Good luck to him and his team. They deserve to win the title"
Terry Neill, Arsenal manager

"Malcolm MacDonald and Frank Stapleton hardly had a kick against Kenny Burns and David Needham. The immensely talented Liam Brady looked little more than an apprentice alongside Gemmill and McGovern"
– Press comment

Man of the match – Archie Gemmill

February 4, 1978 v Wolverhampton Wanderers (h), won 2-0
Conditions are boggy but Forest win comfortably with goals from Woodcock and McGovern.
Forest: Shilton, Anderson, Barrett, McGovern, Needham, Burns, O'Neill, Gemmill, Withe, Woodcock, Robertson.

Post-match Comments:

"Didn't someone say we would struggle when the heavy grounds arrived? Well, this was one of those days – I wonder what theory they are going to come up with next?"
Peter Taylor

"Forest fought for everything, moved the ball quickly, refused to let the pitch cramp their style – and won in comfort" – **Press comment**

Man of the match – John McGovern

February 25, 1978 v Norwich City (a), drew 3-3
Not many teams come back from three down against Forest and Norwich manager, the experienced and wily John Bond gushes praise for Brian Clough's team. Withe scores his first league goal for more than four months and Forest extend their lead through Barrett and O'Neill. A Ryan penalty, Suggett strike and Keith Robson effort give the Canaries a deserved point. Brian Clough is not present for this game.
Forest: Shilton, Anderson, Barrett, McGovern, Needham, Burns, O'Neill, Gemmill, Withe, Woodcock, Robertson

Post-match Comments:

"We were second best throughout, even when three up. By our standard, I was not impressed."
Peter Taylor

"They are dead certain to win it. They will win it by a mile. This setback won't make any difference. Archie Gemmill will run them there on his own and what about Tony Woodcock?"
John Bond, Norwich City manager

March 4, 1978 v West Ham United (h), won 2-0
This is the first of three crucial home games for Forest and they start off well with goals from Needham and a Robertson penalty. The press are now making references to the fact that Forest remain unbeaten in the league this year. It is a sentiment which is set to run for some considerable time to come. West Ham will join Newcastle United and Leicester City for the drop at the season's conclusion.
Forest: Shilton, Bowyer, Clark, O'Hare, Needham, Burns, O'Neill, Gemmill, Withe, Woodcock, Robertson

Post-match Comments:

Brian Clough:
"You don't win titles against the Liverpools and Man Cities when the grass is green and the sky's blue and the sun's shining. It's out there, on days like this, against teams like West Ham, on pitches like that. That's when titles are won".

Man of the match – John Robertson

March 14, 1978 v Leicester City (h), won 1-0
Wallington, Whitworth, Weller, Webb, and Williams fail to add the 'W' for win to their effort and John Robertson's penalty is enough to keep Forest's championship momentum ticking over nicely. Leicester are destined to finish bottom.
Forest: Shilton, Anderson, Clark, O'Hare, Needham, Burns, O'Neill, Gemmill, Bowyer, Woodcock, Robertson

Post-match Comments:

Brian Clough:
"We won and that's all that matters. Now we have to get 12 players fit to play Liverpool at Wembley" (League Cup final)

Peter Taylor:
"We're going to win the League and the European Cup next season".

March 25, 1978 v Newcastle United (h), won 2-0
Forest are in triumphant mood after John Robertson's penalty beat Liverpool at Wembley in the League Cup final in front of 100,000 fans.
They also make it three out of three in consecutive home league games and are scoring full marks for consistency up front and frugality in defence.
Robertson scores his third penalty in three straight league games, while right-back Viv Anderson scores his third, and final, league goal of the season.
Forest: Shilton, Anderson, Clark, O'Hare, Needham, Burns, O'Neill, Withe, Woodcock, Robertson.

Post-match Comments:

Brian Clough:

"We are still suffering a backlash from all our efforts last week in winning the League Cup.

"Style is important. If you are going to win anything you do it with conviction to show that you really are the best.

"Between now and our last match you will see us put on the sort of style we did in the first half of the season".

Man of the match – Peter Shilton

March 29, 1978 v Middlesbrough (a), drew 2-2

Mills and Cummins earn Middlesbrough a point but they should have taken two, such was their dominance. Forest are very resilient and have not tasted defeat in the league for 16 matches. Woodcock and O'Neill help grab a point.

Forest: Shilton, Bowyer, Clark, O'Hare, Needham, Burns, O'Neill, Gemmill, Withe, Woodcock, Robertson.

Post-match Comments:

Brian Clough:

"I am glad Everton still have to play here. If I was to send Gordon Lee a dossier on Boro, it would frighten him".

Other Comments:

"Cloughie's title favourites twice came from behind to make it 16 league games without defeat" – **Press report**

"The result would have been totally different but for an incredible miss by Middlesbrough's David Mills in the dying seconds" – **Press report**

April 1, 1978 v Chelsea (h), won 3-1

Chelsea are without a win since March 4 when they promised much after beating Liverpool 3-1 at Stamford Bridge. They never look like winning at The City Ground and are swept aside by goals from Burns, O'Neill and a Robertson strike from open play. Langley scores for Blues.

Forest: Shilton, Bowyer, Clark, O'Hare, Lloyd, Burns, O'Neill, Gemmill, Withe, Woodcock, Robertson

Post-match Comments:

Brian Clough:

On replacing David Needham with Larry Lloyd:
"It was a straight selection job. Needham had a bad 'un in midweek so he was out. It happens to them all"

On subbing Archie Gemmill, the driving force behind much of the season's success:
"Archie wasn't with it. Names don't matter. If he's not producing, off he comes, whoever he is".

"I never thought this was one of those days we wouldn't score, because I didn't think Chelsea's defence was good enough".

"Frank Clark was tremendous. He was getting into their box while Archie Gemmill was hanging about in our half".

Other Comments:
"Those who doubted their ability to stay the pace, and people who scoffed at their prospects of coping with heavy grounds, have already been put in their place. Forest produced an emphatic display to complete the statistical details of their title triumph".
John Sadler, journalist

Man of the match – Kenny Burns

April 5, 1978 v Aston Villa (a), won 1-0
Forest suddenly emerged from a match dominated by Aston Villa to snatch a dramatic winner from Woodcock four minutes from the end – and with Everton losing at home to Liverpool, that goal must be worth four points
Forest: Shilton, Anderson, Barrett, O'Hare, Lloyd, Burns, O'Neill, Gemmill, Withe, Woodcock, Robertson.

Post-match Comments:

Brian Clough:
"We have been a very difficult side to beat all season and that is partly because we play for the full 90 minutes".

April 11, 1978 v Manchester City (a), drew 0-0
Manchester City finish the season in fourth place but the dynamism from Barnes, Kidd, Tueart and Hartford is lacking in this game. They have drawn five of their last six matches but even with six wins, they would still fall

short of a runaway Forest side.
Forest: Shilton, Anderson, Barrett, O'Hare, Lloyd, Burns, O'Neill, Gemmill, Withe, Woodcock, Robertson

Post-match Comments:

Brian Clough:
"We don't concede many so we've always got a bit of a chance".

"Give them the title now and send a warning to Europe next year!" – **Press comment**

April 15, 1978 v Leeds United (h), drew 1-1
Leeds win only one of their last seven matches and just manage a top 10 finish. They took the lead through a Frank Gray penalty but Forest struck back with a strike from Withe.
Forest: Shilton, Barrett, Clark, McGovern, Lloyd, Burns, O'Neill, Gemmill, Withe, Bowyer, Robertson.

Post-match Comments:

Brian Clough:
"It was a scramble. Sometimes you have to scramble for a point".

Other Comments:
"At present we are seeing a weary second rate replica of the exciting entertaining side that has led the first division by example".
John Sadler - Reporter

Man of the match – Frank Clark

April 18, 1978 v Queens Park Rangers (h), won 1-0
Incredibly, only 30,000 show up for this win which, barring a mathematical miracle, hands Forest the title for the first time in their history. There are still five games remaining which serves to underline the emphatic dominance of Brian Clough and Peter Taylor's team this season. A John Robertson penalty split the teams.
Forest: Shilton, Barrett, Clark, McGovern, Lloyd, Burns, O'Neill, Gemmill, Withe, Bowyer, Robertson.

Post-match Comments:

Headline: Cloughie's Done it!

Brian Clough:
"I am not accepting a thing. If we get a point at Coventry on Saturday you can buy me a drink".

Other Comments:
"John Robertson's penalty gave classy Clough's climbers 58 points and no team in the land can better that" – Press comment

April 22, 1978 v Coventry City (a), drew 0-0
Nottingham Forest are confirmed as First Division Champions at Highfield Road. They have won the League and League Cup double in a season where they have swept all before them. The rise has been meteoric, spectacular, utterly impressive and has the signatures of Brian Clough and Peter Taylor underneath it.
Forest: Shilton, Anderson, Barrett, O'Hare, Needham, Burns, O'Neill, Bowyer, Withe, Gemmill, Robertson

Post-match Comments:
After this result, Nottingham Forest were confirmed as Champions. After the game Brian Clough and Peter Taylor were asked about their management formula.

Brian Clough:
"No magic – just hard work and pure skill"

"Winning the title isn't the ultimate test. That comes next season with The European Cup".

Peter Taylor:
"I had learned my football under Harry Storer at Coventry and he was the hardest man in the world. Coventry must have been the toughest team in the league but when I saw the Hungarians play I thought immediately that a combination of their skill and Storer's demand for total physical effort must be the right way. I moved to Middlesbrough and met Brian Clough and found that he was on exactly the same wave-length".

Man of the match – Peter Shilton

April 25, 1978 v Ipswich Town (a), won 2-0

It is symbolic of the professionalism Clough has bred throughout the club that they won this game. With their heads still dizzy from this season's achievements it would have been so easy to roll over. But this is Brian Clough's Forest and every game must be won.

Forest: Shilton, Anderson, Barrett, O'Hare, Needham, Burns, O'Neill, Bowyer, Withe, Gemmill, Robertson

Post-match Comments:
Brian Clough:
"It was important to me that we maintained our habit of not losing."

Other comments:
Brian Clough's champions went marching on after destroying cup finalists Ipswich Town – Press comment

April 29, 1978 v Birmingham City (h), drew 0-0

It is party time at The City ground as the championship is celebrated. The happy habit of not losing is maintained but curiously only 37,625 are there to see it.

Forest: Shilton, Anderson, Barrett, McGovern, Needham, Burns, O'Neill, Gemmill, Withe, Woodcock, Robertson

Post-match Comments:

Brian Clough:
"This is a great day for Nottingham Forest football club."

May 2, 1978 v West Bromwich Albion (a), drew 2-2

All the goals came in a frenetic first half. A Robertson penalty and Bowyer's first league goal since October earned a point for Forest. Tony Brown and Wayne Hughes got the goals for the Baggies who cap a fine season by finishing sixth. Not many teams remained unbeaten against Forest this season.

Forest: Shilton, Anderson, Barrett, McGovern, Lloyd, Burns, O'Neill, Gemmill, Withe, Bowyer, Robertson.

Post-match Comments:
Brian Clough:
"West Brom are hard to beat and play good football. We don't like being beaten either and know what the ball is for."

Other Comment:

"Brian Clough's army goes marching on. Forest were in top form in a thriller at West Brom which defied terrible conditions." – Press comment

May 4, 1978 v Liverpool (a), drew 0-0
Anfield is expectant but Forest are not in any mood to relinquish their 26 game unbeaten run. It is a gutsy performance and secures their seventh clean sheet in nine games. This and many other statistics herald the brilliance of Peter Shilton and his defence.
Forest: Shilton, Anderson, Barrett, McGovern, Lloyd, Clark, O'Neill, Gemmill, Withe, Bowyer, Robertson

Post-match Comments:
Brian Clough:
"It is always good to come to a place where football is played properly, and leave there with something!"

Other comments:

Headline: "Shilton is king of the Kop".

"Super saves by Shilton from Souness, Hughes and Kennedy kept Forest level and with only Withe and Gemmill playing forward Forest were happy to settle for a point" – **Press comment**

Clough and Taylor parade the League championship trophy in May 1978.

1978-79

August 19, 1978 v Tottenham Hotspur (h), drew 1-1

Forest are fresh from their 5-0 pasting of Ipswich in the Charity Shield and are the form pick for the new season. Tottenham parade their two new Argentinian stars while Forest are largely the same team as last season. Trevor Francis will soon be joining them. Ricky Villa scores on his debut and O'Neill opens his seasonal account early.

Forest: Shilton, Anderson, Barrett, McGovern, Needham, Burns, O'Neill, Gemmill, Withe, Woodcock, Robertson

Post-match Comments:
Brian Clough:
"It will be six months before the best is seen of Spurs' new stars Ricardo Villa and Osvaldo Ardiles. It took Archie Gemmill as long as that to settle down with us and he only moved 12 miles down the road from Derby.
I was happy for Ricardo Villa when he scored. All right so his goal cost us a point. But I always feel happy for goalscorers because they have the hardest job in the business."

August 22, 1978 v Coventry City (a), drew 0-0

Once again Coventry almost defeat Forest but once again Forest survive. Incredibly there is still very little being made of the astonishing achievement Brian Clough and Peter Taylor are performing at The City Ground.

Forest: Shilton, Anderson, Barrett, McGovern, Needham, Burns, O'Neill, Gemmill, Elliot, Woodcock, Robertson

Post-match Comments:
Brian Clough:
"It was hard for us today. We don't look like scoring at the moment and will have to wake up soon."

Other comments:
Forest's performances have not picked up from where they signed off last season and surely cannot expect Shilton to perform miracles every game –
press comment

August 26, 1978 v Queens Park Rangers (a), drew 0-0

Once again Forest cannot find the back of the net and appear to have left their scoring boots at Wembley. Clough is on the lookout for a striker. QPR eventually get relegated.

Forest: Shilton, Anderson, Barrett, McGovern, Needham, Burns, O'Neill, Gemmill, Elliot, Woodcock, Robertson

Post-match Comments:
Brian Clough:
We are looking to bring in a player or two. Maybe it is time for a change.

Other comments:

"Brian Clough has dropped an almighty clanger in selling striker Peter Withe to Aston Villa for £200,000." Alex Montgomery, **journalist**

September 2, 1978 v West Bromwich Albion (h), drew 0-0
Already the home crowd has dipped below 30,000 as a goal drought stretches into its third game. West Brom rarely lose to Clough and should have carried off all the points today such was the quality shown by Bryan Robson, Cyril Regis, Laurie Cunningham and John Wile.

Forest: Shilton, Anderson, Barrett, McGovern, Needham, Burns, O'Neill, Gemmill, Elliot, Woodcock, Robertson

Post-match Comments:
Brian Clough:
"Hey Ron (Atkinson), 7 points out of 8 isn't it? I hope you get 77 points – you deserve to with the attitude your team has. Hey, I mean that – I thought they were smashing.

"Any team that comes here and is prepared to play with four forwards will do for me. They were exciting, they came at us all the time and that is what the public love to see. We had our hands full and were more than happy to settle for a point

"My team have lost confidence because they haven't been scoring goals. Mature players who have known success can ride this sort of situation because they know it will some right eventually. These lads haven't known success until last season and they don't know how to cope with it."

Other Comments:
"Peter Shilton should have a licence for the saves he makes! We would have won it comfortably but for him." – **Ron Atkinson.**

Man of the match – Peter Shilton

September 9, 1978 v Arsenal (h), won 2-1

Forest are back among the goals although things were becoming a little restless once Liam Brady had given Arsenal a half time lead. But Forest are nothing if not gutsy and a Robertson penalty and Bowyer strike brought their first win of the season.

Forest: Shilton, Anderson, Barrett, McGovern, Lloyd, Burns, Mills, Bowyer, Birtles, Woodcock, Robertson

Post-match Comments:
Brian Clough:
"If our fans don't cut out the swearing I'll close the Trent End. They can't take a goal against them, they can't take it when we play badly, they can't take anything. I'm willing to lose 6000 off the gate rather than have young families listen to that. They make me squirm. They make me vomit. I had my wife and two kids there today and I'm not having them listening to that filth."

Man of the match – Ian Bowyer

September 16, 1978 v Man Utd (a), drew 1-1

Forest go in at half time a goal up after Bowyer's effort but there is to be no repeat of last season's fantastic achievement as Jimmy Greenhoff restores parity for United. Forest are still buzzing from their first leg defeat of Liverpool in the European Cup two days earlier. Forest have now gone 32 games without defeat despite a slow start to the season which will eventually cost them the championship.

Forest: Shilton, Anderson, Barrett, McGovern, Lloyd, Burns, Gemmill, Bowyer, Birtles, Woodcock, Robertson

Post-match Comments:
Brian Clough:
"It has been a good week."

Other comments:
"We have learned a lot from last year." – Dave Sexton, Manchester United manager

September 23, 1978 v Middlesbrough (h), drew 2-2

Once again the attendance drops and surrendering a two goal half time lead is not the best preparation for the return visit to Anfield in the European Cup. Birtles and O'Neill set Forest on their way but Middlesbrough got

back into it with goals from the two Davids; Mills and Armstrong.
Forest: Shilton, Anderson, Barrett, McGovern, Lloyd, Burns, O'Neill,
Bowyer, Birtles, Woodcock, Robertson

Post-match Comments:
Brian Clough:
"Larry Lloyd and Kenny Burns must take the blame – nobody else. They
showed a lack of talent in the professional stakes. The trouble is we thought
we had won at half-time.
"They will be OK. This lesson will have done them the world of good. Let's
be fair to the opposition. It was typical Middlesbrough. They don't know
how to pack it in."

Man of the match - David Mills (Middlesbrough)

September 30, 1978 v Aston Villa (a), won 2-1
Forest are flying after overcoming Liverpool in the European Cup and
gaining their first away win of the season. The streak is now at 34 games
and is at last capturing the imagination of the the world outside the East
Midlands. A Craig penalty had given Villa a half time lead but goals from
Woodcock and a Robertson penalty took the points back to the Trent.
Forest: Shilton, Anderson, Bowyer, McGovern, Lloyd, Burns, O'Neill,
Gemmill, Birtles, Woodcock, Robertson
The fact that Forest equalled the record of 34 unbeaten League games was
the last thing manager Clough was worried about.

Post-match Comments:
Brian Clough:
"I'll only acknowledge that when they have gone another 34. All I'm
bothered about now is going home to a meal, putting my feet up and
thinking about how we are going to beat Oxford in the League Cup on
Wednesday."

Man of the match – Larry Lloyd.

October 7, 1978 v Wolves (h), won 3-1
Forest have created a new record for remaining unbeaten in top flight
football. Brian Clough will often say it was his proudest achievement.
Furthermore they do it in style.
Wolves struggle all season and never look like getting anything out of this
game despite a goal from Mel Eves. Forest were well in command and are

flying at the moment. Two from new star Garry Birtles and another from O'Neill meant Wolves' manager, John Barnwell left empty handed. He won't be the last.

Forest: Shilton, Anderson, Clark, McGovern, Lloyd, Burns, O'Neill, Gemmill, Birtles, Woodcock, Robertson

Post-match Comments:
Brian Clough:
"We have written our name in the record book – probably for all time – and I mean all time. We haven't finished yet. We'll probably go on to reach 49, I don't think it is on to make 50."

Ferenc Puskas was at the game checking Forest for his new club AEK Athens in preparation for their European Cup tie.

October 14th, 1978 v Bristol City (a), won 3-1
Bristol City are once again no match for a stylish Forest side. Only a Ritchie penalty in the first half keeps Alan Dicks' men in the game but two penalties from Robertson and a goal from in-form Birtles inch Forest ever closer to the land mark of a 40 match unbeaten run.

Forest: Shilton, Anderson, Bowyer, McGovern, Lloyd, Burns, Gemmill, O'Hare, Birtles, Woodcock, Robertson

Post-match Comments:
Brian Clough:
"I am a bit disappointed we didn't keep a clean sheet but City put us under more pressure than anyone for a long time. We needed a good result to settle us down for our visit to AEK Athens and we got it."

Man of the match – John McGovern

October 21, 1978 v Ipswich (h), won 1-0
Having trounced Ipswich in the Charity Shield by five goals without reply Forest enjoy the psychological advantage. However, they have to settle for just the one goal but it is enough to beat Bobby Robson's men who go on to finish sixth in the division ahead of Arsenal and Manchester United. O'Neill got the goal.

Forest: Shilton, Anderson, Clark, McGovern, Lloyd, Burns, O'Neill, Bowyer, Birtles, Woodcock, Robertson

Post-match Comments:

Brian Clough was on holiday

Other comments:
If Ron Greenwood doesn't pick Peter Shilton in goal for England in Dublin on Wednesday there is no justice – Press comment

"We came here not to lose but that goalkeeper made some saves he had no right to make." – Bobby Robson, Ipswich Manager.

While Forest were wrapping up their win, manager Brian Clough was lazing on a Majorca beach. His partner Peter Taylor said: "I've just told him the result on the phone. He said the sun was shining."

Man of the match – Kenny Burns

October 28, 1978 v Southampton (a), drew 0-0
A below par performance but Shilton once again refuses to open the door. He will keep 19 clean sheets in the league this season.
Forest: Shilton, Anderson, Clark, McGovern, Lloyd, Burns, O'Neill, Gemmill, Birtles, O'Hare, Robertson

Post-match Comments:
Brian Clough:
"I'm pleased because we survived without playing well."

Other Comments:
"Forest are like a machine which never breaks down and it goes all the way back to Peter Shilton. He is formidable" – Lawrie McMenemy, Southampton Manager.

At the end of the game Brian Clough led his team on a 10-minute walk to the station for their train instead of using the coach.

Man of the match – Peter Shilton

November 4, 1978 v Everton (h), drew 0-0
Clough and Taylor are still looking to sign a striker and given that this is the fifth occasion they have failed to score this season it is a wonder they remain unbeaten for an incredible 39 games.
Forest: Shilton, Anderson, Bowyer, O'Hare, Lloyd, Burns, O'Neill, Gemmill, Birtles, Woodcock, Robertson

Post-match Comments:
Brian Clough:
"I couldn't help smiling. There we were pinned down, shots peppering our goal like machine-gun fire and the fans pick that moment to chant: 'Everton are boring'. Boring! It was like the Third World War in our penalty area. I don't know how Everton have been playing all season but they certainly didn't bore me. They walked all over us in the first half and I could put it in stronger terms than that but you wouldn't print it!
"Our back four were diabolical and gave Everton more room than they would find in an empty car park. Kenny Burns looked as though he had been off for a year instead of a week.
"We haven't bought a player in over a year now so we'll have to do something soon."

Man of the match – Trevor Ross (Everton)

November 11, 1978 v Spurs (a), won 3-1
Forest were without 5 first team players and still overcome a spirited, hard working Spurs side. At half-time and 0-0 it looked as though another goalless encounter was on the cards but Anderson's first league goal of the campaign plus efforts from Robertson and Birtles could not be matched despite a strike from John Pratt.
Forest: Shilton, Anderson, Bowyer, O'Hare, Lloyd, Needham, Gemmill, Mills, Birtles, Woodcock, Robertson

Post-match Comments:
Brian Clough:
"Our composure impressed me more than anything else."
Peter Taylor:
"It didn't worry us. All our players, from the youngest apprentice to the oldest professional are taught to play a certain style. If a player cheats on us, doesn't pull his weight, we show him the door.
"If you can't give players reasons that make sense they won't go out there and do it for you. In my opinion English football stagnated for 14 years under Walter Winterbottom because he taught players to do things a certain way but when those players eventually asked: 'Why?' Walter didn't know what to tell them."

Other Comments:
"I could weep for my players. To lose after playing so well is a real sickener. But if we can play like that against the best team in the country

THE LIFE OF **BRIAN**

there's not much wrong with us." – **Keith Burkinshaw, Tottenham Hotspur manager**.

Forest have now gone one year without losing.

Man of the match – Peter Shilton.

November 18, 1978 v QPR (h), drew 0-0
Two goalless draws against QPR but Forest once again refuse to lose. Just when it seems the streak is at an end they bounce back and add another few games to it. It has now been one full year since Forest last lost a game – away at Leeds United by a solitary Ray Hankin strike on November 19 1977.

Forest: Shilton, Anderson, Bowyer, Needham, Lloyd, O'Hare, Mills, Gemmill, Birtles, Woodcock, Robertson

Brian Clough did not appear for the press conference.

Other comments:
"Frankly, I can't help thinking that it will be a good thing for the team and for the game when somebody ends Forest's unbeaten run which is now a phenomenal 41 games." John Sadler – Reporter.

"It wasn't very exciting, but it was a good team performance. We refused to play into Forest's hands by knocking high balls at their defence. We played it around expecting them to come at us but they didn't." – Steve Burtenshaw, QPR manager.

Man of the Match – John Hollins (QPR)

November 25, 1978 v Bolton (a), won 1-0
Forest remain in fourth position after John Robertson's goal bags both points at Burnden Park. A trip to Anfield is next and the streak will come under a severe challenge once again. The memory of losing to Forest in the European Cup will no doubt be fresh in the memory.

Forest: Shilton, Anderson, Clark, Needham, Lloyd, Bowyer, O'Neill, Gemmill, Birtles, Woodcock, Robertson

Post-match Comments:

Nottingham Forest stretched their unbeaten run to a mind boggling 42 games – the equivalent of a full season's programme – Press comment

Even Brian Clough must know that Peter Shilton cannot go on performing heroics of this order every week to keep Forest in the top four – Press comment

"If Ray Clemence is better than him it can only be by a hair's breath" – Ian Greaves, Bolton Manager.

The End of the Streak

December 9, 1978 v Liverpool (a), lost 0-2
Most things are lost at Anfield and Brian Clough will not be unhappy to end his team's streak at the home of Bill Shankly and now Bob Paisley.
Forest: Shilton, Anderson, Clark, Needham, Lloyd, Bowyer, Gemmill, McGovern, Elliot, Birtles, Robertson

Post-match Comments:
Brian Clough:
"Even a blind man must fancy them but no English title was won in December. They played us off the park. We never had a kick. They murdered us – particularly in midfield. We never got any rhythm and though it is a bit of a relief that the run is over we'd have preferred to have won."

Other Comments:
"For two-goal destroyer Terry McDermott it was a day to savour. It was the day he ended Forest's fairy-tale run of 42 games without defeat and a day for personal justice". Frank Clough – Reporter.

"The amazing thing was that this was one of our easiest games of the season. Our defence had nothing to do all afternoon. I scored twice against Forest in the League Cup last season and they were both disallowed. We overran them but they finished winners. There must be something about my birthday. Last year I celebrated with a hat-trick against Hamburg in the Super Cup and now these two today. I can't wait for next year." –Terry McDermott.

Man of the Match – Terry McDermott

Peter Shilton and John Robertson were the only two players to appear in all 42 games.

Chapter 10
Nottingham Forest
European Kings

Forest will be the biggest threat to us retaining the
European Cup next season
Bob Paisley, 1978

Skegness was Europe to Nottingham
Brian Clough

You will win in Cologne!
**Peter Taylor in the dressing room after the 3-3 draw at
home to FC Cologne**

We won two European Cups and we never practised a free kick.
'Just give it to Robbo' was the cry
Martin O'Neill

On his arrival at the City Ground in January 1975, Nottingham Forest were described as the "Sagging Reds" and Brian Clough endured a 12-match league run with only one victory. The 1974-75 season saw Forest finish in 16th position, their lowest second division placing since 1948-49.

Mid-table security seemed a long way off, let alone the unimaginable feast of two successful European Cup campaigns.

The 18 European games, which resulted in two European Cups, remains to many the greatest achievement of any manager in the history of the game.

It fulfilled the dreams of all who carry Nottingham Forest in their hearts and for those fans who had their trips to Hull, Carlisle and York replaced with tours of Amsterdam, Cologne, Munich and Madrid, there will never be anything like it. It was the best of times and it all started at home against the European Cup holders, Liverpool . . .

1978-79

September 13, 1978 v Liverpool (EC 1, 1st leg) (h), won 2-0

Forest: Shilton, Anderson, Barrett, McGovern, Lloyd, Burns, Gemmill, Bowyer, Birtles, Woodcock, Robertson
Scorers: Birtles and Barrett

Pre-match Comments:

"If we have to meet them sometime – and we probably will – it may as well be now as later".
Brian Clough

"The City's Match of the Century"
Nottingham Evening Post, September 13, 1978

Post-match Comments:

"Garry Birtles last night suddenly emerged from the obscurity of the Central League to star in Europe's premier competition. He scored the first of Forest's priceless goals and had a hand Colin Barrett's second".
Press Comment

"We have again done the city of Nottingham proud. I would hope that the people of Nottingham will respond to our achievements and if they raise

THE LIFE OF **BRIAN**

Peter Shilton earning his corn to deny Terry McDermott in the goalless draw at Anfield.

their standards at the same amount as we did to beat Liverpool, the city will have no problems at all".
Brian Clough

September 28, 1978 v Liverpool (EC 1, 2nd leg) (a), drew 0-0
Forest: Shilton, Anderson, Clarke, McGovern, Lloyd, Burns, Gemmill, Bowyer, Birtles, Woodcock, Robertson

Pre-match comments:

"It will be like coming face to face with Rommel and his panzers. Liverpool will throw things at us the like of which have never been seen on a football field before. What we have faced before in this season will seem like paper cups compared to what Liverpool have got prepared for us. But we'll be ready".
Brian Clough

"I want all the players to roll up their sleeves an inch or two higher and win for Colin Barrett (injured)".
Peter Taylor

"The tempo will obviously be a lot higher to what I have been used to in the Central League but that's no problem really".
Frank Clark (Colin Barrett's replacement)

"If we are knocked out it will be the biggest blow of my career"

CLOUGHIE Forest

Emlyn Hughes, Liverpool

"Everybody has got their tails up again and we believe we can do it"
Phil Thompson, Liverpool

"It is time for the flannel to stop and the action to start. I know how desperate Brian Clough is to win the European Cup, because I remember how desperate I was myself".
Bob Paisley, Liverpool manager

Post-match Comments:

"At the final whistle Brian Clough could not restrain his emotions and leapt from the dugout to acclaim his team".

"I thought we played better at Anfield than we did in Nottingham. We did not just set out to defend, because we knew the value of scoring. Europe is still something new to us but we are learning all the time".
Brian Clough

"You have got to fancy Forest to win it now".
Bob Paisley

October 18, 1978 v AEK Athens (EC 2, 1st leg) (a), won 2-1
Forest: Shilton, Anderson, Clark, McGovern, Lloyd, Burns, Bowyer Gemmill, Birtles, Woodcock, Robertson

Pre-match Comments:

"I know that whoever pulls on the Forest shirt will do themselves, me and the club proud"
Brian Clough

"I would have loved to have played Martin O'Neill and Ian Bowyer but it just isn't possible"
Brian Clough

"The team are 100% relaxed and I am 1000% relaxed".
Ferenc Puskas, AEK manager

Post-match Comments:

THE LIFE OF **BRIAN**

"The press lost this game for AEK. They expected them to win 3-0 and the players froze from fear when they soon realised this was not going to be the case".
Brian Clough

November 1, 1978 v AEK Athens (EC 2, 2nd leg) (h), won 5-1
Forest: Shilton, Anderson, Clark, O'Hare, Lloyd, Needham, Bowyer Gemmill, Birtles, Woodcock, Robertson
Scorers: Needham, Woodcock, Anderson, Birtles (2)

Pre-match comments:

"If the Nottingham people do not come along tonight we may as well go and play our football where it is more appreciated, at Mansfield or Doncaster, or perhaps maybe Sunderland".
Brian Clough

Post-match Comments:

"They were supposed to be weakened without McGovern, O'Neill and Burns but I hate to think what they might have done at full strength. From our point of view it will be better to go out to the eventual winners, so I hope they can win it. I can't see any team capable of beating them".
Ferenc Puskas

March 7, 1979 v Grasshoppers Zurich (EC 3, 1st leg) (h), won 4-1
Forest: Shilton, Anderson, Clark, McGovern, Lloyd, Needham, O'Neill, Gemmill, Birtles, Woodcock, Robertson
Scorers: Birtles, Robertson (pen), Gemmill, Lloyd

Post-match Comments:

"Forest Furies fight back to flatten the giants of Zurich"
Press comment

"Four minutes from the end I did not think we were going to get another couple of goals".
Brian Clough

"Forest showed skill and determination"

CLOUGHIE Forest

Ron Greenwood, England manager

March 21, 1979 v Grasshoppers Zurich (EC 3, 2nd leg) (a), drew 1-1
Forest: Shilton, Anderson, Barrett, McGovern, Lloyd, Needham, O'Neill, Gemmill, Birtles, Woodcock, Robertson.

Pre-match Comments:

"I expect to win".
Brian Clough

"Clough knows the big guns like Liverpool, Real Madrid, Juventus and PSV are out of the running and that the European Cup is up to be taken by the boldest, the bravest and the best.
Frank Clough, journalist

Post-match Comments:

"Men and Boys – Half-pace Forest are still too good"
Press comment

"From my seat on the touchline it was never a penalty. I'm just pleased we are through with no injuries".
Brian Clough

April 11, 1979 v Cologne (EC semi-final, 1st leg) (h), drew 3-3
Forest: Shilton, Barrett, Bowyer, McGovern, Lloyd, Needham, O'Neill, Gemmill, Birtles, Woodcock, Robertson.

Pre-match Comments:

"The only way Cologne can surprise us tonight is by suddenly producing a Bofors gun or a doodlebug".
Brian Clough

"Honestly, I do not give a damn what they try to do – whether they intend to alter their style or their tactics or even their players. In my team I have players who have come across everything there is to see in football. We will win".
Brian Clough

"People tell me they have a right-back called Konopka who loves to go flying forward on the overlap. So I get asked daft questions about how we will cope with him. I'll tell you this, there's no way I intend pulling back John Robertson and turning him into the most talented full-back in the world. Robertson is paid by us to create – and that is what he will be doing. So if their chap comes galloping forward willy-nilly, we'll tear him to pieces, just like we did John Gidman at Aston Villa a couple of weeks ago.
Brian Clough

"Forest expect a sell out, which, with TV fees and advertising, could swell the take to around £15,000".
Press comment

Post-match Comments:

Jap Sub Sinks Forest
Headline

"Brian Clough's boys were outwitted, outmanoeuvred and out-fought too often in part one of this semi-final".
Press comment

"The first and third goals were down to me".
Peter Shilton

"Our defence was caught cold but I still think we have a chance.
We caught a cold in the draft they left as they went past us. They had no option but to attack because we left so many open gaps. Shilton can make amends by earning his corn out there.
Brian Clough

April 25, 1979 v Cologne (EC semi-final, 2nd leg) (a), won 1-0
Forest: Shilton, Anderson, Clarke, McGovern, Lloyd, Burns, O'Neill, Bowyer, Birtles, Woodcock, Robertson.

Pre-match Comments:

"If Cologne were in the First Division they would be in the lower reaches. They always look likely to concede goals and there was nothing about them that particularly impressed me. What happened in the first leg was a brain-storm and it won't happen again. I think we will win. Most people

seem to think that we won't – and that suits us down to the ground. We don't like to be on the same plane of thought as other people because we are supposed to be the experts".
Brian Clough

"I fancy us this time. The Cologne players have good techniques but we know that we are a better team. Now it is up to us to prove it".
Tony Woodcock

"We were punished in the first leg but tonight we will have it right again".
Larry Lloyd

"If they stick to the good habits we have drilled into them, there will be no problem".
Peter Taylor

"I have travelled in Europe with different teams for nearly 20 years and I have never seen a side as brimming with self-assurance on the eve of a crucial match as these lads".
Frank Clough, journalist

"They are exciting, they are as good as any team in Europe today. But we have made our plans and we expect to win".
Hennes Weisweiller, Cologne coach

Post-match Comments:

"Bowyer's Beauty Launches Miracle Men Into the Munich Final"
Headline

"That lad's head is worth a million pounds to me right now".
Brian Clough

"It was a magnificent performance and an unbelievable result. Our game fell into place. Our good habits came through and once again we have notched up another clean sheet – and that's what we breed our players to do".
Brian Clough

"Good luck to Forest – they are a fine team. The better team won,

although we were handicapped by the injury to Deiter Müller and Van Gool who played with flu.
Hennes Weisweiller

"In the dying moments Shilton earned his wages with a sensational flying save from Konopka"
Press comment

May 30, 1979 v Malmo (Final) (Munich), won 1-0
Forest: Shilton, Anderson, Clark, McGovern, Lloyd, Burns, Francis, Bowyer, Birtles, Woodcock, Robertson
Scorer: Francis

Pre-match Comments:

"We don't ask questions here. We just put up the team-sheets".
Brian Clough

"In 1972 at Derby, I was responsible for a bad backpass that gave Arsenal the goal that knocked us out of the FA Cup. He never let me forget it. Every single cup tie since he has let me know, very forcibly, that my blunder cost him the chance of leading his team out at Wembley. There was once when I thought I had got away with it but he caught me in the tunnel and reminded me again".
John McGovern

One in a million – Trevor Francis heads in John Robertson's cross in the '79 final.

"Nottingham Forest will win the European Cup tonight – there hasn't
been a bigger certainty in sport since Arkle was in his prime".
Frank Clough, journalist

"We will have to play as well as we have ever done to win. What I really
want is a continuation of the football we were playing at the end of the
season when we beat Leeds and West Brom. I want to see our normal
discipline. I want to see our wide players getting into the game and I want
to see the specialists doing their job".
Brian Clough

"Malmo remind me of that Huddersfield Town team in the 50s. They had
it so well organised in those days, you didn't even see their penalty area".
Peter Taylor

"20,000 Forest Fans warned to behave".
Press comment

"I was shocked to learn that Brian Clough takes holidays during the
league season. That even took the British press by surprise. To me it is
unthinkable".
Bobby Houghton, Malmo manager

"When Brian Clough visited us the other week, I invited him to a game of
squash. I let him beat me 3-0".
Bobby Houghton

Post-match Comments:

Headline:
"Thanks A Million – Nottingham Forest. The babes of Europe just 10
months ago are now the new kings of the Continent!"

"To make your debut in the final and score the winner, that's stuff you
don't even dare to dream about".
Trevor Francis

"He was the best player on the pitch and there has been a lot of pressure
on him and I am pleased he won the game".
Bobby Houghton

THE LIFE OF **BRIAN**

"Trevor has had an outstanding match. He was the best player on the field. This is an unbelievable milestone in my life. To think that four years ago we were near the bottom of the second division and now we are European Champions. I still can't quite believe it".
Brian Clough

Liverpool manager, **Bob Paisley,** watched the final on TV in Jerusalem: "I'm glad Forest won because it's good to keep the trophy in England".

1979-80

September 19, 1979 v Oesters (EC 1, 1st leg) (h), won 2-0
Forest: Shilton, Anderson, Gray, McGovern, Lloyd, Burns, O'Neill, Bowyer, Birtles, Woodcock, Robertson
Scorers: Bowyer, Hallan o.g

Pre-match Comments:

"A successful defence of the European Cup would prove a sight harder than winning it".
Brian Clough

"We hit rock bottom on Saturday at Norwich and it is up to them to go and do their stuff. They are on trial and so are Brian and myself, because it is our job to motivate the team".
Peter Taylor

Post-match Comments:

"We should have come alight tonight. We were worse than on Saturday – and this time we were at home".
Peter Taylor

October 3, 1979 v Oesters (EC 1, 2nd leg) (a), drew 1-1
Forest: Shilton, Anderson, Gray, McGovern, Lloyd, Burns, O'Neill, Mills, Birtles, Woodcock and Robertson

Post-match Comments:

"Success hasn't changed Peter and I. We were arrogant at the bottom of the league and we are arrogant at the top – that is consistency".

148

Brian Clough

"Forest just couldn't put it together and it was left to Woodcock to end Forest's agony".
Press comment

October 24, 1979 v Arges Pitesti (EC 2, 1st leg) (h), won 2-0
Forest: Shilton, Anderson, Gray, McGovern, Lloyd, Burns, Mills, Bowyer, Birtles, Woodcock and Robertson
Scorers: Woodcock, Birtles

Post-match Comments:

"OK, we should have had more goals but a two-goal lead is good enough in any competition. A lot of teams in Europe would swap places with us".
Brian Clough

"I can't teach someone like Garry Birtles how to put a ball between two bits of wood".
Brian Clough

November 7, 1979 v Arges Pitesti (EC 2, 2nd leg) (a), won 2-1
Forest: Shilton, Anderson, Gray, McGovern, Lloyd, Burns, O'Hare, Bowyer, Birtles, Woodcock and Robertson
Scorers: Bowyer, Birtles

Pre-match Comments:

"They kicked us a bit in the first leg and I don't suppose they will be any different in front of their home fans. But the physical side doesn't bother us. It is the teams with talent you look at apprehensively. They showed that they do have quite a bit of skill but I don't think they have enough to skin us".
Brian Clough

Post-match Comments:

Headline: "Cool Forest Tame Hatchet Brigade"

"It was an accomplished win against a bad side".
Brian Clough

THE LIFE OF **BRIAN**

"Woodcock, Birtles and Robertson were magnificent in the way they took the stick. There were no complaints or gestures from them. I only wish skilful players were given more protection by referees".
Brian Clough

"Bowyer is an amazing success story. He cannot claim a first team place when all the Forest personnel are available but every time he is thrown into the European theatre, he hits the net".
Press comment

March 5, 1980 v Dynamo Berlin (EC 3, 1st leg) (h), lost 0-1
Forest: Shilton, Gunn, Gray, McGovern, Lloyd, Burns, O'Neill, Bowles, Birtles, Francis, Robertson.

Pre-match Comments:

"Saturday's result against Bolton (0-1 away) was a disgrace, a disaster. Playing Bolton should have been the ideal preparation for the lads to sharpen their teeth but they were out-fought. Our so-called creative players, Martin O'Neill and John Robertson, gave one the impression they were more concerned about where their wives were going to sit at the League Cup final instead of getting down to business".
Brian Clough

"They apply themselves off the field perfectly with their big houses, fast cars, business agents and picking up their fat wage packets – but some of them seem to have forgotten that they can do all that only because of football".
Brian Clough

"I don't fancy going over there with nothing. A goal or two will help but the priority is a clean sheet".
Brian Clough

Post-match Comments:

"I think we can win the second leg in Berlin. I didn't see anything to frighten us. Strikers are paid to score goals and the midfield to create them. We didn't do either".
Brian Clough

"All I have to show for my time in the game is a memento from our Supercup win against Barcelona, so I want to win a medal with Forest more than anything".
Stan Bowles

March 19, 1980 v Dynamo Berlin (EC 3, 2nd leg) (a), won 3-1
Forest: Shilton, Anderson, Gray, McGovern, Lloyd, Needham, O'Neill, Bowyer, Birtles, Francis and Robertson
Scorers: Francis 2, Robertson (pen)

Pre-match Comments:

"We need a goal to stay alive and I have replaced Stan (Bowles) with Ian (Bowyer), because he is the best bet to get us one. I'll tell you this. If we score one, we'll get another".
Brian Clough

Post-match Comments:

Headline: "Fantastic Forest! Fabulous Francis!"

"Brian Clough toasted his players for one of the most monumental performances in European football history".
Press comment

"I am proud of them all. We didn't survive by sitting back on defence and trying to scramble a goal – we were positive. Man of the match? Trevor Francis".
Brian Clough

April 9, 1980 v Ajax (EC semi-final, 1st leg) (h), won 2-0
Forest: Shilton, Anderson, Gray, McGovern, Lloyd, Burns, O'Neill, Bowles, Birtles, Francis, Robertson.

Pre-match Comments:

"It will be harder than playing Real Madrid or Hamburg, because we won't know what to expect. It is probably the best Ajax team since the 70s but I think Forest must be favourites".
Rudi Krol, Ajax captain

"Holland have appeared in the last two World Cup finals – that is the pedigree of their football. We have won the last three European Cups – that is the mark of English quality. It is an intriguing semi-final but if we are at our best, I think we will win".
Brian Clough

"I think Trevor is trying so hard I actually feel sorry for him. He is putting himself in where it hurts and deserves a change of luck".
Brian Clough

Post-match Comments:

Headline: "Your best yet Trev!"

"If he maintains his present form he won't only get us into the final in Madrid, he'll win it for us. His performance was the best since signing for the club by a distance. He was marked man-for-man but still turned it on".
Brian Clough

"Ajax are a team with good skill and that is what impresses me. We still have a lot of work to do in Amsterdam".
Brian Clough

A French observer at the match said: "You have not seen the best of Rudi Kroll. He goes forward to support the front line a lot more in home games".
To which **Brian Clough** responded: "I just hope he does try that against us. We'll knock it straight into the space he has left and let Trevor Francis and Garry Birtles get on with it".

April 23, 1980 v Ajax (EC semi-final, 2nd leg) (a), drew 0-0
Forest: Shilton, Anderson, Gray, McGovern, Lloyd, Burns, O'Neill, Bowyer, Birtles, Francis, Robertson

Pre-match Comments:

"We are coming up to 70 games this season and if we do make it to the final, I would like to see the players enjoy a good, long rest".
Brian Clough

"I can't see any way we can lose if our approach is right".
Trevor Francis

May 28, 1980 v Hamburg (Final) (Madrid), won 1-0
Forest: Shilton, Anderson, Gray, McGovern, Lloyd, Burns, O'Neill, Bowyer, Birtles, Mills, Robertson.
Scorer: Robertson

Pre-match Comments:

"Bowles would still have had a chance of playing if he had come. But he now won't be playing unless he is hiding in the box with the cup".
Brian Clough

"We have to put Trevor (injured) and Stan (dispute) out of our minds until the battle is over. We won a championship, two League Cups and got to the final of the European Cup without any contribution from them, so we know we can do it".
John McGovern

Post-match Comments:

Headline: "We Love JR!"

"I don't remember being so involved in a game before. It's the greatest moment of my career. We've achieved some things at Forest but I think this was our personal best. We applied ourselves better than I have seen any side for many years. Our centre-forward didn't even have the strength to take his shinpads off".
Brian Clough

"It went in, and it was magic, but I really couldn't care less who scored".
John Robertson

"It was one of the greatest nights of my career. For once I had something to do. It's nice for us to win something and for me to have played a part".
Peter Shilton

Chapter 11
Cloughie – By Friends, Players & Colleagues

Geoff Boycott
Legendary former England cricketer and close personal friend of Clough. This is Geoffrey's reading from Brian's memorial service at Pride Park on October 21, 2004

Over the years I used to go and watch his team play at Derby and Nottingham when I wasn't away playing for England and he would come and watch me at Worksop, Nottingham, Chesterfield or Derby. When I scored my hundredth hundred at Headingley, against the Australians in 1977, I rang him up that night and found out from Barbara that he was sitting in his chair by the fire and that he had called up Nottingham Forest that afternoon to say he wouldn't be in for a meeting, because he was going to watch his mate make a bit of history.

He also used to come to Worksop on a sunny day in his shorts and casual clothes and sit in a deckchair and watch the cricket. He'd get invited to the committee room but it was not for him – he wanted to watch the cricket.

I remember one day he came to watch me at Chesterfield on a gorgeous, sunny day and, on a lovely batting pitch, I got myself out. I was so upset, I stayed in the dressing room. I was so disappointed and downhearted and after about an hour Brian came into the dressing room. He said: "I know you are down but look at your team-mates outside. They are not sure if they will *ever* make runs". He said: "Now *you*, you'll make runs – if not today, tomorrow; and if not tomorrow, then the day after". He said: "You've got talent, young man," and he made me feel 10 feet tall – and yet I had failed.

I always felt that was his real strength. He was a genius at man-management. He had his own style. We all know he was confident, positive and he had great self-belief. He was full of himself to the point that some people were very wary of him. Some disliked the way he said things. They thought him arrogant, brash, forthright, too opinionated – and yes, he was all of those things.

But if they *really* listened to what he actually said when he talked about football, they would have found that he was nearly always right.

He was provocative and passionate and had a great picture of how he wanted his teams to play football – on the floor, passing the ball at pace, with great defence. He never asked players to do what they weren't good at.

When I was watching once, I saw this young lad called Alan Hinton and afterwards I said to Brian: "He's pretty good but he's a bit shy in the tackle".

He replied: "I don't pay him to tackle. I pay him to pass that ball onto my centre-forward's head, so he could get goals – and he's bloody good at that!"

He had a rare judgement of players, all kinds and different types of individuals some of whom had failed at other places. When I was at Nottingham Forest one time, he bought a full-back called Frankie Gray, from Leeds. I said to him: "He's a left-winger, how can you play him as a full-back?" But Brian just chuckled.

Anyway, off I went to play for England and I came back towards the end of the season. We were chatting away after a match and he said: "Hey, by the way, you know that left full-back I bought who can't tackle?" I said: "Yeah". He said:

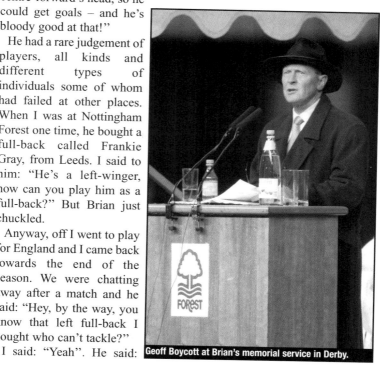

Geoff Boycott at Brian's memorial service in Derby.

155

THE LIFE OF BRIAN

"Our supporters are going to name him player-of-the-year", and he chuckles away because he knows he has got one over me.

All his teams carried great records. Great records about discipline, no troubles with referees because his players were told to respect the officials. His teams often finished top of the fair play league and yet they still won trophies. It wasn't that or luck that brought his teams and himself success. Two league championships with different clubs – Derby in '72 and Nottingham Forest in '78, four League Cups and two European Cups. It was his unique style of management that we had never seen before.

I've been a supporter of Manchester United for 42 years. Denis Law was my boyhood idol and I watched him play there and fell in love with him and Bobby Charlton. It is the richest soccer club in the world and yet they have only won two European Cups – and yet Brian and Forest won it twice in two years. His achievement with just decent-sized clubs was fantastic.

He was the best England manager we've never had and some people say he would have been a public relations disaster. I don't know how they make such assessments or assumptions. I believe he would have done a great job but because the FA was frightened of him, we, the public, missed out on a great experience.

We often had conversations and he always wanted to talk about cricket, while I always wanted to talk about football. I went to see him the day he went to Leeds. The players there never gave him a chance. He liked their football but not some of the things they did, because he told them what they didn't want to hear. I remember him saying that one smart arse had said to him at Leeds: "What can you do for us that we haven't done already?" And as quick as a flash, he said: "I would do the same thing again, only I would do it better".

There were two sides to Brian. People thought he was all talk, brash and outspoken but they didn't really know him. That was the outer crust of him and sometimes a defensive mechanism. Inside he was a warm, genuine person. Caring, kind with a heart of gold. He has spoken at dinners and written articles for benefit brochures for all kinds of sports people.

He sent flowers to wives and canvassed events for charity. One day he just turned up at my home in Wakefield, Yorkshire and he got his gardener to bring a van with white conifers. He planted them in my garden because he thought I would like them and enjoy them. They are still growing today.

When Forest won their first European Cup, he came home and gave me a replica of the trophy in cut glass.

As a kid, I wish he would have been *my* manager. Why? Because he would have made me a better player. I remember asking him when he bought Peter Shilton: "Is he really *that* good?" He said: "Geoffrey, he *is* that good. He is like you. He practices when nobody is there, when the others have gone home, and he hates the ball going into his net as much as you hate getting out".

Brian wasn't perfect. Like us all, he made mistakes. He had his faults and his shortcomings. Perhaps handing in his resignation at Derby; perhaps even going to Brighton or Leeds? But one thing I know he was sad about, and that was falling out with Peter Taylor, his great mate, and not making up before Peter died. There were these instances or moments in his life where maybe he would have liked to have done them differently. But so would we all.

He ran the most disciplined football clubs wherever he managed but there came a time when he couldn't discipline himself and he had a little too much to drink.

But for me he was a rare and special friend, funny and amusing. As a football manager he was a charismatic, eccentric maverick but he had that rare gift for understanding people and knowing how to get the best out of them. For knitting people together and winning. He was very, very clever.

His son, Nigel, used to tell me how he would sit in his rocking chair at home near the fire just thinking.

Can we all remember when he would disappear in the middle of the season for a sunshine holiday, Monday to Friday, leaving the team with Peter Taylor?

I asked him about that once and he said, it's a long season and he needed a rest from football, and the players needed a rest from him. Nobody does that.

I think the one story that really summed him up for me was the European Cup game against Liverpool. Most of the players were quiet and nervous, so he got the driver to stop at the pub so that he could get some crates of beer on for the players. He handed out cigarettes to the smokers and had a sing-a-long, so that by the time they got to Liverpool they weren't frightened of anybody. Identifying the problem, and having the courage to carry out such an unorthodox solution, was what he was all about. Imagine what the media would have done to him had they lost.

I would just like to say to Barbara, Simon, Nigel and Elizabeth, we are all sad that he has gone – probably 10-15 years too soon – but, for me, and I hope for you, too, you try and remember just the good times. The amusing moments and the great football his teams played.

I think that is the way he would like us to remember him.

Bernie Slaven
Former Middlesbrough and Republic of Ireland striker – a Boro legend

Cloughie's gone but he'll never be forgotten. It has been a sad week for football and a sad day for the town of Middlesbrough.

Brian Clough was a wonderful man, and a Boro legend, and I was lucky enough to spend some time with him.

I had the pleasure of meeting him a few years ago when I was doing the *Bernie's About TV* show, and he was absolutely charming. He was great in front of camera and he was such a character.

I admired him greatly because he told the truth.

He was full of confidence as a player and during his time at Boro he would say to his team-mates: "What are you doing having a shot? Give me the ball. I'm the best goalscorer at this club and I will put it in the net".

He was a wonderful finisher, but at Boro he was scoring four in a game at a time when the defence was conceding five the other end.

Some people say he didn't score at the top level, but that's rubbish, he didn't get the opportunity.

He only got two caps for England, which was ridiculous. But he was playing for Middlesbrough, which was an unfashionable club, and in those days there was very much a Southern bias against Northern players.

If he'd been a player in the modern age he would have probably been able to overcome the injury that finished his career.

In those days, if you injured your knee ligaments you were as good as finished.

Cloughie was a very clever man, something that wasn't always appreciated.

A story I heard came from an old mate of mine from Glasgow called Jim McInally. He was a young full-back at Forest, living in digs in the mid-80s.

Living so far from home, he wasn't able to get back to Scotland for Christmas, so he was alone in his room on Christmas Day when he heard a knock on the door.

When he opened the door, in walks Brian Clough who said: "Get your coat on, you're coming with me".

When he got back to Cloughie's house, the great man then proceeded to cook Jim Christmas dinner.

I thought that was a wonderful gesture and something you can't imagine many other managers doing.

It also showed that behind that confident persona was a warm and considerate man. I've heard many similar stories over the years.

He also had his quirky side.

I remember my former Boro team-mate, Peter Davenport, saying that, on one occasion at Forest, Cloughie stuck his head in the dressing room after training to tell the players that he wanted them to come and do some

gardening.

Sure enough, when he got them back to his house, he sat himself down and had a drink while he watched the players get stuck into his garden.

Another thing was that managers in his day didn't have a huge support network like they do now.

Cloughie was a coach, manager, motivator, psychologist and fitness guru all rolled into one. Some of his methods would be frowned upon but they certainly worked. He was famous for forcing his players to have a couple of drinks on the night before a big final to settle their nerves.

People often asked him why he stopped doing the TV work, because he was a brilliant analyst. When I asked him the same question, he answered: "Bernie, I can't pronounce all those foreign names".

What a great guy. He'll be sadly missed.

Courtesy of the Middlesbrough Evening Gazette

Harry Hooper
Formerly with West Ham, Wolves, Birmingham and played with Brian at Sunderland

Brian was a fabulous goalscorer. I have never played with or seen a better goalscorer in my life. He lived for football and was so dedicated. He used to feed off everyone around him and scored goals with either foot. He was a great goal poacher.

If you found one of those cameramen behind the goal at Roker at that time and asked him to show you his photos I bet everyone would have Brian in them. He was everywhere.

He used to visit me and my wife when we lived in Sunderland. Margaret and I were the first couple to have children and Brian would take my boy, Harry, into the garden and kick the ball about with him and bring him sweets. He was a born leader and as a manager he was straight and strict. He stuck to his guns and most players respected him for it.

I was born in Sunderland and as a player I had three good years there and as I have said there was no better goal scorer than Brian Clough. He just had this instinct to be there in the right place. We should have won promotion in his first season there. We drew 1-1 at Swansea on the final day after Brian had put us ahead. That is the worst goal Sunderland has ever conceded. It went through Cecil Irwin's legs. We missed out again the following season by a whisker but that was after Brian's injury. I wasn't playing that day against Bury but I was in the stand. He went for an impossible ball he had no chance of getting. I heard the crack in the stand. Sickening. He did make a comeback but he was nowhere near his former self and packed it in.

I played with him in an England B game against a Scotland B team at St Andrews, Birmingham. I think Dave Mackay and George Herd were playing that day.

We used to see a lot of each other at Sunderland and we were always talking football. Brian didn't drink and I, like so many others were amazed to hear that he became so heavily into drinking. It just didn't sound like Brian at all. He was one of the greats.

Ken Simpkins
Hartlepools United goalkeeper under Clough

I was already at the club when Brian and Peter Taylor arrived.

However, I was Brian's first goalkeeper to appear in the FA Cup for him.

He worked hard at Hartlepools and while it is well known that he learned to drive the team bus, it is not so widely known that he would visit local businesses, social clubs and other organisations asking for financial support for the club.

He wanted everyone smart and well presented and he had a couple of goes at me because of my weight. I worked really hard to improve and Brian put me in a specially designed plastic suit to help sweat off the pounds.

I remember once he fined Cliff Wright, a friend of his from his Middlesbrough days, for calling him "Brian". He said it was now "boss" or "Mr Clough". Anyway, Peter Taylor made sure Cliff was reimbursed.

Taylor left Burton Albion to join Brian at Hartlepools and they brought in George Smith, John Sheridan, Terry Bell, Tony Parry, Mickey Summers and Stan Aston, all of whom were from the Nottingham area.

I think John McGovern was his best signing and he remained the youngest lad to play for Hartlepools until quite recently.

Peter Taylor was good mates with Les Green, another goalkeeper. Les and I shared the shirt, although I think I only played in the cup games because he was cup-tied.

We made it to the FA Cup third round, which rarely happened, and were about 12-1 odds against to beat Huddersfield at Leeds Road. It was a terrific occasion with 3-4,000 Pools' fans creating a fantastic atmosphere. We ended up losing, mainly because the ref awarded a goal that hadn't crossed the line. Not even the linesman gave it and I was obviously nearer than anybody else – and it definitely did not cross the line. We should have taken them back home for a replay.

Bob Murray
Sunderland chairman

I am honoured to have been a Sunderland supporter when Brian played for the club. He is a legend. I saw the match at Roker Park when he suffered the terrible knee injury. The game would never be allowed to take place today, so atrocious were the conditions.

It was so sad that he never had the chance to fulfil his potential at Sunderland. But his achievements as a manager may never again be matched at the type of club he managed.

Charlie Hurley
Sunderland legend
He was a great player for Sunderland and a great individual. I played in the same team as him and against him. It was often my job to stop him scoring and that was never easy.

Mick McCarthy
Sunderland manager
Cloughie was a great football man and a fantastic character. He wasn't just a great manager, his playing record was tremendous.

All Sunderland quotes courtesy of Luke Edwards, The Newcastle Journal

Ian Mellor
Former Brighton & Hove Albion player signed by Clough and one half of the legendary strike-force with Peter Ward
If not for Brian Clough, my partnership with Peter Ward would never have happened. I only signed for the Seagulls because Clough was manager.

My nickname was 'Spider' and I struck up a good relationship with Peter Ward, although, sadly, not until *after* Clough controversially quit for Leeds.

He signed me in 1973-74 for a club record £40 000 from Norwich.
I dropped down two divisions from Norwich because of Brian
Clough. I wouldn't have signed for Brighton if it wasn't for him.

He had such a reputation and I felt he could get my game back together again.

When I walked into his office to sign there were cans of beer all over the desk. It was towards the end of the season and he told me he didn't want me to play with the rabble there, but to report a couple of months later to Heathrow for the club's end-of-season tour in Spain.

When I went over to him at the airport he didn't even say hello. The first thing he said to his record signing was "where is your tie?"

I never had the pleasure of playing for him, apart from in a match against the waiters in our Spanish hotel. He suggested we had a few pints before that game and I scored five goals.

He went to Leeds soon after that. It is one of my biggest disappointments that he signed me and I never played a proper match under him, so I never found out, at first hand, how good he really was.

The guy was eccentric, very knowledgeable about football and a great disciplinarian.

I would have loved to have played for him because I never got booked or sent-off. If you look back at his teams, they were never allowed to retaliate.

Norman Gall
Brighton & Hove Albion's captain under Clough

I had bad knees and was ready to retire the year before under Pat Saward. On his first day Cloughie asked "who is the Geordie?". I put my hand up and he said: "You are captain".

He kept me going for another year and I enjoyed every minute. He knew exactly what he wanted, who was good, who was bad and what they could and couldn't do.

We lost 8-2 at home to Bristol Rovers in front of the TV cameras and I was expecting a rollicking after that. Instead, he told me not to worry about it, go home and have a drink and that I was playing next week.

Steve Piper
Brighton & Hove Albion player under Clough

I remember being carried off injured in a 4-0 FA Cup defeat at home to non-League Walton and Hersham. He didn't believe I was injured, so the trainer, Glen Wilson, had to carry me into his office over his shoulder to prove I couldn't walk.

I remember meeting him for the first time at the White Hart Hotel in Lewes. Everyone was pooping themselves, even the older players were so in awe of him. The first person he picked on was John Templeman with his long hair. He called him "Shirley Temple".

He had unbelievable charisma and he was great for me as a young lad in the short time he was at Brighton.

His training methods were totally different. He would come in an hour before the game on a Saturday, give his speech and then that was it. We didn't see him again then until the following Thursday.

For his first game, against York, he put about 10,000 extra fans on the gate. That was the sort of impact he had. It was like Arsene Wenger coming to Brighton now.

Harry Bloom
The late vice-chairman of Brighton & Hove Albion, who was involved when

Clough arrived from Derby

Although he was only here (Brighton) a short time, his mere presence saw the gates at Goldstone rise from 6,000 to 16,000 and he was the catalyst, along with Peter Taylor, for what followed – Alan Mullery inherited the team that they began and the rest is history.

Duncan McKenzie

Signed by Clough in his brief time at Leeds United

Football will never see anyone like Clough ever again. He was box office wherever he went.

He broke the mould, had a different style of management to anyone else – he was an amazing man.

He looked at the bigger picture and is probably the best manager who ever lived. It's the end of an era. People talk of Shankly, Paisley, Busby, Wenger and Ferguson – Cloughie is up there with them.

Gordon Guthrie

Took over as physiotherapist at the Baseball Ground just weeks after Clough arrived as manager in 1967. After 30 years in the role, he is now kit manager at Pride Park

I was originally coaching at the club when Brian took over as manager, and I'll never forget the impression he made on his first day in charge. He'd arrived at the stadium at 9am to get himself settled before meeting the players an hour later.

The Baseball Ground used to have concrete passages and, with the manager's office situated at one end of the main stand and the changing rooms at the other end, you could hear him approaching a mile off as he paced along the corridor towards us.

The dressing room door flew open and, after saying "good morning", Brian just stood there for what seemed an eternity, looking around at the faces in front of him. Finally, he said: "Well gentleman, some of you are drawing too much money for what you are producing on the football field, while some of you are not receiving enough for what you are producing. Over the coming weeks, I'll be deciding who will be getting a rise, and who will be leaving the club".

Reg Matthews, an England international goalkeeper we had signed from Chelsea in 1961, was sat nearest the door and, on his way out, Brian turned to him and said: "By the way, Reg, I reckon you're probably the only top player I've got here, and I've heard you like the fags. Well, you can have a smoke any time you like, including half-time".

Well, the players didn't know what had hit them – they all just sat there open-mouthed. That was my first experience of him and it was immediately obvious that he was a unique character. Jack Bowers, a Derby County legend, was the physio when Brian arrived, but he suffered a stroke just a few weeks later and, seeing as I had started to take physiotheraphy qualifications, Brian just said to me: "You've got the job".

It was the best move I ever made, and the next few years working for Brian were just a fantastic experience. He was considered by the public as being loud, brash and big-headed, but that wasn't Brian Clough, the person. It was like Jekyll and Hyde in a way. Behind closed doors, he was a very generous, kind and thoughtful person.

If it was your wife's birthday, he would send a big bouquet of flowers or a box of chocolates. The next morning, you'd go in and say: "Thanks ever so much for that boss", and he would say: "Gordon, that's between me and your wife". If it had been someone else, you might take that the wrong way, but not with Cloughie.

It was the same with the kids. My two boys were at school in those days and Brian would always ask how they were. If, perhaps, you happened to mention one day that one of them was sick or under the weather, he would say: "Right, leave a note of things to be done and get yourself off home. If he's still not better tomorrow, give me a call and stay at home with him". I'd say: "But what about the injuries, boss?" He'd just reply: "Never mind the injuries. Family comes first".

That summed him up really. The most important thing in his life was the family and he kept that side of things very private from his football life. I like to think I knew him well and would consider him a friend, but I never went to his house. He would often nip off for breaks during the season with the family and I know that Barbara was a tower of strength to him throughout his career.

When I look back to my time working for Brian, I feel privileged to have known him. What he achieved with Derby County was nothing short of miraculous and, looking at the game today, I can't see how something like that would ever be done again. In terms of his standing in football, I would honestly place him up there with the likes of Shankly, Busby and Nicholson from that era.

The greatest thing I can say about Brian is that I learned something from him every day. Every time he spoke, he said something that was worth listening to, or taught you something. Sometimes you wouldn't realise it until years later, but that was the impact he had on everyone around him.

There will never be another like Brian Clough.

John McGovern
Former Derby County and Nottingham Forest skipper, who also played under Clough at Hartlepools United and Leeds United before lifting the European Cup in two consecutive seasons at Forest

Brian's best quality was being able to keep your feet on the ground. I remember one match where I had marked Alan Ball – who had just helped England win the World Cup – out of the game. **(Continued over)...**

Brian said to me "well done lad, you didn't let him have a kick. He is a very good player and you are not".

I could have been with him at five clubs but I turned him down when he took over at Brighton after leaving Derby under a cloud. When I told him I preferred to stay where I was, he slammed the phone down on me.

Archie (Gemmill), Kenny (Burns), the two Johns (Robertson and O'Hare) and I were players who gave maximum effort whenever we took to a football field. We possessed the grit and determination that were qualities which tended to be features of Scottish players.

Although I left Montrose as a seven-year-old, I had very strong ties with my homeland, and as a footballer probably developed in a similar way to my countrymen. Brian not only appreciated this commitment, but demanded it. I don't think he would actively go seeking Scottish players because of their natural characteristics, though. He would play players from China, Mongolia or wherever if he thought they could do a job for him.

Together, Peter and Brian were unbeatable, the perfect partnership.

Individually, the light of brilliance did not shine from them quite so dazzlingly. Brian's great trick was making the game simple for players, and supplying them with the confidence and self-belief he possessed to a Muhammed Ali degree.

He needed players who had the talent to carry out his instruction, and it can sometimes be forgotten just how good the players at Forest were in his time. John O'Hare and I were never favourites with the fans. John was the nicest man that I ever met, but when the going got tough, he and I would get stuck in. Brian knew that, and because of that he would remain behind us 100 per cent, even when things weren't going well for us.

Comparing Forest's record-breaking side with the Arsenal team that eclipsed their achievement in 2004, McGovern told the Sunday Telegraph's Trevor Haylett:

I've seen it written that we did not have the flair and imagination that Arsenal possess and that's absolute tripe. If it were possible to put the two teams up against each other it would be like one of those classic tennis matches that switches first one way and then the other and finally goes to five sets. There would not be a gnat's whisker between us in terms of ability.

The game did not attract the coverage it does now and it was only when we sat in the dressing room, having just lost to Liverpool, that we realised we had gone 42 games unbeaten. There was no big celebration when we passed the previous record of 29 games set by Leeds. That was not Cloughie's way. It was all about looking forward rather than back.

We were not Manchester United, Arsenal or Liverpool so we did not attract as much publicity. But remember that Clough took over a Forest team who were near the foot of the Second Division (now the 'Championship') and within five years had steered them to two European Cups, two League championships and two League Cups.

It's an achievement that will never be repeated. When Sir Alex Ferguson took over at United it took him seven years to win the title.

What's more, Clough did it with a small-town club and at a time when our league was stronger than it is today. In those days English teams lifted the European Cup six years in succession but on only one occasion since 1985 has it happened.

People go on about the pace of Thierry Henry but Trevor Francis was just as quick. We had John Robertson out on the left who was a genius with the ball and who worked back harder than Robert Pires does. And we had a right-sided midfielder in Martin O'Neill who could match Freddie Ljungberg for goals.

Jeremy Keith
Derby County Chief Executive
He was this club's greatest-ever manager and, in the eyes of Rams supporters, the best the world has ever seen. The contribution he made – not just to Derby County but to the country itself – will remain as a lasting legacy to the man who made Derby his home for the last 30 years.

Peter Shilton
Former Nottingham Forest & England goalkeeping legend
Brian Clough was the main man. He was strong, a great football man and a very honest man. He was one of the all-time great English managers.
I think he was unique, he had his own unique style.

Martin O'Neill
Former Nottingham Forest midfielder and now manager of Celtic
He was such a massive influence, I couldn't thank him enough for what he did for me personally. He should have managed England and he should have been given a knighthood, there is no question of that.

He was absolutely sensational and I don't think Brian would disagree with us either. He would be the first to say that he was the greatest of all-time. But he was like England's version of Muhammed Ali. He had fantastic charisma, unbelievable charisma. Outwardly he had this fantastic self-belief and self-confidence but, in truth, I think sometimes he was as vulnerable as all of us.

One of the great myths of all-time was that he was a manager and not a coach and seldom on the training ground. The very fact is that every day was a coaching lesson from Brian Clough and when he did come down to the training ground for a 20-25 minute spell, you'd pick up enough in that time to do you a life-time. He coached *during* the course of games.

His memory was phenomenal. John Robertson and I were lucky that, probably in that spell from 1975 to 1980, he was at his very best. He was bright, he was everything.

John O'Hare
Former Derby County and Leeds United striker under Clough

I last was with him at the 25-year reunion. He looked as good as I had seen him for some time. He was incredible, he had the audience in the palm of his hand.

I first encountered Clough at Sunderland, where he was coaching the youth team after retiring through injury. He was an idol in Sunderland even then.

He could grab our attention in a couple of seconds. He had presence.

Trevor Francis
Clough made Francis Britain's first £1m footballer when he signed him for Forest from Birmingham City in February 1979. Three months later he repaid that faith by scoring the winner in the European Cup final

It was a privilege and a pleasure to play under Clough. He put me in the

Making football history by signing Trevor Francis for £1million in 1979.

170

reserves as soon as he signed me.

He was very grudging in his praise, even *after* we won the European Cup in Munich. Cloughie and Peter Taylor were very subdued, it was all very low key. But we went from strength to strength after that.

We all took stick – it didn't matter who you were, whether you cost £1m or came on a free transfer. He treated everyone the same.

There were times his behaviour bordered on eccentric but that was part of his pure genius. We all had the greatest respect for him.

I thank God that I had the privilege of playing for the best manager in the business and look back on my time at Forest as an honour.

Alan Hill

A key member of Clough's backroom staff at Forest, he admits he will always regret not patching things up with Clough. Hill had no option but to testify against Clough in court when he became embroiled in the much publicised 'bung' case involving Teddy Sheringham's transfer from Forest to Tottenham Hotspur in 1992. Clough never forgave Hill and the 60-year-old conceded it will haunt him for some time.

It will stay with me for the rest of my life that I never made up with Brian. Of course I'm full of regret and disappointment. I became involved in the bung case and had to tell the truth. Brian never forgave me.

John Robertson

Former Nottingham Forest left-winger who scored the winning goal in the 1980 European Cup final. He is now assistant manager to former City Ground team-mate, Martin O'Neill, at Celtic.

He is a genius, he is the best. I will never meet anybody like him again. One lifetime does not produce two Brian Cloughs.

When I played for Brian, I just used to want to get a 'well done' from him. When I was playing, if ever I did anything right, he always used to get his little hand up and when that happened, I used to feel 10 feet tall.

He'd take the players away on trips and leave the wives moaning, but bunches of flowers would arrive at their doors and he became the hero.

It should be said that this was not the case with Larry Lloyd's ex-wife. She threw the flowers down the toilet!

For me, he is at the top of the list because of what he has achieved. There have been some brilliant managers but Brian Clough achieved it at two clubs which were totally provincial, not very big and not very fashionable, yet he went on to win two European Cups. As far as I'm concerned he is definitely the best there has ever been.

The classic story was the one about Tony Woodcock. He had decided to

THE LIFE OF **BRIAN**

grow a beard, but the gaffer pulled him to one side. Brian asked: "What's that on your face?" Tony replied that he was growing a beard.

Brian asked why, and Tony replied: "I want to be different". Quick as a flash, Brian retorted: "Son, if you want to be different, try scoring a hat-trick on Saturday". It just summed up the real Brian Clough.

To win two European Cups with Nottingham Forest and reach another semi-final with Derby County says everything about the man. We won the old Second Division title one season, the First Division championship in the next season and the European Cup in the season after that. Five players who weren't getting a game when Brian arrived at Forest – myself, Martin (O'Neill), Tony, Viv (Anderson) and Ian Bowyer – all won the European Cup just four years later.

Nobody would have touched Kenny Burns at that time because of his reputation. But Brian signed him, converted him from centre-forward to centre-half and turned him into Footballer of the Year.

Simplicity was the great thing about Brian. There was nothing complicated about what he told you. To be honest, I loved the guy.

He took us for a drink the night before the 1979 League Cup final against Southampton. It was done with the best intentions, though, and it settled all our nerves. He could be extremely charming, too. We were extremely lucky to work with someone so talented and so brilliant.

He could have stepped into any given job. People talk about Sir Clive Woodward moving into football, but Brian could have coached the English cricket team without a problem.

John Robertson was talking to Roger Hannah (Daily Mail)

Garry Birtles
Former Nottingham Forest striker under Clough
We thought he was indestructible. When I heard he'd died, it was just like a bolt from the blue. Brian's son, Nigel, phoned me. He was upset, I was upset and it's just been a major shock.

When somebody like Brian Clough dies, it's hard to explain how you feel. It's like a member of your family dying. He was immense, the best manager this country has ever seen.

What can you say about Cloughie? They broke the mould when they made him, there will never be anyone like him again.

Arsenal deserve great credit for what they've done but I don't think they've done it until they've won a trophy in Europe.

And it has taken Wenger five or six years to mould that team. Cloughie got us promoted in 1977, we won the First Division in our first year and then two European Cups.

Neil Webb

Former Nottingham Forest midfielder Clough signed from Portsmouth and sold to Manchester United for £1.5m

It was a great honour to work for him, you never knew what would happen. He gave you the confidence to be better than you probably were.

Kenny Burns

Former Nottingham Forest centre-half whom Clough developed to become Footballer of the Year in 1978

Cloughie is the greatest English manager ever. He saw things that nobody else could see – that was his beauty.

Sir Alf Ramsey won the World Cup but what Clough did was more impressive.

He was a great manager and a great man. He put me back on the straight and narrow and enhanced my career. He was like an adopted father to me.

Larry Lloyd

Kenny Burns' central defensive partner who proved another great Clough bargain signing for Nottingham Forest

I didn't find him a very nice man. He was difficult to work for. And I think he fined me.

However, Clough was also an extremely perceptive manager and he knew instinctively which players needed what kind of treatment. John (Robertson) needed that "well done", a pat on the back. I couldn't give two monkeys whether he said "well done" to me, but he knew that and used to go the other way and give me a rollicking. Clough knew I used to fall for it, and running through that tunnel, my attitude was 'I'll show that big so-and-so'.

I have got a lot to thank him for. He rescued me from Coventry and it was a gamble for both of us. But all I needed was five minutes in his company to know he was a man who was going places.

Viv Anderson

On the verge of breaking into the Nottingham Forest first team when Clough took over, he went on to become the first black player to be capped by England

We were just lads when he took over and he was marvellous to us. He taught us how to conduct ourselves on and off the pitch.

I was always in absolute awe of him and I will always be indebted to him.

Frank Clark
A veteran left-back for Clough's Nottingham Forest who went on to manage the club himself
His greatest strength was man-management. He was just a natural. He hadn't learned it from books, or from going on courses, he was just a natural. He had a gift of getting 100 per cent from everyone who played for him.

One match that always sticks out was my 500th appearance. I had never scored a goal and he put me up front at half-time against Ipswich. It is the only time I have ever heard players laugh out loud in a dressing room.

As it happened, I scored my only ever goal and it was all down to the boss.

When he walked through the door, the atmosphere was electric.

Sean Haslegrave
Clough's first signing at the City Ground when he bought him from Stoke City, but hit by injuries
Brian Clough was sometimes egocentric, sometimes a bully but he was a managerial genius.

I'll never forget the moment he told me he was going to make me his first signing at Nottingham Forest. I was playing for Stoke in a UEFA Cup tie against Ajax of Amsterdam, and the manager, Tony Waddington, had substituted me in the second half. I wasn't happy, so afterwards I went to speak to the gaffer. Before I could say anything, out of the corner of my eye I could see Clough marching towards me. I was completely gobsmacked. Cloughie had travelled to Holland for the tie and he was saying "You'll do for me, young man. That was a fantastic performance. I want to sign you, youngster".

Sure, enough, a few months later Clough snapped me up for £50,000.

I met him at a travel lodge on the M6, and it was typical Cloughie I suppose. I walked in and he just said: "Right, son, I'm going to France tomorrow on holiday with the wife and kids, and I'm not leaving here until you sign. You can talk about anything you want – the weather, pop music or shopping – but just sign there, lad". I did, and I was a Forest player as Brian Clough began to assemble one of the greatest club sides in Europe.

I'd gone down to Stoke at 15, knocked on the door and asked for a trial. But there I was, signing for a managerial legend. I was a kid from a council estate in Stoke who just wanted to play football. When I left school I was an apprentice welder on £12-per-week, but when I became a professional I thought I'd died and gone to heaven.

There are those who still dismiss Clough as a loud-mouthed tyrant, while

others saw him as a managerial talent to rank alongside Bill Shankly, Sir Matt Busby, Jock Stein and Sir Alex Ferguson. I think his secret was that you never knew what he was going to be like from one minute to the next – that's how he operated. He was totally unpredictable and always kept you guessing, and that was his massive strength.

Brian could be terribly hard and quite ruthless, and I've seen big men hide in corridors to avoid him, but I'll never forget him helping out one of his ex-players at Derby. The guy had lost everything in a failed business venture, and had to auction his house and most of his possessions to pay the debt. When Cloughie heard about it, he went to the auction, bought everything and gave it back to him. It was an unbelievable gesture of true kindness, but he always used to say: "If you do it for me, son, I'll see you right".

Brian built an incredible football team at Nottingham Forest but, unfortunately, I injured both my ankles soon after I signed. I felt guilty that I'd let Brian down, because he had put great faith in me and it didn't work out. Things had moved on by then, though, and Brian signed Archie Gemmill.

I left Nottingham Forest with an empty feeling but I never regretted joining a wonderful club like Preston, a place that has been my home for more than 25 years now.

Stuart Pearce
Former Nottingham Forest and England legend who was the last player at to captain Forest under Clough

He was one of the big characters in the game. I can't name anyone bigger.

It was different every day. He brought simplicity and the main thing was respect. I'm eternally grateful for what he did for my career. I earned 76 England caps in my time at Forest under Brian, which says it all really. He *made* me as a player.

I think he was a man for all seasons. He had a reputation for being a hard taskmaster, which he was when it was needed. But there were other times, like when I came back from the 1990 World Cup under a bit of a cloud, and he was there with an arm around the shoulder. He knew exactly what to do at the right time.

You can talk about him for hours in terms of stories you've got but the bottom line is, just go and have a look in the trophy cabinet he brought to different clubs around the country. That says it all basically.

No matter what team we played, whatever the competition, he would want to win it. I remember we took a team to Notts County for a testimonial. He played the full side only four or five days before the FA Cup final, but that was him.

THE LIFE OF BRIAN

Football will remember him, that's for sure. There's a part of Brian Clough in all of us, make no mistake about that.

Chris Woods
Former young goalkeeper at Nottingham Forest
I often recall the only time I ever had the nerve to say "no" to Brian Clough!
We played squash regularly and they were quite competitive affairs. One afternoon, the legendary cricketer, Colin Milburn, was watching Clough and I from the spectators' gallery. During a rally, I heard something fall from above onto the court – and when we stopped playing Cloughie checked it out and asked me to pick it up.
It was Colin Milburn's glass eye! I refused!
It's the first, and last, time I defied him – and he had to pick it up himself!
Cloughie took his squash very seriously and there was a time I couldn't go with him to play because I was training.
He gave me a rollicking!

Peter Davenport
The former Forest striker, and now Bangor City manager, recounts a typical

Clough tale

Normally, players at Forest never saw the boss from Monday to Thursday (other coaches took care of football and fitness training). Fridays and Saturdays were Cloughie's days for motivating his chosen team and selecting their tactics for the coming game.

But this particular week, the players got a message to turn up in the club trophy room at 10 am on Thursday. When we arrived promptly, there was a horseshoe-shaped line of chairs for them to sit on, with one in the middle – for Mr Clough – that remained empty.

Half-an-hour passed and no-one else turned up.

Another 15 minutes went by as the players fidgeted and wondered what was going on. Just before 11am, the door opened and in came . . . not Brian Clough, but a huge, freshly broken branch from a tree, with Cloughie holding the other end of it out of sight. All that the players could see at first were bunches of green leaves (it was Nottingham Forest, of course).

The manager paraded into the trophy room with the branch thrust out in front of him. He went round all the players, poking each of them in the chest with the bushy end and giving individual messages to everyone. He said to me: "You'll go before me". Clough then left without further ado.

In the evening of the same day, I got a phone call from my mother: "How's it going, son?"

"It's been a bit of a strange day, actually, mum".

"Well, I've had a lovely day. At 10 o'clock this morning, the most beautiful

bunch of flowers arrived by courier from Mr. Clough. There was a little card with them. You are so lucky to be working for a man who cares about his players so much".

I was dumbstruck. The point of the story is the principle it illustrates, not the actions. (You could hardly get away with Cloughie's

behaviour in either the office or the football club these days.)

How do you "kiss em and kick 'em" at the same time? Use your imagination! That's what the great managers do.

He was the best manager I ever played for – the best of the lot. I have played under the likes of Ron Atkinson and Alex Ferguson, but his man-management was unique. He could get the best out of any player in the dressing room.

He made you feel special when you went out on the pitch.

Joe Kinnear
Current Nottingham Forest manager

He is a football legend and as a manager he was simply a genius. The

success he had here speaks volumes. To win the kind of things he did while competing against the likes of Liverpool, Manchester United and Arsenal was a staggering achievement. To go on and conquer Europe was even more remarkable.

Nigel Doughty
Nottingham Forest chairman

Over the years he was always recognised as one of the outstanding English managers and should have been boss of the England team but that was never going to happen. He ran the club from top to bottom and could never do that with the FA.

He ruffled feathers everywhere, that was part of his make up, but there was always a sense of amusement before the brashness. He *was* Nottingham Forest Football Club. The success he had here goes down as one of the great football achievements of all-time. Wherever you go in the world, the city has become synonymous with Robin Hood and Brian Clough and there is no doubt he has touched the lives of so many people in the area.

He would be the first one to say he was the greatest of all time.

The Mayor of Nottingham

Brian Clough reached the pinnacle of his remarkable career in Nottingham and was one of the greatest ambassadors in the city's history. His association with Nottingham over 18 years as manager of Forest was so strong that he became as synonymous with the city as Robin Hood.

Arsene Wenger
Manager of the mighty Arsenal team that emulated Nottingham Forest's undefeated league record that had stood for 26 years

I remember watching his teams play and I would say that the Forest side of the late 70s will go down in history as one of the all-time greats.

Whenever I have met Martin O'Neill and the other European coaches they told me about it. They were a team more based on a solid defence which they used to go forward.

What Nottingham Forest did under Clough was unbelievable because of the size of the club. I rate highly what Clough achieved. It's huge, incomparable. It is great to beat their league record but, of course, it's even more of a challenge to win two European Cups like they did.

I never had the chance to meet Brian Clough but I know he was a special character.

It's not an exaggeration to say that I was truly touched when he complimented the way the current Arsenal side (season 2003-04) played and that we deserved to break his record.

People use the word legend too freely but Brian Clough is a true legend of English football and his success in this country and in Europe is a legacy for which he will always be remembered.

Arsene Wenger respects Cloughie's achievements.

Chapter 12
Cloughie – By The Press

John Vinicombe
Former Chief Sports Reporter, Brighton Evening Argus. Now 75, he recalls the day he broke the news of Clough's arrival at the Goldstone Ground in November 1973

Brighton were in a dreadful position just before Cloughie took over – 20th in the third division with home gates having fallen to around 6,000.

They were away at Hereford United one Saturday and, at half-time, I went downstairs from the press-box to the toilet, which was also used by the directors and their guests.

Anyway, while I was standing there going about my business, Brighton's vice-chairman, Harry Bloom, just happened to pitch up right next to me. After the usual acknowledgement he turned to me and said: "Hey John, you'll never guess who we are going to see tonight".

When he told me that he and the chairman, Mike Bamber, were planning to meet Brian Clough and Peter Taylor at a London hotel, I almost lost control of what I was doing!

I said: "You must be barmy, you'll never get him", but Harry was adamant it was happening and so I nipped back up to the press box to try and get the story over to the office. Of course, this was in the days long before mobile phones or lap-top computers, so I had to somehow find a space in the small and confined press box in order to phone over copy without being heard by those around me.

I eventually managed to get the story over as a lead and it appeared in our classified section that evening – before the meeting at the hotel had even taken place.

Cloughie's appointment was duly announced a few days later and they rolled out the red carpet and gave him a terrific reception.

They held a press conference but that didn't offer an opportunity to speak to him one-on-one, so it wasn't until a couple of days later that I actually met him for the first time.

I would go down to the ground almost every single day and, on this occasion, I was invited into his office, where he was sat in the chair with his feet up on his desk.

The first thing he did was to tell me how dead-beat and tired he felt after running up and down the pitch during the tough training session that had just finished.

"You bloody liar," I said, "there isn't a bead of sweat on you and the bottom of your boots are perfectly clean!"

He just turned round to me and said: "You c***!"

"Takes one to know one," I replied, and with that he agreed, invited me to sit down and from then on I don't think there was ever a cross word between us.

I was a few years older than Brian, so I wasn't scared of him, and I wasn't going to bow down at his feet. I like to think he respected me for that and we got on well. There was such a candour about him and he was incisive and analytical about the game – he could judge a player after watching him for just a couple of minutes.

We talked a lot – not only about football, but also about politics and everyday life. If you talk to someone about one subject only, you get a distorted view of the person, and talking to him on a personal level was how I got to know and like the man.

He had his eccentricities, of course. After home games he would be out of the Goldstone Ground and in his silver Mercedes on the way back to Derby by 5.30pm, and he only spent a few days a week down in Brighton. Indeed, I often spent my time commuting between Brighton and Derby in order to talk to him. He was always accommodating, though, and often asked if my wife and I would like to stay overnight at the hotel up there.

I occasionally sat next to him on the train for away games – I can remember drinking champagne at 9am on the way to York! – and I gradually came to realise that Brian certainly wasn't a cruel man. He was in fact a very kind man.

I can recall an evening away game on a freezing cold night at Walsall, when I rushed down to the dressing room at the final whistle to get some instant quotes so that I could make a quick get-away.

Anyway, I burst through the door and there was Brian Clough, on his hands and knees, helping to untie the laces on the players' boots because their own hands were so cold and stiff.

He turned to me and said: "You're not supposed to be in here," and I thought: 'You're not supposed to be untying boot laces', but that just summed up the legend of the man.

People may say that he used Brighton as a stepping stone but, when the club appointed him, he was very grateful to be given a job and didn't go there just to sit around waiting for a better offer.

From Day One, he introduced a very drastic regime. He saw players in a black and white sense – good and bad – and he quite rightly came to the conclusion that Brighton had been struggling because they *had* a lot of bad players.

Before his first match in charge, he took the entire squad out to dinner at the White Hart Hotel in Lewes, just to see how they behaved *en masse* in that kind of social scene – who ate peas with their knife, who pinched the waitress' bum, that kind of thing.

He didn't like the long hair that was fashionable among players at the time and ordered many of them to have haircuts, which didn't go down too well. He was suspicious of any player who would pack a white tuxedo for a pre-season tour or club break.

It all led to a virtual transfer merry-go-round and the influx of new players was quite phenomenal for a club of Brighton's size and status – it wasn't unusual to see two or three players arriving on the same day.

The results weren't instant, however, and Brian had to endure a horrendous period when the team lost 4-0 in the FA Cup against Walton and Hersham and were then beaten 8-2 by Bristol Rovers. That left everyone stunned but, in effect, Cloughie actually enjoyed it. He knew he had a real challenge to get his teeth into and would turn it around.

Sure enough, the results started to go his way and we began to see the best of personality and motivating techniques. The public adored him, other managers were in awe of him and the players were scared stiff of him.

He was invited by the Shah of Iran to go and manage over there for a ridiculous amount of money, but he turned it down, and I think we reported that it was because there wasn't room for two Shahs in Iran!

I also remember him deciding to fly over to New York one weekend to watch Muhammad Ali fight – something he had always wanted to do.

He basically had a free hand to do whatever he wanted and there was no doubting that Cloughie was the boss – I think that's why he later said that Mike Bamber was the best chairman he had ever worked for.

I was very close to Mike, who was very upset when Brian departed for

Leeds, but I think he realised that he was such a hot property and it was never going to be a long and lengthy relationship.

There's no doubt in my mind, though, that Brian laid the foundations for the success that Brighton subsequently went on to enjoy. He tore down the old order and put the structures in place that allowed Peter Taylor, and then Alan Mullery, to take it on and lead the club into the top flight. He may have only been there for eight months but he made the kind of impact on Brighton and Hove Albion that no-one else possibly could have done.

Mel Henderson, *chief sports writer, Ipswich Evening Star*

Everyone who met Brian Clough has a favourite recollection and I am no different. He was brusque, outspoken, controversial and, when you consider his achievements as a football manager, something of a miracle worker and didn't he know it!

When I plucked up the courage to knock on his office door, the last thing I expected was to be sat down, poured a drink and for him to make my football-mad son's dream come true.

It was March 7, 1981, and I was preparing to depart for Ipswich's FA Cup quarter-final clash with Nottingham Forest at the City Ground. My son, Derek, who was six at the time, suddenly piped up: "Daddy, can I be mascot at the game today?" Talk about being put on the spot! Thinking I had the perfect escape route, I quickly replied: "No, it's an away game today. And anyway, with daddy working at the football club, it wouldn't be fair on all the other boys and girls who want to be Ipswich mascots."

I was the public relations officer at Portman Road and had wrongly assumed that my son wanted to be the Town mascot. But he informed me: "I want to be Forest mascot – remember, Trevor Francis is my favourite player."

Stuck for an answer second time around, I told him: "If it's a draw today, there will be a replay at Ipswich and I will ask if you can be Forest mascot."

Later that day I witnessed a 3-3 thriller and, realising there was no way I could return home that evening without a firm answer for my son, I made my way in search of the great man. About an hour had elapsed after the final whistle and a Forest employee told me he would be in his office. I located it, took a deep breath, knocked and there was no doubting the identity of the person who shouted: "Come in." I entered and explained who I was, whereupon Cloughie invited me to sit down and asked if I would like a drink. Then, having poured two generous measures, he asked: "What can I do for you?" He listened intently and a smile broke across his face as I relayed the story. "So here I am," I said, "to pop the question."

Cloughie didn't appear to stop to think about his answer. "No problem," he said. "Bring him along to our hotel on Tuesday at tea-time and we'll look after him."

You can imagine my son's reaction when I returned home and relayed the news. When I took him to the Copdock Hotel at 6pm, Cloughie shook his hand, assured me he would be fine and said: "We'll bring him down on the bus."

It all seemed too good to be true but, sure enough, as the Forest coach drove into the stadium, there was my son perched proudly on Cloughie's lap, right at the front in his all-red strip. He was taken into the away dressing room and reappeared for the pre-match kickabout – warm-ups were less intense in those days – with his hero. Trevor looked after my son, who was allowed to fire the ball past Peter Shilton, and then he joined skippers Mick Mills and Kenny Burns, with the Ipswich mascot and the match officials, on the centre spot. ITV were broadcasting highlights of the game and Derek's proud grandparents, having been tipped off, were able to hear commentator Gerry Harrison tell a nationwide audience: "The Forest mascot is actually the son of the Ipswich PRO."

Town won the replay, 1-0, thanks to Arnold Muhren's goal, but Derek remained a Trevor Francis fan, even switching his allegiance to Manchester City when he moved there. Now a DJ in Amsterdam, he remains a City fan, but he has never forgotten Brian Clough's generosity all those years ago.

Sure, Cloughie was a hot-head – some would even describe him as a bit of a bully – and he was most definitely confrontational, no more so than when he gave those pitch invaders a slap or 10. But underneath a public persona to which, I believe, he deliberately played up, he was an uncomplicated character and a thoroughly nice man who treated Derek like a grandson, providing him with a lasting memory he will never forget.

I know it has been said before, but we will never see his like again. Cloughie really was a one-off. Not so many years ago, after he had slipped into retirement and was said to be an alcoholic, I was in the Caribbean when I met a couple who happened to live close to him and his wife. They relayed a story about him staggering down the middle of the road, not far from his home, when they came upon him. As good neighbours, they helped him and the woman said: "Brian, you're going to have to be careful. If a car comes round that bend, and you're in the middle of the road, you won't have a chance."

He looked her straight in the eye, appeared to sober-up instantly, winked and replied: "They'll stop for me, love!"

Trevor Frecknall

Sports editor of the Nottingham Evening Post from 1979-92

My first audience with Brian Clough ended with him easing me out of the City Ground with his foot, accompanied by a growled "F*** off".

My final match as the Nottingham Forest correspondent of the local paper ended with the manager insisting that I carry the League Cup out of Wembley.

It goes without saying that I obeyed both instructions. Anyone required to remain in regular contact with the most mercurial manager football has ever known knew there was a simple rule: Cloughie gets what Cloughie wants.

And so when I, as the newly-appointed sports editor of the *Nottingham Evening Post*, went to tell him, in December 1978, that his favourite journalist had just been sacked for joining a strike, he listened carefully to why, asked a few questions that highlighted the ideological differences between his socialist beliefs and my employers' Thatcherite tendencies, then escorted me to the exit, saying: "You're banned. Don't take it personally. I think me and you could have got on. Hey – all life's a game."

"I'll be playing to win as well," I retorted.

"Good lad," he replied. "Now f*** off!" And his boot, on my backside, propelled me into the car park of the City Ground.

So the rest of the 1978-79 season was spent covering Forest matches without ever talking to the manager. The task was made easier by the club's committee members – the equivalent of today's directors – smuggling me into the ground for home matches and by the *Post* owner having a six-seater jet that propelled a photographer and myself around the Continent to European Cup ties, culminating in Forest's victory over Malmo in the final in Munich.

Come the following season, the plane could not take us to Sweden for a tie against Oester Vaxjoe. We were not going to be able to fly pictures back for the following day's paper – until Cloughie ended his ban by coming to our rescue.

"I'm not having any mates of mine stuck in a cold hole like this another night," he said, insisting he pack us on to the club's charter plane back to East Midlands Airport.

Mates of his? It had been nine months since he had spoken to either myself or our photographer. Apparently we had won him over by the way in which we had overcome the difficulties. He always appreciated wholehearted effort.

From that point on, Clough allowed me into his inner circle. Although he was only too aware of his status as Britain's most famous manager, he made a point of being available to the local paper and talking directly to the fans. We would talk most days, after training, often with him in his famous green sweatshirt and his incongruous flat cap.

Of course, he knew the value of a story, but frequently preferred to give the big ones to me for free. In 1989, when he lashed out at a couple of supporters who invaded the pitch after Forest had beaten Queen's Park Rangers in the League Cup, we found the fans and engineered a reconciliation. Our view was that the louts had headed his hand, but the FA fined him a record £5,000.

The morning after the disciplinary hearing, the whole world wanted to know his reaction, but Cloughie grabbed me by the ear and led me past his first-team squad, took me into his office, poured me a huge whiskey and ginger (it was 10.10am), sat behind his desk wearing his trademark flat cap, waited for me to sup it and then gave me the story that the whole football world was begging for.

"The FA did me proud," he said, and as I waited, pen poised, for the next quote, he picked up his phone and dialled my office. "You make up the rest," he said. "Twelve pars – and if I don't like it, I can always cut you off."

After I had dictated the copy, Cloughie's digit closed on the telephone rest. "Now let me get to work," he said. "And if I hear any of that on the radio before I see it in the *Post*, I'll know you can't be trusted."

Clough knew all our deadline times and edition times, and he also knew how newspapers worked. For long periods he banned most of the nationals from the City Ground, allowing just myself and John Sadler (who wrote his column in *The Sun*) into the inner sanctum.

He rarely took umbrage at criticism of his team, so long as it was constructive. Criticism of him was more difficult, but also very rare. As the local paper, we knew all too well what he had done for the team and the area, and we knew how popular he was with our readers.

I was banned once, when I reported (with perfect accuracy) his quotes casting doubt over Peter Shilton's continuing suitability as the England goalkeeper. Shilton was by then a Southampton player, and Clough's assistant, Ronnie Fenton, pointed out that my quotes would provide the perfect incentive for him to play a blinder against Forest when the two teams met in a fortnight's time. Clough decided to deny the story completely, and back it up by refusing to talk to me.

We soon got over it and resumed our relationship. In 1990, I was trying to give up my 30-a-day smoking habit and he promised me a story every day so long as I succeeded. He was as good as his word – and even let me sit on the front seat of the coach with the League Cup when they retained it at Wembley.

Chapter 13

Cloughie – By The Fans

Lilian Baker *(grew up in Brian's street, 13 years his senior)*
I used to live in Valley Road when Brian was a young lad. I was friends with his mum. Brian was always kicking a tin can around the street and his dad was often asked: "Will you get that boy a ball?"

My mother, Jessie Tunelty, was quite involved with local politics and would often help the Labour Party during local and national elections. She would ask Brian to go 'number snatching', which entailed asking people their voting number outside the polling booth. They would then be able to identify those people in the street who hadn't voted, and would knock on their doors and get them along.

My mum was a very clean, respectable lady and she would expect the same from others. She often told Brian to go inside and wash his hands, which he always did.

It was hard to stay clean and tidy playing in the street and I always remember Brian in his green velvet jacket with snot stains on the arms!

He was a lovely boy from a lovely family.

Marcus Alton, *editor, www.brianclough.com*
(non-profit-making tribute website) – Nottingham Forest
I once met him at a fete in a community hall in Derby, a little while after he'd retired from management. They'd set-up a little table for him to sit at and sign autographs. I'd taken along a photo of the Forest team in the changing room after the FA Cup semi-final win in 1991. All the players had signed it, and I just needed the signature of the Great Man.

He looked at the photo and his face lit-up instantly. After he'd signed it, I said: "Thanks, Mr Clough, that's made my day." He then got up out of his chair and gave me a hug and a kiss on the cheek. "Young man, it's made *my* day too," he told me. That moment will live with me forever.

Another special time was when my partner and I met him again when we queued for five hours (from 5.45am) to be first in-line at his first-ever book signing for *Walking on Water*. It was worth waiting every single second. He lavished his time on us, signing everything we asked him to, and chatted all about his grandchildren and his times at Forest. He even presented us with a bottle of champagne for being first in the queue. "We used to bathe in this stuff," he joked. A few days later he signed the label of the bottle for me. I can guarantee it will never be opened!

When the paperback version of his book came out, I felt privileged to interview him for BBC Radio Nottingham. He thanked me for all the get-well messages I'd passed on to him following his liver transplant. I'd received them through my tribute website, www.brianclough.com. We were then taken into a private room for the interview. I was so nervous as I knew that Cloughie could be unpredictable. But the quotes he gave me were pure gold-dust.

I asked him how he was feeling after the operation. "I'm in good nick," he told me. Then he joked: "I'd like to take you around with me for the next few weeks, because you definitely make me better looking than I am." And I was flattered! We chatted after the interview and I left feeling like a king.

That was the mark of the man. Whether you met him for 30 seconds or 15 minutes, Brian Clough made you feel special. You were his friend, and he was yours.

When I stood on the steps of Ten Downing Street this October, presenting the petition signed by thousands of people calling for a posthumous honour for the Master Manager, I felt so proud I was representing all those fans who wanted to say 'thank-you' to their friend.

And as I stood there on that late October day outside Number Ten, the sun shone brilliantly and the sky was a clear blue. Just right for a man born on the first day of spring. And I think that gorgeous weather was a sign of Cloughie's approval – he was giving us his famous thumbs up. That made my day too.

Simon Siegel, *Nottingham Forest*
On meeting the Master Manager in Nottingham, a friend of mine said: "Hello, Mr Clough, it's a pleasure to meet you." To which he replied: "It's a pleasure to meet you, young man – take your hands out of your pockets."

Will Mather, *West Bridgford, Nottingham*
Cloughie should have been knighted. He made many a Saturday afternoon a magic experience down at the City Ground, as well as all over the country when Forest played away.

I looked forward to five to three to see him walk out and applaud us in the Trent End when we chanted his name (causing much amusement when he got confused between the 'Brian Laws' and 'Brian Clough' chant!).

I do miss him now. There is no-one in the game who produces the same presence and we're much the poorer for that.

Eric Kirton, *Farndon, Nottingham Forest*
In the early 80s, when I was working close to the City Ground, I came into contact with Brian Clough on many occasions and in the course of conversation I mentioned that I was getting together ground equipment for a brand new bowling green in my home village of Farndon.

As soon as Brian knew of my involvement in groundsmanship he asked the groundskeeper at the time to sort out any old equipment that the club had no longer any use for.

My trailer was loaded up and in due course I sold what we had no use for, to bowling and football clubs, to increase our funds, which at the time was badly needed.

I, as well as Farndon Bowling Club, will be eternally grateful to Brian for his generosity. Brusque, though he may have seemed at times, his heart was always to other people's advantage.

Daniel Mounser, *editor of www.nottinghamforest-mad.co.uk and writer for the Nottingham Forest fanzine, Blooming Forest*

How can you begin to describe Mr. Clough? What he said went and anyone who disagreed was wrong. I remember going to my first Forest game, back in 1989, and seeing the great man leaping out of his dugout, shouting orders with his infamous finger pointing.

I was only lucky enough to meet the great man once, at the 25th anniversary of Forest's first European Cup win, in May 2004, but I completely froze. He said: "How are you, young man?" and all I could reply was: "Yes thanks, Brian."

He's the sort of character that can make you feel a million dollars and I'm sure all players who have played under him would agree.

An absolute legend who will never be forgotten by the people of Nottingham.

When anyone asks me if I believe in God, I always say: "Yes, but he retired in 1993."

Chris Horn, *Nottingham Forest*

His other son, Simon, owns the newsagent on Central Avenue in West Bridgford and Clough would sometimes hang around in there when he was over to see Simon.

One day we were in the newsagent with our two young daughters, Rachael and Suzannah. Rachael was only one at the time and still in her pushchair. Now our Rachael is a 'solidly built' girl and was gleefully sticking both legs in the air. Sir Brian grabs hold of her legs, gives them a right good squeeze and said: "She's gonna be a centre forward with legs like that."

Dave Winnett, *Sherwood – Nottingham Forest*

I met the great man once, at Wembley in 1992, when England played against France. The game is famous for Shearer's first England goal (Lineker got the other) and Geoff Thomas' shot from the inside-left position that ended up near the right corner flag.

More significantly for me, England featured in their ranks D Walker, S Pearce and N Clough. All were impressive, with 'Sir Des' immaculate (what's new?). I headed to the car park, already elated, when, standing against a large motor, accompanied by the lugubrious figure of Chairman Mo, was Him, Sir Brian, hands thrust deep into pockets of his long Umbro coat.

"Will you sign this, please?" I asked, thrusting my programme towards him "Er, no, son," was his reply. Bugger. Undeterred, I asked: "What did you think of our boys' performance tonight?" He focussed on the badge on my Reds cap. "Nottingham Forest?" he asked. "Certainly am," I beamed, puffing out my chest. Sir Bri relaxed a little, leant forward and uttered words that have been burned on my memory ever since: "We walked it, son, we *were* the team." I probably could have floated back up the motorway at that point.

I feel like I've lost a family member. Sir Brian gave me more happiness than anyone outside my family and very close friends. It was a privilege to be around in his time.

Robert Nichols, *Middlesbrough - Fly Me To The Moon fanzine website*
As a player he was red-hot, a totally tuned in, ruthless goal machine. His career savagely cut short by injury but still with a record that stands comparison with the very best.

He reinvented himself as a quite brilliant manager. At a time of big personality managers Cloughie was a colossus. Too big a character for the confines of football, Brian Clough was a household name, his voice the most imitated, his quotes legendary. A genius and someone we were always proud to call our own.

When Brian returned to Middlesbrough for book signings, the queues would break all records. He was so popular in a town where everyone seemed to know him or his big family. He always had time to swap anecdotes and reminisce as he signed away. People really cared for him. He was special but still one of us.

My grandma knew his mum and dad. My mum used to be a good friend of his brother, Gerald. My dad sat on the same train as Brian as they travelled to National Service in Dumfries. They never really talked – Cloughie's mind was focussed on his football goals.

He was a man of the people, never forgetting his roots.

Shirley and Frank Smelt, Derby
We were regulars at Derby during Brian's time there but we didn't like what they did to him, so when Brian went, we left, too, and we haven't been back until tonight, to pay our last respects.

Ray Johnson, Stapleford

I've been following Forest since they won the Cup in '59 and went to Wembley about six years on the trot. Wonderful times. We'll never see the likes of it again. Not at a small club. The man was unbelievable.

I remember his last game at Forest. It was an amazing occasion to see the way the fans cheered him off the pitch at the end. What manager, who had just taken his club down, would receive a response like that? It says it all about the man. He was instantly forgiven.

I still bring my grandson along these days but we watch something not quite as good.

Paul Stevens, Olveston, Derby

Fantastic fellow. I've been a Forest fan all my life. He came to us when were doing nothing and gave us the world. I work at Nottingham Forest as a host in the hospitality lounges and saw him only recently. He signed my programme and noticed my name badge and dedicated it "To Ron", which I thought was a nice touch.

My favourite memory has to be winning the European Cup twice, especially the first one as we beat Liverpool on the way and they were the holders. All the memories are happy ones.

Sean Hanrahan and Tony Martin, Mansfield

I only met him once, at a book signing, and I'll tell you something everyone else will tell you – he called me "Young man!"

I come from Mansfield and you tended to support any team that was doing good. In the early 70s Derby were that team. I must say that it has been a huge cross to bare over the past 30-odd years!

Eileen Morrisroe, Derby

I was over at Derby during the glory days and although I never had occasion to meet Brian, my late husband did. It was an old boys' reunion at Derby school and my husband picked him up and they went together. Brian was the guest of honour. My late husband adored him and if he was here now he would give you chapter and verse on everything he did.

Pat and Beryl Ratcliffe and grandson Jack, Olveston

We were watching Derby in the late 60s and 70s when the likes of David Nish, John McGovern, Roy McFarland, Colin Todd, and Alan Hinton were playing . Brian was a great bloke. Down to earth. What I liked is that he just came straight out with it. He knew what he wanted and that was it.

Jack: I met him once in town and he asked me how I was and who I supported. I said Derby and he said: "Well, thankyou. Now be on your way," and walked off.

Rams Trust – David Mortimer

I've been a fan for 30-odd years and was at the Baseball Ground during the Cloughie era. I was very proud to give Brian an award on behalf of the Rams Trust last year.

The fans had never really had a chance to show their feelings when he left all those years ago, so The Rams Trust members struck up a crystal chalice and presented it to him on the day he became a freeman of the city of Derby, on May 4, 2003.

Basically, it was an idea brought about by my brother and I, so I was very honoured to be the chap to present it to him. Brian took it from me and said: "Thankyou very much. It is beautiful".

The man was genius. You will never replace Cloughie.

Steve Goldby – http://www.ComeOnBoro.com

When the announcement came, it was difficult to believe it because common consensus said that he was indestructible. I don't think that he ever actually said that he was indestructible but if he had, we'd probably all have believed him.

The news of Cloughie's death hit hard and when the realisation sunk in, the admiration and respect that had built up over many years of high profile media appearances and unparalleled footballing achievement was brought to the fore by the most heartfelt, sincere and overwhelming tributes that I have ever experienced being paid to anyone.

Since that sad day, everything that can be said about him has been said several times over, and powerful and stirring stuff it is, too. And it is all a fitting testament to the great man, because legends don't come along very often during the course of a lifetime. Cloughie was a legend not just because of his remarkable achievements in football, but because of the person that he was.

Although many stories of outspoken behaviour, sometimes bordering on the offensive, are very easy to come by, people forget that this was only a small part of his character. Critics will often overlook the hundreds of favourable anecdotes that you will come across in this and other books written about Brian Clough.

Does anybody remember how gracious he was in defeat when Liverpool ended Forest's record unbeaten run in 1979? You would never catch Cloughie saying that he didn't see a controversial incident.

The man was a hero because he spoke his mind about the establishment and that is something that the majority of people are afraid to do. It inevitably cast him as a leader and a man of the people and it also cost him the England job. That job was his by right, because of his success at club level, but the FA were never going to appoint somebody who was not afraid to tell them what he thought of them.

But he possessed far greater qualities than those required by the FA top brass. He was above political correctness and transcended diplomacy. He was bigger and better than anyone at the FA and that scared them senseless. They would simply not have been able to cope with the World Cup and European Championship successes that Cloughie would have delivered, and preferred to appoint managers who would create the right impression when overseas.

To Cloughie, making the right impression in football meant winning matches and he utilised his huge personality to lead his teams to victory. Making the right impression in life meant being true and standing up for what you believe in. Images of his altercation with pitch invaders late in his career will stay with me forever.

He was the greatest manager who ever lived.

And many times during the course of his managerial career, I hoped that he would come back and manage Boro but, unfortunately, it was never to be. Derby and Forest were the ones with the foresight to make the controversial appointment and just look at the dividends that it paid.

During his memorial service and many written and spoken tributes and obituaries, several former players and Clough understudies all spoke of the "Clough magic".

What exactly is that "magic?" It is getting the best out of people; coaxing average achievers into producing excellent performances and turning a disenchanted organisation into a set of world beaters.

And how do you achieve the above? Well, you can't formulate the theory, you can't bottle the recipe and you certainly can't write a book about the methodology. The qualities required to pull off miracles and write legends are only found in heroes and when those heroes turn on the "magic", the world takes notice.

Cloughie, you will be missed.

Matthew Major

I have been an Arsenal fan all my life. Having started going to Highbury in the 70s, I was – like everyone else – fully aware of the presence of that man, Brian Clough.

Although I have many memories of football then, I look back on those years and always seem to think of Cloughie. I can't think of another

An emotional farewell at his final league match in charge of Forest in 1993.

character from that era whose words are still quoted today.

Neale Callender, Ilkeston

I wrote a thesis on Nottingham Forest for my degree at Humberside University, which can now be found at the Institute of Football Studies in Preston. I have followed them since 1977 and met Mr. Clough in 1992 before a pre-season friendly. It was a lasting pleasure.

David Humphries

I met Mr Clough when I was a young boy. I can remember how scared I was, but he was great. I still have the autograph. As a Sunderland fan, I have come to admire his scoring achievements.

Paul Rose, Middlesbrough

I was born and bred in Middlesbrough and live a couple of minutes away from the street in which Cloughie lived. My grandad lived opposite him and I remember, as a child, my father recounting stories of him kicking a ball about in the street with Cloughie.

He played for Boro and scored two-hundred goals at a rate of almost a goal a game (Cloughie that is, not my dad!). What would he cost in today's market?

Joan Jones, Sunderland

When he played for Sunderland, we all loved him – not only for his playing skills, but also for his outspoken comments to all and sundry. He proved his class by overcoming that horrendous injury which stopped him from playing football, and showing everyone that he was also a class manager.

Andy Newman – the following is extracted from the website: www.socialistunitynetwork.co.uk

What are we to make of the often repeated claim by Brian Clough that he was a socialist? Just earlier this year, commenting on a community day for pensioners run by Derby council, he said: "It's a wonderful concept and fits in right with my socialist ideals, and there aren't many good socialists left these days!"

In 1961 players broke through the maximum wage of £20 a week through their union, the PFA, led by Jimmy Hill. And throughout the 60s many players were badly paid. This was the world that shaped Clough, the former engineering fitter. This was football when provincial clubs were not just businesses, but vanity projects run by autocratic local businessmen for their personal prestige. In the stifling social conformity of small towns, so brilliantly shown in the 1960 film, Saturday Night, Sunday Morning, a confident and outspoken working class man like Brian Clough would learn that there is them and us, and he was us.

There is no doubt that it was Clough's hatred of the establishment, its cronyism and fawning to money and privilege that prevented his talent being recognised (by the FA).

He cared not at all for reputation or money value. There is an excellent story of how, in 1979, Clough signed Trevor Francis from Birmingham City, as the game's first £1million footballer and promptly put his new signing in the reserves. It got 'worse' as the manager, instructing his new player ahead of his first team debut, told him: "Don't worry too much about what to do, just give the ball to John Robertson and he'll do the rest". When Trevor pointed out the blatantly obvious – "but you've just paid a million pounds for me", Brian replied: "Yes, but he's a better player than you".

But his mercurial outspokenness also damaged the left. Having been one of the first (and biggest) celebrity sponsors of the Anti-Nazi League, he was also one of the first to publicly distance himself from the ANL in 1979, in the wake of violence with the NF. Other celebrities, notably boxer Henry Cooper, stayed the distance with the ANL.

So returning to the first question. Was Clough really a socialist? He had a hard life, of early disappointment as a player, and frustration that his genius never gained recognition. Clough lived his whole life in a closed sporting world where money and power hold sway. He never accepted that wealth means you are right. In that sense of instinctive class consciousnesss, he probably was a socialist. He wanted a fairer world.

Finally, Clough would probably have liked the cartoon on the front of the Daily Telegraph. It showed a gravestone, and the words: "The greatest manager of all time, even if I do say so myself".

Gordon Brown is a Royal Sculptor who was commissioned to create the

The Cloughie Bust.

commemorative bronze bust of Brian Clough (left) that stands at Nottingham Forest's City Ground. He runs the Longdale Craft Centre in Ravenshead, Nottinghamshire (www.longdale.co.uk) that also houses The Gallery Restaurant, where Brian often used to dine...

I first got to know Brian when I worked on the Freedom of the City of Nottingham award box that he was presented with. He would often eat at the restaurant here and I am actually in the process of creating a plaque for the chair that he always used to sit in – we've had a few fights between people wanting to sit in it in recent years!

It was a wonderful honour to be commissioned to produce his bronze bust in 1999 and we have also produced a limited edition of miniature versions that are available from here for £495. There are only 350 worldwide and a percentage of all sales will go to the Brian Clough Memorial Fund.

I got to know Brian well and always found him to be a lovely man who was polite and had time for a chat whenever he came here.

There was a public view of him as big-headed and arrogant, of course, but that wasn't Brian Clough, the person. He had to have a different way of life at work – in much the same way as someone like Tony Blair does – but when he was away from football and relaxing with his family and friends, he was a true gentleman who was respected and admired by everyone who knew him.

Bill McAvinue, Jersey

My fondest memory of Brian Clough came in July 1970 when I was playing football on a beach in Jersey with the former Arsenal full-back and my best man, Bob McNab. Bob and I had known each other from schooldays.

Anyway, Brian Clough, who often took his teams to Jersey for a pre-season break, was chatting with Bob, who called me over and introduced me.

On hearing that I was getting married the following day, Mr Clough, who didn't know me from Adam, put his arms around me and said: "That's the best thing you'll ever do". I've never forgotten it and was a keen observer of his career from that time on.

Brian was a man who spoke his mind. Whether you were a chairman or a new apprentice, he would treat you the same. He was controversial because if you speak your mind, a lot of people don't like you.

I remember a few years back when he went into hospital, I think for a heart-related complaint. I sent him a good luck message and was astonished to receive a signed picture of the great man. I still have it to this day. It speaks volumes about the man.

Although I am originally from Huddersfield, I have spent the past 40 years in Jersey and the cuddle from Brian Clough – he was a very tactile man – is something I will never forget.

Stuart Johnson, *Middlesbrough*

I met him at the signing of his new book in Canary Wharf. The queue was enormous, I joined at 1.40pm with two copies of *Walking on Water*. Even as I bought the books, the staff told me: "Mr Clough is on the lower floor, but there is little chance of you getting these signed now, it's going very slowly."

THE LIFE OF **BRIAN**

They closed the queue two places behind me, at 1.45pm. The variety of those in the queue fascinated me – builders in shorts and hard hats, City types, middle-aged, middle-class women, Boro, Forest, Derby and no doubt Hartlepool and Brighton fans (bet there's none from Leeds, I thought).

Mr Clough had his son, Simon, and his grandson, beside him, and he was as alive as a newly-struck match. The reason it was taking so long was because he gave time to everyone, laughing and joking, kissing the lasses' hands, pointing the infamous finger, taking meticulous care of the spelling of names to be written before his signature.

I lost it a bit, though, when there were lasses going up with four copies, and you just knew he was gonna take ages charming and flirting. There were old gadgies with, I imagined, no end of tales about "I met you at the bus stop just after you signed for Sunderland" and "Would you just sign this christening card for me granddaughter?"

I told those in front to scrunch up a bit, to make the queue look smaller in case The Man took a sly look. He'd hopefully think there weren't many left, and stick with the signing.

After a very long wait, I stumbled up and said: "Thanks for waiting, Mr Clough" and he looked up. "It's a pleasure, Sir," he said, making me feel more terrified and uncomfortable than any former teacher with bamboo in his hand had.

I put the *FMTTM* in front of his grandson and said pathetically: "I brought you this article I wrote, about Lindy Delapenha."

His face lit up: "Ooh lovely, thank you."

"Of course, it refers to you a bit, and I tried to get it to you via Forest, but…"

Mr Clough said: "He was always welcome in our house, never even had to knock the door, he'd just come in and sit down in the armchair."

Someone was shouting over my shoulder. Mr Clough looked past me, direct and focused. A large bunch of banknotes was thrust forward past my arm, and a Southern voice said: "Sorry, Brian, but I haven't got a brown paper bag!"

Cloughie was onto him like one of his shots. "Thank you," he said, reaching out to grab it. But the hand withdrew smartly, and the fella took several steps back. "GIVE IT TO ALAN SUGAR!" Cloughie shouted after him (accompanied by an entirely appropriate curse or two).

I recovered a bit, time was precious, but my heart was thumping,

"Anyway, you were saying that Lindy would just walk into your house, before we were interrupted?" I said.

"Aye, and I'd shout to Barbara, 'I 'ope you've got ice cream in the fridge, 'cos Lindy's here! He'd sit there and eat a whole bloody tub of the stuff!"

"He spoke well of you," I offered.

"Oh, I met up with him, what? . . . 12 month ago.

"When he came to the Riverside?" I said.

"No, he came to see me in Nottingham. Bloody hell, I couldn't believe how well he looked, so fit and tanned, and so smart in his dress sense," said Cloughie.

"What names go on these books, anyhow," he said. I gave him mine, and asked him to do one for my brother-in-law, Tim, a Forest fan, and he concentrated on his writing and I just gawped at the world in silent respect (he poked his tongue out a little as he wrote, and I thought how much effort he was putting in to ensure there wasn't the slightest mistake in what he wrote, even though he'd been doing the same thing for hours).

As I finally gave in to 'Redca' (who was waiting for me) and stepped back, he said: "I'll read that thing later, thank you, you should go home!"

As I stood half-listening to the exchange with our man from the coast, I wondered what Cloughie meant. Did I look rough? I'd remembered to wear a suit, and be perfectly polite. I dreaded the finger and the 'young man' routine. I craved approval from a man my Dad revered (and he was a hard judge of Boro players, fans and the club). I hoped he was referring to the antics of the cockney 'bung boy', and the contrasting warmth of our exchange.

Signing for the fans.

But he was saying to Redca that his wife's family are from Marske, and that when he was a kid and his parents took them on the train to the seaside, it was the same fare from Middlesbrough to Redcar or Marske, or Saltburn, but Saltburn was considered really posh, so that's where they were taken. "The kids that got off at Redcar had two patches on the arse of their trousers, but I only had one!"

At some point, he said to me: "I used to be nobody, and now I'm nobody again, and I said: "But you've been a real *somebody* in between," or somesuch nonsense.

Brian Clough is not a has-been. He is a Boro legend, a man who was scared of nothing and no-one, with the warmth of an angel, the wisdom of ancients, the humour of the devil – and seemingly endless patience with ordinary fools like me.

Martin Cloake, *Spurs season ticket holder and co-author of We Are Tottenham – Voices from White Hart Lane*

Cloughie's classic Forest side were one of the reasons I became so hooked on football. I was already a committed Spurs fan by the time Forest were promoted to the old Division One, but the fact that a newly-promoted team could win the title in their first season, then go on to win the European Cup – twice! – demonstrated what magic the game held.

That example still helps me retain my enthusiasm for a game which we're now told can spring no surprises. I also liked the confidence with which he expressed himself, eschewing the false modesty seen as polite in British society, his honest approach to how football was played and his willingness to identify himself as a socialist – although very much a socialist of his time.

Darren Nunn, *York*

When I proposed to my girlfriend at the City Ground, both Brian Clough and David Platt spent time before a TV interview chatting and posing for photographs with us both.

He also signed our photographs of the occasion with personal messages, making the occasion extra special. Whilst being an excellent football ambassador, he also spent time with, and cared about, his fans.

Mr. Broad, Ockbrook, Derby

About 24 years ago my brother's daughter was very poorly and, at the age of 16, was dying of cancer. Brian took his three kids along to the City Hospital to see her. He spent an hour or two with her and two days later she died.

That was the kindest thing he ever did in my book and you don't ever forget kindness like that. He did a lot of things like that which people didn't know about.

I never met him but I wish I had. I've been a Derby supporter for years and that's the best I've seen.

Richard Rushworth, *Spondon, Derbyshire*

Of the 40-50 years I've been watching football, Brian Clough gave me the best 10-15 years. Many big occasions watching semi-finals, finals, trips to Europe and so much more we wouldn't have had without him.

I went to the 1980 European Cup final in Madrid, a fantastic occasion. It was a nailbiting match towards the end but Brian did it for us and that was the most exciting football experience I have had.

I would go to those Derby games in the early 70s because the atmosphere was tremendous and I know Derby fans who came to Forest in the late 70s for our cup runs. We just loved the occasions and the football.

Tom Wheeler, *Derby*

My mother was meeting Kathy, my sister-in-law (who was about 14) off a train in London from Derby in the early 70s.

She was at the gate when Kathy walked up from the train with two men. The one who was carrying her case said: "I believe you are meeting this young lady?" My mother replied: "Yes."

To which the man replied: "I will leave her with you then."

My mother said to Kathy: "I know those men's faces . . ."

Yes, it was Brian (with the case) and Peter Taylor.

He was always a "gentleman" in the eyes of my mother after that, but she hadn't liked him before.

Charlie Simpson, *Draycott, Derbyshire*

I was a season ticket holder in the early 70s when Derby won the championship and made it to the semi-finals of the European Cup. The full house at the old Baseball Ground for the Benfica match will take some beating.

That was the night when he watered the pitch. He knew all the tricks and we benefited from that. In those days you could walk around the pitch to change ends at half-time, which we did, and I remember my feet disappearing in the mud around one of the corner flags. Eusebio had no chance!

For me, not only did he do wonders for Derby County, but the atmosphere when you were at work, in the town, in the pub or in your own home . . .

The Nottingham Forest team of today pay their respects to the legend.

everything felt alive and we were at the centre of everything. When your football team is doing well, life feels good. And Brian's teams always did well.

Chris Yoell, *Nottingham*

Derby had been messing around for years before Brian arrived and even before he won anything you knew that he was going to do something.

My favourite memory was when we beat Chelsea in the League Cup. What a night that was. To be losing with 30 minutes to go and then to see us suddenly score three goals, was unbelievable. I've never been to a match like it. It was absolutely rivetting.

It is a funny thing, football. If it's down, you're down and if it's up, so are you, and I take a ride on that. Those were great times at Derby and it was very upsetting when Brian left. Mackay kept it going for a bit but it has really been down hill for most of the time since then.

My favourite Cloughie player was Colin Todd, although my all-time favourite was Kevin Hector, but he was already here when Clough arrived. Tim Ward signed him. I even go back further than him, to Harry Storer, when we were in the Third Division North. In fact, Storer did a bit of a 'mini Clough' at the club, getting us promoted to the second division.

Derek Mannion ("as in Wilf!"), Ripley

I met Brian quite a few times when he lived in Quarndon, near the cricket ground. I used to drive the bus that went by his house and when the women had been to visit his wife, he would always come to the bus and say: "Look after these ladies, driver. Get them home nice and safely." He was a true gentleman.

Anonymous, *Derby fan*

I used to drive a taxi and I would pick Cloughie up when he was at Forest.

I would collect him from the hotel at Stapleford and drive him home. He was always a proper gentleman and when he came to pay the fare, which at that time was ten pounds, he would hand over a £20 note and I would give him £10 change.

Then he would hand it back to me and say: "That £10 is for you, young man."

Mick Kerry, *Holbrook, near Belper*

I used to help a friend of mine at a garage in Allestree. Brian would come in for his petrol in the late 60s and 70s and I used to serve him. He was always very chirpy and all I can say is that he was a big character and we're all going to miss him.

John Midgley, Burton-on-Trent

I've been a Derby fan all my life and stood on a box at the Baseball Ground when I was six.

I wrote to Brian once, prior to Roy McFarland's testimonial game, to ask him if I could take some photographs. I was both a keen Derby supporter and photographer at the time. The club said 'yes' and sent me the pass.

On the night of the game, the official club photographer suggested to me that rather than sit behind the goal, I should sit near the tunnel to get some 'different' pictures? This was good advice and I settled myself down on my camera box and started taking a few shots.

All of a sudden I heard a voice say: "Hey, young man, get yourself back from out of that tunnel. Not even the directors sit that close!"

On another occasion I was walking to the Baseball Ground one day and it was when he had been poorly at some stage a few years back. Anyway, he came off the car park – it was a night match – and I said: "Good evening Mr Clough, how are you?" and he replied: "Good evening, young man. How are *you?*" I said I was very well, to which he replied: "Well, that is all that matters, then."

Paul Walker, *Derby*

THE LIFE OF **BRIAN**

I saw Brian Clough in Derby town centre one day. He was struggling with his knees so was using sticks, but still wearing his green sweat shirt.

He asked a group of lads, aged about 18-19, the way to a book shop. "Up there on the right, Brian," one of the them said.

I thought that Brian had let it go but as he was walking off, he said: "Mister Clough!"

The lads just apologised and he walked off. Typical Clough.

Desmond Page, *Derby*

I first went to see Derby play in 1948 and, even though I'm an ex-Army officer, I still called Cloughie 'Sir' whenever we met. That's a measure of the respect I had for him. The last time I saw him was at Burton Albion quite recently. He was a bit of a God to Derby fans and I'm devastated by his death.

When he was young he was a bit impetuous and easily got upset. He became a bit too big for his boots but his signing of Dave Mackay was a masterstroke. Mackay was the centre-pin of promotion to the first division and all the players respected him.

Peter Guildford, *Derby*

Under Cloughie, Derby played the best football I've seen at the club, either before or since.

My son, Martin, played for Allestree Juniors under-15s and he received his player-of-the-year award from Brian back in 1983. Cloughie came along to the presentation and behaved like a gentleman, talking nothing but common sense to the kids.

He was a man for ordinary people.

Phil May, *Shelton Lock*

I've heard it said that, near where he lived at Quarndon, Cloughie would often help out old ladies who had trouble paying for their shopping at the local supermarket. If the old dears didn't quite have enough money on them, Brian would give the cashier at the checkout a wink and pay the lot out of his own pocket.

Dave Mackay was just what we needed to get us out of the old second division, but Roy McFarland was Cloughie's best-ever signing at Derby. He had class.

But then again, Brian made lots of really good buys, such as Archie Gemmill, who was tremendous for both Derby and Forest.

Howard Sprenger, *Derby*

GODS
BOSS
MR
CLOUGH

I used to see Cloughie around Allestree, especially in the early days, shopping with his kids at Park Farm now and then, but I'd never really spoken to him until I got into a conversation with him earlier this year, ironically as it turns out, at a funeral.

He wasn't actually at the funeral – he just happened to be meeting some business associates at the hotel where were eating our cucumber sandwiches after the service at Markeaton Crematorium.

He looked very well and I started chatting to him, because in a situation like that he was somebody you could just approach and have a chat with. He treated me like a long, lost friend, shook my hand warmly, and then spotted my black tie and the obvious gathering of a funeral party. "Was he a relation?" he asked. "Yes," I replied, and then as a hasty correction, I added: "But not one of mine!" We both laughed at my awkwardness, and then for some reason I felt compelled to point out that the deceased had been a Swindon Town supporter. "Oh!" said Cloughie, "he didn't have much luck then, did he?"

We laughed again, and he said: "Bring the family over for a chat." To my eternal regret, he did not finish the sentence with "young man!" He then spent several minutes chatting with the family of the deceased – the widow, the daughter and son.

I don't think anyone could make a funeral 'special', and the truth is that the family will remember more about that day than the fact that Brian

The City Ground became a sea of floral tributes as soon as Brian's death was announced.

Clough talked to them, but he didn't do it for effect. He did it out of genuine concern that they'd lost a loved one, and it was just a natural thing for him to do to express his condolences with utmost sincerity.

Neal Cresswell, *Toronto, Canada*

I remember Cloughie's last league game at home. The entire ground was on its feet, with a wonderful ovation from the Sheffield United fans.

Sadly, it seems the people in football power have made a point of ignoring Brian throughout his career – ignoring him or fearing him.

Ray Harford, Leeds United fan

I am still waiting for our club to fully recover from that tragic day when Brian was dismissed.

Joe Appleby, *Lookout Mountain, Georgia, USA*

As a young boy living on the next street to the Clough family, I remember Brian very well. We played against each other in competing street teams on Clairville Common. It was Valley Road v Eden Road.

I also remember that in our family you couldn't say a bad word against Brian Clough. My late mother was a cleaner at the school Brian attended and she had nothing but praise for the Head Boy of Marton Grove School.

I left England in 1963 for Canada and USA but I kept up on Cloughie's career. He certainly added a little Boro spice to the game, and the game is all the better for it. He may have called himself 'Big 'Ead', but he wasn't really. Just full of confidence in his abilities.

Why not a knighthood? He deserved one.

John Ansbro, *Brighton*

It was around the time he was staying at the Courtlands Hotel in Hove – he never moved to Brighton – and he brought Forest down for a game.

I was a youngster waiting outside the hotel for autographs of the team – they used to meet and eat there. It was a rain-sodden night and as they arrived, Brian asked what I was doing there and said I was not to bother his players by asking for autographs, especially as it was raining.

I waited and after about an hour Clough came to the front door, wanting to know why I was still there. Being cheeky, I said I was waiting in the hope that he would be in a better mood when his players were leaving.

With that he invited me into the dining area and instructed all his players to sign my book. I was in heaven!

Tony Millard *(radio and TV broadcast), Hove*

When Clough was in charge at Brighton I worked as an electrical engineer and as a part-time sports freelance for BBC Radio Brighton. I had no direct dealings with Brian, although I did interview Peter Taylor when he was in charge after Clough had departed.

When Brighton chairman Mike Bamber announced Clough was coming following the sacking of Pat Saward, most supporters had to pinch themselves. The pair (Clough and Taylor) arrived and, very shortly, so did an assortment of players from all over the country – some of them not very good. The pair brought in coaches and scouts – Ken Gutteridge and Bryan Daykin, colleagues from the Midlands – and people started to come and go at a great rate.

Bamber announced, at the start of 1974, that he would have Brighton in Division One within five years. They actually got there in May 1979 No-one had believed him but, in retrospect, the introduction of Clough and the publicity it generated probably gave impetus to Bamber's aim. He was greatly helped by fellow director Keith Wickenden, then Chairman of European Ferries, and that's where the money came from.

Clough spent little time in Brighton – he never had a home there and used the Courtlands Hotel in The Drive as his headquarters. He usually came down from his Derby home on Thursdays and went back north on Saturday evening each week. If the team was playing up north, he might not even come to Brighton at all during the week.

Only two local journalists appeared to get reasonably close to Clough – John Vinicombe of the Evening Argus and Neil Coppendale of BBC Radio Brighton. Peter Brackley, later of BBC Radio, and also ITV and Channel 4 football commentator, as well as being a great after-dinner speaker, was in charge of his station's sport. He occasionally talked with Clough and later earned his respect. Peter also did a marvellous impression of Clough!

Nigel Clough (a tiny lad then) used to join his father in the dugout at Brighton.

Taylor's time in the manager's office alongside Brian was mostly spent studying the racing pages of the dailies. One had the impression that a winner of the 3.30 was more important than a Brighton result.

Brian Clough –
Gone but not forgotten
A poem by John Robson,
A Love Supreme, Sunderland

My very first hero
Red and white Number nine
Prolific goalscorer
In rain or sunshine

When he was injured
I wrote him a letter
Hoping that soon
His knee would be better.

But in my note pad
The letter stayed
But every night
I prayed and I prayed.

Mrs Barbara Clough reads a poem at Brian's memorial service held in the pouring rain at Pride Park.

Injury curtailed his time
As my playing hero
His opinion of Stokoe
Was rated at zero

He took pictures of him
Then ranted and raved.
To threaten his children
If they misbehaved

He was successful
He was nobody's fool
He brought some success
To old Hartlepool

When he moved to Derby
He stole Todd and O'Hare
They were the champions
While he was there

Twice European winners

From the City Ground
A better manager
Will never be found

He did not like
The long ball played up high
"If God had wanted that
He'd have made grounds in the sky"

He was the law
Though hoodlums were tough
They were no match
For that man Brian Clough

Now he has gone
We are all sad
He's the best manager
England never had.

Nigel, Simon and Elizabeth Clough at their father's memorial service.

Andy Hallam, *Tollerton.*

Over the past few years (before I moved recently to Tollerton), I always used to pop into Central News of West Bridgford, which is the newsagents owned and run by Brian's son, Simon.

The bonus of doing so was the chance to chat many times to Mr. Clough himself, who was always great value for money, and was always willing to talk all things football.

One pre-season Saturday morning, a couple of years ago, I was picking up my newspaper when a voice bellowed from the bottom of the shop: "What are you up to today, young man?" to which I replied: "I am going to Rushden and Diamonds, Mr Clough. I have never been to the ground before and we are playing them today in a friendly."

Cloughie went quiet for a couple of seconds and then shouted in the direction of two elderly ladies at the counter: "Oi, missus, let that young man jump the queue, please. He has a bus to catch to watch his team. The daft bugger helped pay my wages for 18 years and if he is still watching that rubbish now, he deserves to be served first!"

Typical and, as always, priceless.

A sad fan at the first Forest home game following Brian's death in Septmber 2004.

KPF, *Charlton*

There cannot be many football supporters who didn't have some affectionate regard for Brian Clough. Even supporters of clubs that he never managed are saddened by his death.

He had always seemed indestructible and to have a short, sharp answer to every problem. Yet we hadn't heard much from him for some years and we now know that he had two serious illnesses. He did appear briefly on television a few weeks ago but he looked, and sounded, quite unlike the Cloughie of old and we realised that something was badly wrong.

I only met him once. I was a

guest of Gillingham's then chairman, Dr. Grossmark, and had been invited for a cup of tea at half-time. It must have been just after Christmas, because instead of the usual neat sandwiches, there were cakes and pastries. Gillingham's opponents were drawn against Nottingham Forest in the third round of the FA Cup a few days later. I didn't want to stare but I was surprised to find myself a few feet away from the famous manager and his assistant, Peter Taylor.

Suddenly, I heard a peremptory command in the unmistakable voice: "Young man!" Everybody froze. I realised instantly that he was speaking to me. "Pass me the sugar, please."

It wasn't said impolitely but there was something in his tone that made it clear that he expected his request to be carried out promptly and accurately and even a hint of a suggestion that, if I had been paying attention, I would have anticipated his need. Blushing with embarrassment, I did what he requested and he nodded in acknowledgement. I knew immediately how his players must have been motivated.

Another thing that struck me was that although Forest were still in the relegation zone at the bottom of the old second division, he and Taylor were completely relaxed and confident that they had the situation under control. They were right. Forest stayed up comfortably and were promoted the following season.

There is a story that, when he arrived at Brighton, he met his new players and greeted them with the words: "You all know who I am. Don't bother to tell me your names because most of you won't be here next week!" This sounds like typical arrogance from "Old Big Head (OBE)", a name he gave to himself, but, like everything else, he had done it with a purpose. As he made this harsh greeting and established his dominance, he watched the players closely. He could see immediately, from their responses, which would be willing to accept his autocratic style of management. Those who didn't, weren't there for long.

He started with some terrible results but by the end of the season Brighton were going well. His brief spell and a longer one before Peter Taylor left Brighton to join him at Forest, laid the foundations for a long period of success for Brighton.

The shock announcement of his death was accompanied by a 'sound-bite'. It was of His* deploring defences lofting high balls up to a bean-pole centre-forward: "If football was meant to be played in the clouds, God would have put grass up there". It was appropriate. It is difficult to believe that Cloughie has gone anywhere that hasn't a football pitch and a team to motivate.

*The capital letter is intentional.

A visitor to Nottingham once asked him: "What is that water near the stadium?" Clough replied: "That is the Trent. That is the water I've been walking on for the last few years!"

Alan Stevens, Charlton Athletic

At a referees' meeting many years ago, I was told this by a Class One referee, who covered the first division (as it was then), about Brian's encounter with a referee who was having a bit of a bad game where the decisions were going against Forest.

Brian: "Ref, you've got to be bloody joking?"

Ref (who had now come over to the dugout): "Who do you think is refereeing this game?"

Brian: "Well, it is certainly not you!"

Dave M. Thomson, *Charlton Athletic fan*

One of the tabloids ran an article about a schoolboy who had decided to write to the famous names of the day, asking for their recommendations about how to make a success of life.

The responses were published in the paper. Several celebs were criticised for not responding and others praised for their responses – e.g. "hard work," "belief in yourself," "never giving in", etc, etc.

Cloughie's letter of response was printed and I am para-phrasing the reply:

"My advice to you, Young Man, is that you should enclose a stamped-addressed-envelope if you expect a reply. Yours sincerely, Brian Clough."

Andrew Thompson, *Royal Navy, Plymouth, a Derby County fan*

As a young kid living in a Derby children's home, I used to see Brian most Sundays, walking his dogs in Darley Park.

I was always in trouble with the Police and other people, but one day Brian had a little kickaround with me, then we sat down and had a chat. His words of wisdom really sank in and changed my life.

He was the only person who has had any effect on my life and turned it into a good life. He stopped me going to prison.

Thanks for saving me from ruin, Brian Clough.

And thanks for making football what it is today, the beautiful game.

"From Enid the tea lady, Cliff, Cedric and Barrie Wilson. With deepest sympathy, Brian. Simply The Best".
Message placed on Brian's seat at Eton Park, Burton Albion FC, the first game after he passed away.

Brian Clough OBE
Factfile

Full name: Brian Howard Clough
Born: March 21, 1935. **Died:** September 20, 2004
Birthplace: Middlesbrough
Job before football: Clerk at ICI
Signed professional: For Middlesbrough in May 1952

As a player
Clubs: Middlesbrough 1952-61 and Sunderland 1961-65
Goals: 197 league goals for Middlesbrough, 54 goals for Sunderland
International appearances: Two full England caps (v Wales and Sweden); one England 'B' cap; and three England under-23 caps

As a manager
Hartlepools United 1965-67
Derby County 1967-73
Brighton & Hove Albion 1973-74
Leeds United 1974
Nottingham Forest 1975-93

Honours

Derby County
1968-69: Division Two champions
1970-71: Watney Cup winners
1971-72: Division One champions
1971-71: Texaco Cup winners
1972-73: European Cup semi-finalists

Nottingham Forest
1976-77: Promotion from Division Two
1976-77: Anglo-Scottish Cup winners
1977-78: Division One champions
1977-78: League Cup winners
1978-79: Division One runners-up
1978-79: League Cup winners
1978-79: European Cup winners
1979-80: European Cup winners
1979-80: League Cup runners-up
1979-80: Super Cup winners
1980-81: Super Cup runners-up
1980-81: World Club Championship runners-up
1988-89: League Cup winners
1988-89: Simod Cup winners
1989-90: League Cup winners
1991: FA Cup runners-up
1991-92: League Cup runners-up
1991-92: ZDS Cup winners

Timelines
1935: Born March 21 in Middlesbrough.

1952: Joins home-town club.

1955: Makes his League debut v Barnsley. Went on to score 204
goals in 222 games.

1959: Wins England caps against Wales at Ninian Park and Sweden at
Wembley.

1961: Signs for North-East rivals Sunderland for £45,000 and nets 63

THE LIFE OF **BRIAN**

goals in just 74 appearances for the Rokermen.

1962: Knee injury against Bury on Boxing Day forces an early end to his playing career at the age of 26.

1965: At 29, becomes the youngest manager in the Football League with Fourth Division Hartlepools United (as they were then known).

1967: Becomes Derby County manager.

1969: Derby win Division Two title.

1972: Derby win Division One title, the first League championship in the club's history.

1973: Clough guides the Rams to the semi-finals of the European Cup. In October resigns from Derby, with assistant Peter Taylor, after long dispute with club directors. In November, becomes Brighton manager.

1974: July – Appointed manager of Leeds, but sacked after 44 days because of player unrest.

1975: January – Appointed manager of Nottingham Forest.

1977: Forest promoted to the First Division.

1978: Forest win the League Cup, before going on to be crowned Division One champions at the end of the season. Clough is named Manager of the Year. Forest win the Charity Shield, beating FA Cup winners Ipswich 5-0 at Wembley.

1979: February – Signs Trevor Francis from Birmingham City,   Britain's first £1million transfer.
March – Forest retain League Cup.
May – Forest finish second in Division One, but are crowned kings of Europe when Malmo are beaten 1-0 in the European Cup final.

1980: March – Forest are beaten in League Cup final by Wolves.
May – Forest retain European Cup when they beat Hamburg 1-0 in Madrid.

1989: February – Clough is charged with bringing the game into disrepute; fined £5,000 and banned from touch-line of all Football League grounds for the rest of the season for lashing out at unruly fans after a home League Cup quarter-final against QPR.
April – Forest beat Luton 3-1 to win League Cup.
December – Clough celebrates his 1,000th league game as a manager.

1990: Forest retain League Cup, their fourth success under Clough, with a 1-0 win over Oldham.

1991: Forest reach the final of the FA Cup, the only major domestic trophy Clough had not won, but are beaten by Spurs.
Clough receives an OBE in the Queen's Birthday Honours.

1992: Forest win the Zenith Data Systems Cup against Southampton at Wembley. Clough takes Forest to the League Cup final at Wembley again, but they are beaten 1-0 by Manchester United.

1993: January – Clough, soccer's longest-serving boss, celebrates the 18th anniversary in charge at the City Ground with Forest bottom of the Premiership.
April – A photographer captures Clough giving the Forest fans a V-sign during a 1-1 draw against Leeds at the City Ground.
It is announced he plans to retire at the end of the season.
May – a tearful Clough watches on as Forest lose 2-0 to Sheffield United, and are thus relegated from the top flight, in his last game at The City Ground. Loses his final game in charge of Forest at Ipswich.

1998: Charged with misconduct by the Football Association for allegedly accepting an unauthorised payment on the transfers of players.

2002: January – Clough, a one-time heavy drinker, undergoes a liver transplant.

2003: May – Made an honorary Freeman of Derby and given the freedom of the city.

2004: Monday, September 20 – Brian Clough dies of stomach cancer in Derby General Hospital.

Clough quotes . . . and all that type of thing

Brian Clough was never short of a word or 10 during and after his colourful career...

On the importance of passing to feet: "If God had wanted us to play football in the clouds, he'd have put grass up there."

On the influx of foreign players in the British game: "I can't even spell spaghetti, never mind talk Italian. How could I tell an Italian to get the ball? He might grab mine."

On the number of French players at Arsenal: "I bet their dressing room will smell of garlic rather than liniment over the next few months."

On how he rated himself: "I wouldn't say I was the best manager in the business. But I was in the top one."

Explaining his nickname: "On occasions I have been big-headed. I think most people are when they get in the limelight. I call myself 'Big Head' just to remind myself not to be."

On Martin O'Neill: "If he'd been English or Swedish, he'd have walked the England job."

On the streaker who appeared during a Derby game against Manchester United: "'The Derby players have seen more of his balls than the one they're meant to be playing with."

On dealing with Roy Keane: "I only ever hit Roy the once. He got up, so I couldn't have hit him very hard."

On his drinking: "Walk on water? I know most people out there will be saying that instead of walking on it, I should have taken more of it with my drinks. They are absolutely right."

On dealing with a player who disagrees: "We talk about it for 20 minutes and then we decide I was right."

On not getting the England manager's job: "I'm sure the England selectors

thought if they took me on and gave me the job, I'd want to run the show. They were shrewd, because that's exactly what I would have done."

On too many managers getting the sack: "If a chairman sacks the manager he initially appointed, he should go as well."

Referring to Sir Alex Ferguson's failure to win two successive European Cups: "For all his horses, knighthoods and championships, he hasn't got two of what I've got. And I don't mean balls!"

On women's football: "I like my women to be feminine, not sliding into tackles and covered in mud."

On then England goalkeeper David Seaman: "That Seaman is a handsome young man but he spends too much time looking in his mirror, rather than at the ball. You can't keep goal with hair like that."

On the late Peter Taylor: "I've missed him. He used to make me laugh. He was the best defuser of a situation I have ever known. I hope he's all right."

On Eric Cantona's infamous *kung fu* kick at a fan: "I'd have cut his balls off."

On how he would like to be remembered: "I want no epitaphs of profound history and all that type of thing. I contributed – I would hope they would say that, and I would hope somebody liked me."

Bibliography

Sources and recommended viewing and reading...

Videos

Champions of Europe: 25 Years On. 2003. Directed by Andrew James. The Media Group.

The Story of The League Cup: Glorious Years. Memorable Goals. 1991. The Football League ITV, BBC and British Pathe News: Granada Television.

Cloughie. The Brian Clough Story. 1990. Watershed Pictures.

Nottingham Forest's Greatest FA Cup Victories. Watershed Pictures WSP1095 (55 minutes) 1992 Narrated by Tony Francis

Cloughie. The Brian Clough Story. Watershed Pictures WSP1001 (80 minutes) 1990 **The Inside Story of a Football Genius, in his own words**. Presented by Brian Moore.

That Championship Feeling 1977/78 (A nostalgic look back to a unique year in the history of Nottingham Forest FC) Produced by Andrew Dollaway for LKA Communications

Match of the Day: Nottingham Forest. BBC Video BBCV4740 (74 minutes) 1992 Written and narrated by John Motson.

The Official History of Nottingham Forest FC Castle Vision (Watershed Pictures) CVI1097 (60 minutes) 1989.

The Official Season Review 92-93 Nottingham Forest. PolyGram Video 086 448 3. (80 minutes) 1993.

Nottingham Forest: The Golden Goals Collection PolyGram Video 6332003. (60 minutes) 1994.

The Pain & the Glory PolyGram Video 6346703. (60 minutes) 1995.

Books

Albion A-Z: A Who's Who of Brighton & Hove Albion FC
by Tim Carder and Roger Harris (Goldstone Books, ISBN 0 9521337 1 7, Goldstone Books)

Seagulls! The Story of Brighton & Hove Albion FC
by Tim Carder and Roger Harris (ISBN 0 9521337 0 9, Goldstone Books)

Jones, R., 2002. **The Essential History of Middlesbrough**. Headline Book publishing

Taylor, P.,1980. **With Clough By Taylor**. Sidgwick and Jackson

Rollin, G and Rollin, J., 2001. **Rothmans Football Yearbooks** 1973-1981. London: Headline Book Publishing

Clough, B and Sadler, J, 2002. **Cloughie: Walking On Water. My Life.** London. Headline Book publishing

Murphy, P., 1993. **His Way: The Brian Clough Story**. London: Robson Books

Cockayne, M.,2004. **Derby County Champions 1974-75**. London. Breedon Books

Cockayne, M.,2003. **Derby County: The Clough Years**. London. Breedon Books

CLOUGHIE Sources

Camillin,P and Weir, S.,2001. **Albion: The First 100 Years.** London. Sports Pavillion.
Glynne Jones.,2003. **Game of Two Halves: Football Yesterday and Today.** London.

Charlton Books
Hamilton, D.,1988. **Nottingham Forest Football Club.** London. Archive
Lawson, J.,1979. **Nottingham Forest Football Club.** London. Wensum Books
Hayes,D.,1998. **Nottingham Forest Football Club: An A-Z.** London. Sigman Press.
Attaway, P.1991. **Nottingham Forest: A Complete Record 1865-1991.** London.
Breedon Books
Mortimer, G and Wilson, M., 1984. **Derby County: The Complete Record, 1884-1984.** London. Breedon Books.
Edwards, G., 1970. **Derby County Football Club.** London. S Paul
Glasper, H.,1993. **Middlesbrough: A Complete Record.** London. Breedon Books.
Hayes, D.,1993. **Middlesbrough Football Club.** London. Aureus Football Club.
Jovanovic, R., 2003. **Forest Giants: The Story of Nottingham Forest 1975-1980.**
Up the Pools 1991 – Neil Watson and Roy Kelly take a look at the promotion seasons
of 1968 and 1991
The History of Sunderland AFC 1879-1986 Graham, Bob & Bill Simmons
Wearside Publications, 1995
THE LADS Thirty Memorable Matches – A Sunderland Echo special 1988

Websites

Brighton and Hove Albion Football Club, 2004. Available from http://www.brighton-hovealbion.rivals.net
Brighton and Hove Albion Football Club, 2004. Brighton and Hove Albion Fanzine.
Available from http://www.brightonfans.com
Hartlepool United Football Club, 2004. Hartlepool United Fanzine Online. Available
from http://www.Bizz.hufc.net
Hartlepool United Football Club, 2004. Hartlepool United Fanzine Online. Available
from http://www.monkeybizz.net
Sunderland Football Club, 2004. The independent Sunderland Football Club Fanzine.
Available from http://www.a-love-supreme.com
Middlesbrough Football Club, 2004. Middlesbrough Football Club online. Available
from http://www.comeonboro.com
Middlesbrough Football Club, 2004. Fly Me To The Moon: The Boro Fanzine Online.
Available from http://www.fmttm.com

Newspapers

Apart from the books and videos above, the quotes from this book were extracted from
the following sources:
Brighton Evening Argus – 1973.1974; The Yorkshire Post – 1974; The Yorkshire
Evening Post – 1974; The Middlesbrough Evening Gazette – 1955 – 1961; The
Sunderland Echo – 1961 – 1965; The Northern Daily Mail – 1965-67; The Derby
Telegraph – 1967-1973; The Nottingham Evening Post – 1975 – 1993; The Sun; The
Times, The Mirror, The Guardian, The Daily Telegraph, and Sunday equivalents
between 1970-1980.

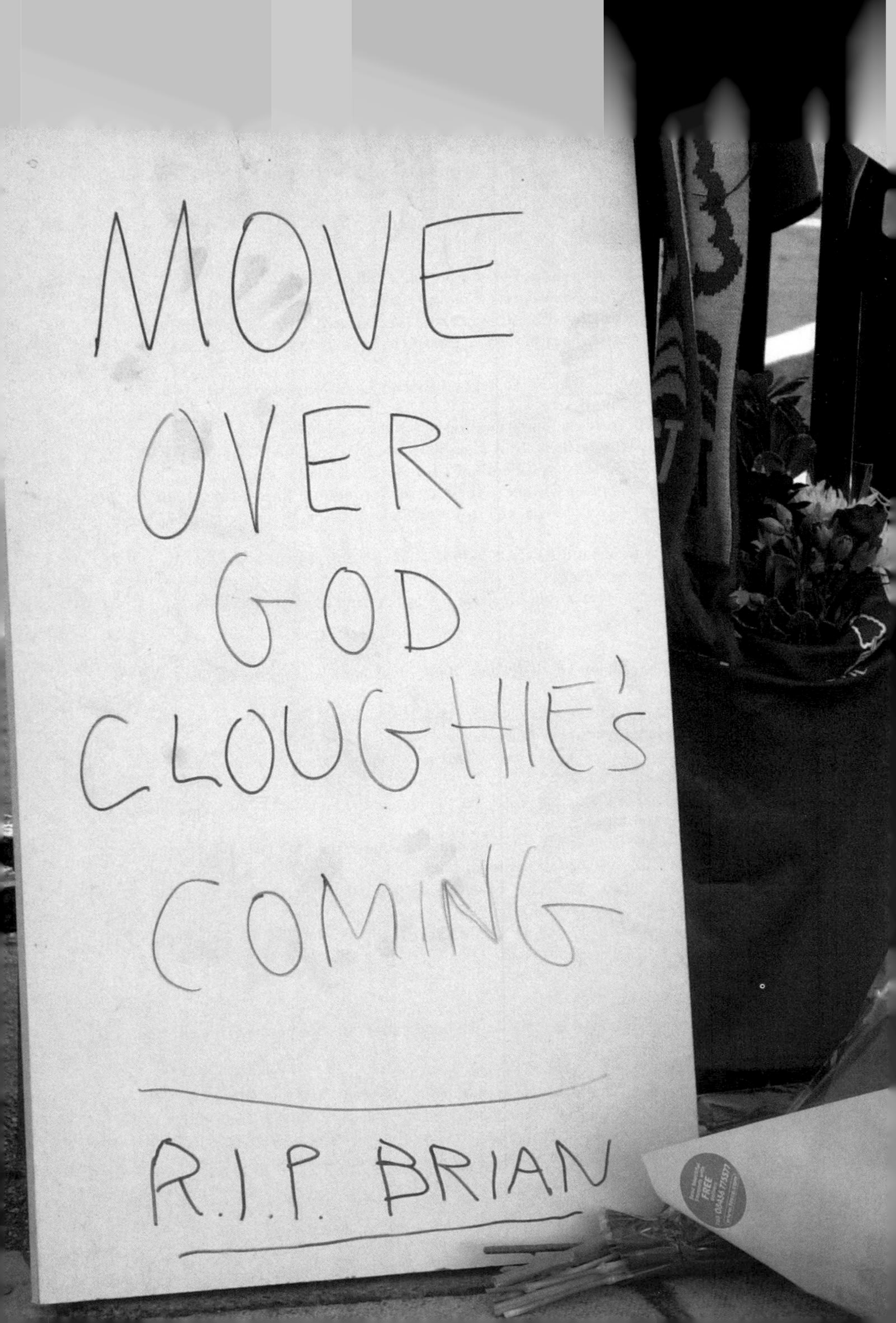
MOVE
OVER
GOD
CLOUGHIE'S
COMING
R.I.P. BRIAN